Clash of empires

Europe 1498–1560

Martin D. W. Jones

CAMBRIDGE
UNIVERSITY PRESS

For Chris and Emma

PUBLISHED BY THE PRESS SYNDICATE OF THE UNIVERSITY OF CAMBRIDGE
The Pitt Building, Trumpington Street, Cambridge, United Kingdom

CAMBRIDGE UNIVERSITY PRESS
The Edinburgh Building, Cambridge CB2 2RU, UK
40 West 20th Street, New York, NY 10011-4211, USA
10 Stamford Road, Oakleigh, VIC 3166, Australia
Ruiz de Alarcón 13, 28014 Madrid, Spain
Dock House, The Waterfront, Cape Town 8001, South Africa

http://www.cambridge.org

© Cambridge University Press 2000

First published 2000

Printed in the United Kingdom at the University Press, Cambridge

Typeface 10.5pt Minion   *System* QuarkXPress®

A catalogue record for this book is available from the British Library

ISBN 0 521 59503 7   paperback

Text design by Newton Harris Design Partnership

Map artwork by Kathy Baxendale

The cover shows part of *The triumph of death* by Pieter Bruegel. Painted in the early 1560s, it illustrates vividly the violence and uncertainty of sixteenth-century Europe.

ACKNOWLEDGEMENTS
Unless otherwise specified, all translations of sources are by the author.
The author is grateful to Peter Browning and Emma Jones for their very helpful criticisms of the draft text, and to Trinity College, Oxford, for a period of Schoolteacher vacation study in July 1997.

theartarchive: p. 25; The Bodleian Library, University of Oxford, 4° C21 Art (1): p. 104; *Portrait of Charles V* (Charles I of Spain) (1500–58), 1516 (oil on panel) by Bernard van Orley (*c.*1488–1541), Louvre, Paris, France/ Bridgeman Art Library: p. 42; *Portrait of Francis I on horseback, c.*1540, by François Clouet (*c.*1510–72), Galleria degli Uffizi, Florence, Italy/Bridgeman Art Library: p. 88; Various pikes, European, 15th–16th century (iron), Wallace Collection, London, UK/Bridgeman Art Library: p. 97; *The mass of St Giles, c.*1500 (oil and egg on panel), by Master of St Giles (*fl.*1490–1510), National Gallery, London/Bridgeman Art Library: p. 130*l*; by permission of The British Library: pp. 126*r*, 132, 166; © The British

Museum: p. 55; Mary Evans Picture Library: p. 79; Hulton Getty Picture Collection: p. 121; Kupferstich-Kabinett Dresden: p. 130*r*; Musées Royaux des Beaux-Arts de Belgique: p. 17; Pierpont Morgan Library/SCALA: p. 8; Alte Pinakothek/SCALA: p. 99; Pieter Bruegel, *The ambush/ The assault*, oil on panel, signed and dated 1567, Stockholm University Art Collections, photo: Per Bergstrom: p. 118; V & A Picture Library: p. 126*l*.

The woodcut on p. 157 is from *The German single-leaf woodcut, 1550–1600: a pictorial catalogue*, vol. 1, ed. W. L. Strauss, Arbaris Books, 1975.

We have been unable to trace the source for the picture on page 163 and for the diagrams on page 103. We would be grateful for any information that would enable us to do so.

Picture research by Sandie Huskinson-Rolfe of PHOTOSEEKERS.

Contents

1

The Holy Roman Empire 1517–59

Focus questions

◆ How and why did Charles V's political relations with his German subjects change?

◆ In what ways, and with what consequences, did the German economy and society change during the period 1517–59?

◆ Why was Germany divided by the Protestant Reformation?

◆ Why, and with what results for the Holy Roman Empire, was Charles V at war for so much of his rule?

Significant dates

1517 Luther writes the Ninety-Five Theses.

1519 Charles agrees to the Capitulation of Election to win the imperial crown.

1521 Luther is excommunicated by the pope and made an outlaw by the emperor (Edict of Worms).

1522 Ferdinand becomes regent of the empire.
Charles splits the Habsburg lands with his brother Ferdinand (the Compact of Brussels).

1525 Charles defeats the French at the Battle of Pavia and captures Francis I.

1526 At the first Diet of Speyer, Ferdinand allows German princes to adopt Lutheranism.
Ferdinand becomes king of Bohemia and begins his long struggle to become king of Hungary.

1529 The Ottoman siege of Vienna fails.
In the Treaty of Cambrai, Francis I surrenders all claims to Burgundian and Italian territory.
Second Diet of Speyer: some evangelical states and cities protest against Charles's order that they enforce Catholicism (the 'Protest' or 'Protestation' of Augsburg).

1531 Evangelical princes and cities form the Schmalkaldic League.
Ferdinand is elected king of the Romans.

1533 Ferdinand starts to pay annual tribute to the sultan for his Hungarian lands.

1534	The Schmalkaldic League invades Württemberg and imposes Lutheranism.
1538	Ferdinand tries to settle the succession to the Hungarian throne in the Treaty of Oradea with János Zapolyai.
1541	The Turks occupy eastern Hungary and put János Zsigmund on the Transylvanian throne.
1542	The Schmalkaldic League invades Brunswick and imposes Lutheranism.
1543	Charles crushes the duke of Cleves.
1544	In the *alternativa*, Charles offers Burgundy or Milan as the dowry for a Habsburg–Valois marriage and a joint crusade against the Turks.
1546–47	Charles fights and wins the Schmalkaldic War.
1548	In the Interim of Augsburg, Charles demands the restoration of Catholicism across the empire.
1550–55	In the 'brothers' quarrel', Charles and Ferdinand struggle to decide the imperial succession.
1551	Ferdinand fails to conquer Transylvania.
1552	Henry II invades and takes Metz, Toul and Verdun. In the Princes' War, Maurice of Saxony leads the revived Schmalkaldic League and drives Charles out of Germany. In the Peace of Passau, Charles is forced to abandon the Augsburg Interim.
1553	Charles delegates to Ferdinand the task of reaching a religious settlement in the empire.
1555	In the Peace of Augsburg, Ferdinand gives legal status to Lutheranism in the empire.
1556	Charles V abdicates as emperor and is succeeded by Ferdinand.
1557	The French suffer major defeat at the Battle of St Quentin.
1559	The Peace of Câteau-Cambrésis ends the Habsburg–Valois Wars.

Overview

Charles V inherited a multitude of crowns. The family tree on page 3 shows how this happened. In 1506 he became duke of Burgundy at the age of 6 and, as such, ruler of the rich trading towns of the Netherlands. In 1516 he inherited the separate Spanish kingdoms of Castile, Aragon, Navarre and Naples. Three years later his paternal grandfather died, leaving him duchies and counties in central Europe that made up the extensive lands of the House of Austria. Together, these domains were an exceptional legacy, but the roll call did not end there. The grandfather who died in 1519 was Emperor Maximilian I and Charles won the election to succeed him. Between the days of Ancient Rome and Napoleon, Europe saw nothing comparable to such a political grouping. For 40 years he was the most potent ruler in **Christendom**.

Christendom is the word they used to mean the Christian world. In the Middle Ages, that meant Europe (a term almost never used).

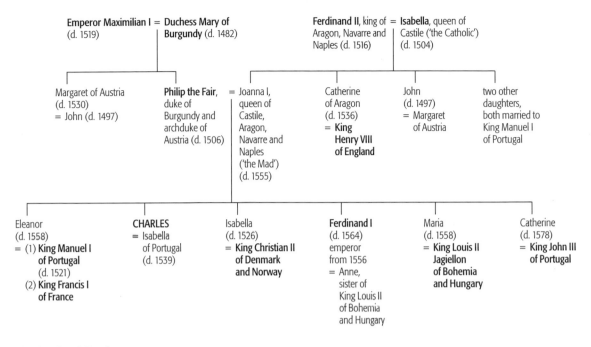

The family of Charles V.

Charles's twin-stated aims were religious: to defend the Catholic faith from the internal threat of the new Protestant heresy, and to guard Christendom from the external Islamic assault of the Ottoman Empire. Alongside both, however, Charles was ever alert to the protection of the **patrimonial** crowns and lands of his inheritance. All these goals brought him into conflict with others. His astonishing position did more than arouse envy. It raised great fears and upset the balance of power. What to the emperor looked like the hand of God seemed in France as an encircling, threatening concentration of hostile power. Most popes and many kings agreed. So too did the German princes. From their perspective, his use of the old title ***caesar invictissimus*** had sinister overtones. More than a few believed that his real ambition was to destroy their sovereign independence. While Charles always argued that he sought only peace, his enemies accused him of naked aggression.

This chapter examines the constitutional and religious politics of Germany, the economic and social condition of Germany and, finally, imperial foreign policy. Overall it seeks to assess the ambitions and priorities, the triumphs and disasters of Charles V. His prospects did not look rosy in 1519. The position of the emperor had been weakening for two hundred years. Imperial supremacy did not exist. The German princes were self-governing. Real power lay with the individual states; central authority barely existed. Charles's long absences

Patrimonial literally means 'belonging to the family'. As well as having various thrones, Charles was lord over extensive estates that were the private property of his family – see the map on page 7 for the lands of the House of Austria. These were Charles's not because he was emperor, but because he was head of the Habsburg family.

Caesar invictissimus means 'undefeated emperor'.

Philipp of Hesse
(1504–67), 'the
Magnanimous', was count
of Hesse and a leading
Protestant prince. He was
the architect of the
Schmalkaldic League
(1531) and a perpetual
advocate of co-operation
(preferably union)
between rival forms of
Protestantism (e.g. he
hosted the 1529 Colloquy
of Marburg). At the same
time, he was driven by
deep hostility to the
Habsburg family and was
always behind schemes to
undermine the emperor.
His dominant position was
undermined when Charles
V discovered he was
bigamously married.
Charles blackmailed him
to keep out of the
Schmalkaldic War and
then imprisoned him
(1547–52).
For Philipp's role in
German politics and the
Reformation, see also
pages 140 to 141.

did not help. Between 1519 and 1542 he was in Germany for less than four years. Only from 1543 did he give Germany his proper attention. That anything at all was achieved is tribute to the regent, his brother Ferdinand, who faced the determined political and religious opposition of some states, led by **Count Philipp of Hesse**. Success in German constitutional and religious politics depended on striking the balance between ruthless opportunism and pragmatic compromises. For all Charles's flashes of brilliance, Ferdinand proved more effective in such a climate. Ferdinand's achievements have not been sufficiently recognised.

General European economic changes hit Germany hard. The Baltic economy was in decline. The Spanish discovery of silver in America undermined German mining and banking. More fundamentally, Germany was unable to cope with the effects of inflation and a rising population. The real value of wages fell while prices rocketed. Rural poverty and unemployment grew worse. Many peasants flocked to the towns, but the influx was beyond their resources. Peasant grievances were very real. Their lords, themselves seeking to survive tough times, tightened the screw in every way they could. East of the River Elbe, they did this by reviving serfdom, tying their peasants to the land and making them little better than slaves. West of the river, they raised rents and seized common land. Most of these problems crystallised in the 1524–26 Peasants' War. But these uprisings were more than simple clashes of poor peasants and rich lords. To a significant degree, the war involved prosperous peasants fighting off both the swarms of poor peasants and the greedy fingers of poor lords. Sections of the German peasantry showed a sophisticated self-confidence and an astute awareness of the need to gain access to new sources of wealth.

Habsburg war in Italy and the Mediterranean is dealt with in Chapter 2. Here, imperial conflicts over Burgundy and Hungary are examined. The first was the continuation of a 50-year-old dynastic dispute with the Valois kings of France over who was the rightful duke of Burgundy and lord of its rich territories. The first breakthrough came in 1529 when, after a string of defeats, Francis I agreed that Artois and Flanders should be transferred to the empire. The French continued to plague Charles along the imperial frontier – most critically in 1552 when Henry II seized control of Lorraine (see the map on page 29). Twice Charles attempted to solve the feud by proposing a marriage between the warring families, to which the Burgundian lands held by each side would be given as dowry to the princely couple. But France rejected such schemes and eventually lost nearly everything after crushing defeats by the Spanish in 1557–58. When Charles abdicated, he had Burgundy (and Milan) transferred to Spain. Spain, not the old Holy Roman Empire, would be the new superpower of Europe.

In Hungary, Ferdinand faced an uphill struggle to establish his kingship. Hungarians rejected him and, to keep their state intact as much as to prevent a German takeover, preferred Ottoman to Habsburg rule. Ferdinand never had the resources to drive out János Zapolyai, his rival for the throne, who was recognised by both the Hungarian nobility and the sultan in Constantinople. Ferdinand only ever ruled the western edge of Hungary. Its heavily fortified frontier kept the Turks out, but *neither* side could advance. Militarily, the war was frozen in stalemate. Politically, however, the Ottomans always held the upper hand – an unpleasant fact recognised by Ferdinand from 1533 when he began to pay annual tribute to the sultan as his overlord.

How and why did Charles V's political relations with his German subjects change?

1519	Capitulation of Election.
1522	Compact of Brussels.
1526	First Diet of Speyer.
1531	Formation of the Schmalkaldic League. Ferdinand elected king of the Romans.
1534	Dissolution of the Swabian League. Schmalkaldic League invades Württemberg.
1541	The Recess of Regensburg.
1546–47	Schmalkaldic War.
1548	Failure of Charles's scheme for imperial leagues.
1550–55	The 'brothers' quarrel'.
1555	Peace of Augsburg.

Nowhere else in Europe could match the complexity of the political jigsaw that was the Holy Roman Empire. Stretching from the Baltic to Tuscany, and from Brussels to Vienna, the empire was a maze of about four hundred self-governing states gathered in a loose federation.

Emperors did not inherit their crown but were **elected** to it. Under the Emperor Charles IV's Golden Bull of 1356, **seven princes** were responsible for electing each emperor. The Bull also gave each electoral prince sovereign independence in the government of his state and immunity from the emperor's jurisdiction. Over the next 150 years that same autonomy was granted to (or taken by) the other territorial princes. They too became sovereign inside their borders. There was no central imperial government, treasury or army. While a small inner council of advisers was introduced in 1527, the institutions that did exist were designed to strengthen the federal constitution and bind the

The kings of Bohemia, Hungary and Poland were also **elected** (as were the popes).

The **seven princes**, given the title 'elector', were: the king of Bohemia, the duke of Saxony, the margrave of Brandenburg, the count palatine of the Rhine and the archbishops of Cologne, Mainz and Trier. Only a simple majority was required.

Technically, Charles was only elected king of the Romans in 1519, making him emperor designate. Coronation by the pope alone would make him **emperor**. That ceremony took place in 1530.

Summarise the power and position of the emperor.

The **diet** was the parliament of the empire.

The **Swabian League** was an association of the states of south-west Germany. It could put more than 12,000 troops into the field.

As head of the House of **Habsburg** (or Austria), Charles was archduke of Austria, duke of Styria, count of Görz and count of the Tyrol. As duke of Burgundy, he was also duke of Brabant, duke of Limburg, duke of Luxembourg, count of Flanders, count of Hainault, count of Holland, count of Namur, count of Zeeland, count of Zutphen and lord of Friesland.

emperor to the states. This was the political reality Charles faced. Indeed, to secure election Charles had, in an agreement known as the Capitulation of Election, to promise to uphold the rights of the states.

With Charles V there seems to be a great paradox: the power he actually wielded never came close to matching the total resources available to him. But by looking at the situation in that way we misunderstand his position. In any modern sense, Charles never ruled a great empire – its component parts like Burgundy and Aragon were too separate and his powers as sovereign over them too varied. Within the Holy Roman Empire itself he reigned but did not rule. 'Germany' did not exist politically. In place of one country there were four hundred, and the religious divisions of the Reformation increased the fragmentation. Whereas in France or England historians point to developing political integration at a national level, creating what we now call 'nation states', scholars of the empire highlight growing political strength at the local level. The 'state-building' that historians describe was going on in Germany too but, whereas elsewhere kings were busy subjugating their nobles, in Germany it was the individual great magnates who were setting up professional bureaucracies and the other ingredients needed for their own state. In Germany local divisions became stronger. In Germany the nation state was not established.

The Holy Roman Empire might be less than the sum of its parts, but Charles was not powerless. As emperor he was supreme judge, and disputes involving princes and nobles gave him considerable influence. Although the Imperial Chamber Court was supposed to limit the emperor, Charles turned it about and with great skill used it against the princes. As emperor he also presided over the **diet**, controlling the agenda and holding a veto. Furthermore, he was never without allies among the states. The princes were unable to present a united bloc. Princely feuds were often bitter; some ended in war. There were always states only too keen to shelter under imperial protection. So aggressive was the duke of Württemberg that the neighbouring **Swabian League** expelled him in 1519 and sold his state to the emperor. Charles was expert at exploiting opportunities such as disputes within a princely family. And Charles was himself the single most powerful territorial prince. The **Habsburgs** had vast territories in Austria and the southern Netherlands (see the map on page 7). To these Charles added Milan and much of what is now the northern Netherlands, while his brother secured Bohemia and a fragment of Hungary. Charles might be weak in Germany, but the empire was larger than Germany. As head of the House of Austria, he dominated the non-German parts of the empire.

Charles took imperial government to a level not seen for centuries. His difficulties with princes and diets over Reformation disputes must not blind us

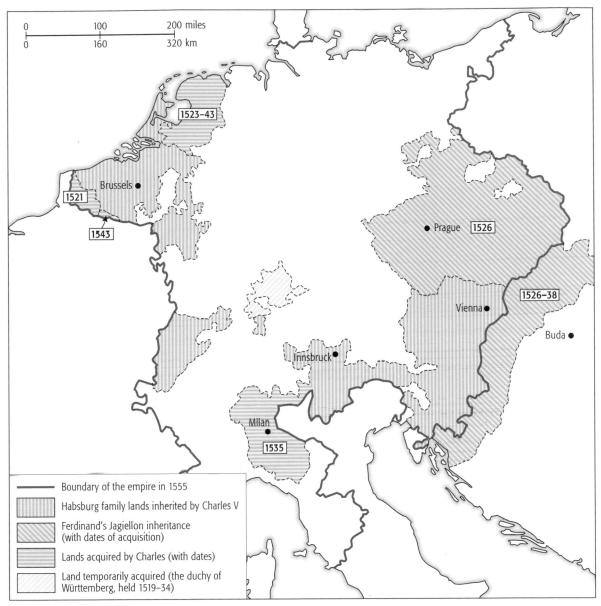

100   200 miles
0   160   320 km

1523–43

1521
Brussels ●
1543

1526
● Prague

1526–38
Vienna ●
Buda ●

Innsbruck ●

Milan
●
1535

Boundary of the empire in 1555

Habsburg family lands inherited by Charles V

Ferdinand's Jagiellon inheritance
(with dates of acquisition)

Lands acquired by Charles (with dates)

Land temporarily acquired (the duchy of
Württemberg, held 1519–34)

The patrimonial lands of the Habsburgs.

to his effectiveness in other areas. At his first diet (Worms, 1521), for example, the states were outflanked over arrangements for the regency to cover imperial government during Charles's forthcoming absence in Spain. Charles won the right to name his regent and ensured that every member of the regency council swore an oath, not to the diet or their state, but to the emperor. Given his own need for a regency, the bargain struck was distinctly advantageous. Charles pulled off another master stroke. How could his family's interests best

The meeting of Charles V and Ferdinand, by Hans Daucher, *c.*1527. How amicable were relations between these Habsburg brothers?

Assess the importance of the Compact of Brussels.

John 'the Constant', elector of Saxony
1525–32. Unlike the previous elector (his brother Frederick 'the Wise'), John explicitly supported Lutheranism. In imperial politics, however, he was more cautious than his ally the count of Hesse in opposing Charles V.

be protected in his absence? Charles's solution was radical and ingenious. He had already appointed his brother as regent. In the Compact of Brussels (1522) he abdicated from the Habsburg patrimonial states and transferred them to Ferdinand. Nine years later, Charles reinforced Habsburg interests and his brother's authority by securing his election as king of the Romans (thereby guaranteeing Ferdinand's future succession to the imperial crown without a contest). The significance of the compact is easily missed. It strengthened the regency, prevented a political vacuum (from which only the states could benefit) and protected the Habsburgs' position. The price Charles paid for that stability was, however, high. He was not yet married but any future son of his had been disinherited before birth – which explains the way in which he later divided his crowns on his abdication.

During Ferdinand's first regency (1521–30), he sustained the momentum of advancing imperial authority until about 1526. To a large extent, he did this by maintaining close links with the Swabian League. Twice he used it to keep the peace, crushing the rebellious imperial knights (1522–23) and the Peasants' War (1524–26). Some began to suspect that he aimed to use the Swabians to govern alone. Ironically, they had let him become powerful. During 1521–24 the princes were amazingly careless. Sustained pressure could have turned the tables, but they rarely bothered to attend his council and, by default, threw away their opportunity. From c.1526, however, Ferdinand's fortunes changed. The imperial knights had once given the emperor considerable influence across south-west Germany, so their destruction removed a valuable arm of imperial authority; when from 1531 the crown wanted to strike against the Schmalkaldic League, the crown lamented the loss of the most obvious weapon. Then there was the very success of the Swabian League. This alarmed the princes. Finally, the public adoption of the **evangelical** cause by seven princes during 1524–26 created a bloc opposed to a core part of imperial policy; Philipp of Hesse led the way.

Imperial cities too were abandoning Catholicism and, as the number of states supporting the Reformation grew, traditional political relationships were rearranged. The Swabian League was neutralised by the defection of Strasbourg; by 1534 religion had shattered the once great league. Around the same time, Ferdinand encountered obstruction at the Diet of Speyer (1526). Philipp of Hesse and **Elector John of Saxony** (see note on page 8) showed what was to come by forming an evangelical alliance which, together with every imperial city present, refused to implement the 1521 Edict of Worms declaring Luther an outlaw. The regent had no choice but in the **Recess** to let each state decide its own policy on the matter 'as they hope and trust to answer to God and his Imperial Majesty'. Three years later, the Protestant states, still a minority, went further and repudiated Ferdinand's decree at the end of the second Diet of Speyer, abolishing the freedom granted at the first. The year 1531 saw the inevitable outcome of such divisions – a military alliance, the Schmalkaldic League, to defend the Reformation. The Protestant princes and cities had formed a separate corporate identity within the empire, whose basis was not a state's obedience to the emperor but its duty to conscience.

Was Ferdinand helpless before such developments? He understood that events were spiralling out of control and from 1525 urged Charles repeatedly to quit Spain and in person stamp his authority on the unruly Germans. Regularly the emperor replied that shortly he would return, yet he did not do so. Simultaneously, Charles failed to give any strategic advice while inhibiting his brother from developing clear priorities of his own. In these critical years, Charles sacrificed the needs of Germany to the interests of Castile and the conquest of Milan. As for Ferdinand, he was preoccupied with his accession to the thrones of Hungary and Bohemia and with the ominous Ottoman advance. The empire looked east as well as west and south. Maximilian I had negotiated a double dynastic marriage with the **Hungarians**; Ferdinand was one of the bridegrooms. In 1526, the Turks smashed the Hungarian state at the Battle of Mohács. King Louis was killed and, as he was childless,

Why did the imperial position weaken between 1526 and 1529?

Evangelical was the original descriptive label used by the reformers and their early followers. The word 'Protestant' was not invented until 1529 (see next marginal note).

Legislation needed the consent of the states and the emperor. At the end of a diet, laws agreed were published in their joint names in a decree called the **Recess**. The refusal by 6 princes and 14 cities in 1529 to enforce the 1521 Edict of Worms and abandon the 1526 Recess was called the 'protest' or 'protestation'. From that title the term 'Protestant' was developed. The word in its Latin original carried none of the negative undertones of the modern word 'protest'. Rather, it meant 'to bear witness' by a declaration of positive belief.

Maximilian hoped to bring **Hungary** and Bohemia back under Habsburg rule. Under the 1515 Treaty of Vienna, two of the emperor's grandchildren, Ferdinand and his sister Maria, respectively married King Wladislaw's daughter Anne and her brother Louis (he became King Louis II Jagiellon of Hungary in 1516).

How justified were the fears of the princes?

Ferdinand won by 6 to1. Charles bribed the electors and only the Lutheran elector of Saxony voted against (as king of Bohemia, Ferdinand could vote for himself). Since Maximilian I had repeatedly failed to secure Charles's election to the kingship, Ferdinand's election was a Habsburg triumph for, as king of the Romans, he was assured of succession as emperor. He had only recently become king of Hungary and Bohemia (with which came the dukedoms of Silesia and Croatia, and the margravates of Lusatia and Moravia). For the Habsburg patrimony, 1526–31 seemed miraculous years.

'The Württemberg campaign was Philipp's most significant stroke against the Habsburgs ... [because] it deprived them of the territory they needed to bridge their Austrian and Burgundian lands.' (Hans Hillerbrand, *Landgrave Philipp of Hesse 1504–67*, 1967)

Ferdinand put himself forward as heir. In 1529, Ferdinand himself had to face the Turks when they crossed the frontier and besieged Vienna. At the very time the regent needed to face down defiant **German** princes, he found himself in need of their assistance (financial and military) to drive back the infidel.

Charles finally returned in 1530 and the diet was summoned to Augsburg. Nothing went to plan. With Vienna just saved, the emperor wanted to advance and liberate Ferdinand's Hungarian kingdom. The states would have none of it, insisting the Protestant problem was more urgent. Given the recent breakdown in imperial government, surely the states were right? As Charles discovered that 'words and negotiations get us nowhere', he decided 'only a strong fist will bring results'. Yet he could not impose that either. Although a majority of the diet was Catholic, it opposed any use of force because the prime casualty of imperial victory must be princely independence. Thus although the 1530 Recess threatened stern action, none was possible. Divided in religion, the states remained united in common defence of their sovereignty. Behind Charles's emphasis on duty to God and the evil of heresy, they feared his constitutional ambitions.

From 1532 to 1543, Charles was never in Germany. Before he left, he obtained **Ferdinand's long-promised election** as king of the Romans. That election, however, alienated three influential princes. Philipp of Hesse and the new Saxon elector John Frederick were Protestants, but religion was not the issue for Duke William of Bavaria, a Catholic. All three were stout opponents of the Habsburg family and objected to what they saw as a blatant perversion of the Golden Bull, designed (they believed) to make the imperial crown the hereditary possession of the House of Austria. To make matters worse, ten princes and ten imperial cities reacted to the 1530 Recess by forming a defensive Lutheran military federation, the Schmalkaldic League. That league was always more than a German religious coalition. The Bavarian duke allied himself almost immediately. Henry VIII of England and Francis I of France established links in 1535–37, while Christian III of Denmark joined in 1538. Around the Schmalkaldic League gathered the political opponents of Charles V. Its power was demonstrated in 1534 when, organised by that most anti-Habsburg of princes, the count of Hesse (and funded by that most anti-Habsburg of kings, Francis I), the league invaded the duchy of Württemberg, overthrew the puppet imperial government and introduced Lutheranism. Paralysed by Turkish war in Hungary, Ferdinand had no choice but to accept this. Imperial power had lost its one pillar in southern Germany while Philipp of Hesse had struck **an incisive blow** for the rights of territorial princes. Within Germany, imperial authority never faced a more resolute enemy than Count Philipp.

Exploiting Charles's absence and Ferdinand's dependence on them to fund Hungarian campaigns, the princes pushed Ferdinand into accepting the so-called 'Standstill' of 1532 (suspending the 1529 and 1530 Recesses), into confirming it in 1539 and finally into granting broad toleration of Lutheranism in the Recess of the 1541 Diet of Regensburg. Ferdinand was even induced to suspend the Imperial Chamber Court (1543). These were golden years for princely power. The diet was permanently divided. The empire had an organised opposition. The emperor could no longer turn to the imperial knights or the Swabian League; both had been destroyed by Protestantism. Religion had become a corrosive force, but the march of events was about imperial politics too. With a foot in both camps, the Bavarian duke stirred his fellow Catholics to distinguish between the interests of their religion and the personal advantage of the Habsburg emperor. Outside Austria, imperial power was weaker than at any moment since 1519.

What inspired the strength of princely power during the years 1531–43?

In and among such endless difficulties, Ferdinand and Charles did find the opportunity to create, with princely approval, a committee system for the diet and a common criminal legal code (the *Carolina*, 1532). Imperial government had not collapsed, but the frustrations were enormous and the idea of war against the princes grew in Charles's mind. But when would he be free to follow it through? Peace with Denmark (1543) and France (1544) finally offered him the chance. Pope Paul III offered him money and papal troops (1545). Yet he did not go to war until July 1546. Why? The answer presumably lies in the timing. Habsburg influence in south-west Germany had already collapsed. Now Charles faced the same in the north-west. For 80 years the Habsburgs and the counts of Hesse had been rivals for dominance in the region. Hessian policy had already secured control over a string of bishoprics in Westphalia. In 1542, **Count** Philipp of Hesse had used the Schmalkaldic League to oust the emperor's prime local ally, the duke of Brunswick-Wolfenbüttel. Each of these factors harmed Habsburg interests, but none compared to the disaster that loomed when in 1546 Elector Frederick II, count palatine of the Rhine, became a Lutheran and joined the league. The onward march of heresy alarmed Charles, but his mind was exercised by two other factors: the rise of the overmighty House of Hesse and the revolution that had silently taken place in the imperial electoral college. Four of the seven electors were now Protestant so the next election would presumably produce a Protestant emperor – which would rule out a Habsburg. Would the college honour its choice in 1531 of Ferdinand as king of the Romans? In 1546, Charles V faced a dynastic crisis of the first magnitude.

Luther said that 'when the **count** burns, nothing can stop him'. William Wright argues that Philipp, as 'the lay defender of protestantism', was the 'lay counterpart to Luther'. (*Philipp of Hesse*, 1996)

Use the events of 1543–46 to work out Charles's priorities. What do these tell us about the emperor?

Imperial politics and the interests of the Habsburg family were (at least) as important as religion in taking the emperor to war. Once the decision was made, Charles began to exploit weak spots among his opponents and with typical skill detached four main players from the league: Duke Maurice of Saxony, Philipp of Hesse, the elector of Brandenburg and the duke of Brandenburg-Kulmbach. The Brandenburgers had always tried to keep a political foot in both camps, commitments to Lutheranism notwithstanding. The cases of the Hessian count and the Saxon duke, however, illuminate Habsburg tactics. Charles had discovered that Philipp was bigamously married (a capital offence). Under threat of execution and the confiscation of his lands, the emperor forced the count to remain neutral. As for Maurice, he offered a prize that could not be resisted. Ever since Saxony was split in 1485, the **two duchies** (ruled by different branches of the House of Wettin) had been rivals. The rivalry was exaggerated further during 1517–39 when electoral Saxony supported Luther while ducal Saxony continued Catholic, the conversion of Maurice's father to Protestantism making little difference. Maurice himself had shown a marked ability to juggle Protestant commitment with friendly imperial relations; he was another German prince with interests crossing the Reformation divide. Married to a daughter of Philipp of Hesse, he had none the less opposed the Schmalkaldic invasion of Brunswick. His major involvement with Ferdinand at the battlefront in Hungary made him well known in the imperial party. Charles used those complex relationships to secure Maurice's neutrality. Then, playing on Wettin jealousies, the duke was enticed to fight on the emperor's side in exchange for his cousin's electoral title. The ruthless neutralising of Count Philipp and the audacious seduction of Duke Maurice must be the finest examples of Charles V's remarkable ability to keep some control in Germany.

Victory in the Schmalkaldic War (1546–47) went to the emperor. Philipp of Hesse was imprisoned. Charles appeared (and felt) invincible. The war, however, proved counter-productive. The scale of Charles's success alarmed the princes. He wasted no time, restructuring the Imperial Chamber Court so that religious cases had to be tried by the emperor's judges, and forcing new constitutions on imperial cities so the majority of their councillors were Catholics. At the Diet of Augsburg (1547–48), he proposed major changes to the constitution by establishing imperial leagues linking all the states into a series of 'circles', each with its own diet, taxes and army (under the direct command of the emperor). Hitherto, leagues had symbolised imperial weakness. This scheme would have turned the tables so, regardless of religious position, the states would have none of it. Led, significantly, by the duke of Bavaria, they saw only a devious **scheme** to undermine their autonomy. For eight months the princes resisted every proposal. By March 1548 Charles's bid to strengthen his position was defeated.

The hollowness of victory in the Schmalkaldic War became even clearer in 1550–52 as Maurice of Saxony and the emperor drifted apart. Ever bold, the

The split of 1485 created **two duchies** of Saxony, often called 'Ernestine' and 'Albertine' Saxony. The ruler of Albertine Saxony was also one of the imperial electors, so his state is also referred to as 'electoral' Saxony. See page 136 and the map on page 137.

Why was Philipp of Hesse so important to German politics during the 1530s and 1540s?

Charles's parallel religious **scheme** (the Interim) fared little better (see below on pages 24–25). The princes were deeply suspicious of the involvement of Austria and Burgundy (both Habsburg states) in the new circles.

elector negotiated his way back into the Protestant camp and by 1551, aged only 30, he was their leader, constructing an alliance with Henry II of France. New war was ruled out by Charles's chronic financial position. He failed to revive the Swabian League and could not even put together an alliance of Catholic dukes and bishops. Meanwhile, **Maurice** was forging a renewed friendship with Ferdinand. Who knows where this might have led, had the elector not been killed in 1553? With Charles increasingly crippled by gout and a dark depression created by his self-torturing conviction of his many 'failures', Ferdinand became the political focus. Very much a realist who was only too aware of the political and religious stalemate, he began to put together a definitive settlement that also involved his own personal interest. About 1547, Ferdinand became aware that his brother was having second thoughts about the imperial succession. Charles regretted the decision made a quarter of a century before which now disinherited his own son Philip. By 1550 Ferdinand and Charles were in direct dispute. For five years the 'brothers' quarrel' disturbed imperial politics. Both agreed a pact, the **Augsburg Agreement** (1551), but this did little to take the heat out of the feud. Its ingenious plan for an alternating sequence of Austrian and Spanish Habsburg emperors was never liked by either side. In 1552 Ferdinand blocked his nephew Philip's election alongside him as 'coadjutor' king of the Romans. Matters were only resolved when Charles came to accept that his territories must be split. In 1555, therefore, Philip renounced all claim to be king of the Romans. Within Germany, the cost of the 'brothers' quarrel' had been high for, as Charles and Ferdinand campaigned for princely support, the House of Habsburg submitted itself to manipulation as never before. All disliked Philip as too Spanish and the Augsburg Agreement because it made the electors puppets of the emperor. But all could see the advantage of not endorsing Ferdinand too quickly.

Once the crippled emperor retired from active politics in 1554, he delegated authority to Ferdinand to determine the German problem. The issues behind the negotiations leading to the 1555 **Peace of Augsburg** were wider than Ferdinand's need for aid against renewed Ottoman threat. He was also making a bid to unite the imperial crown and the thrones of Bohemia and Hungary with the patrimonial lands of the House of Austria into what historians term the 'Danubian monarchy'. The famous peace with its legendary compromise – the constitutional acceptance that each ruler could choose whether his state would be Catholic or Lutheran – was the price Ferdinand was willing to pay to win the 'brothers' quarrel' and secure his own dynasty.

'**Maurice** achieved success because, more than anyone else, he understood the need to divorce political decisions from religion.' (Günther Wartenberg, *Moritz von Sachsen*, 1994)

The **Augsburg Agreement** provided that (a) Ferdinand would succeed as emperor, but then (b) would secure the election of Philip as king of the Romans, who then (c) on succession as emperor would arrange the election of Ferdinand's son Maximilian as king of the Romans, and so on:

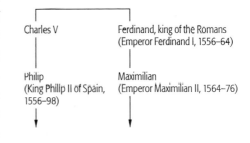

Charles V

Philip (King Phillip II of Spain, 1556–98)

Ferdinand, king of the Romans (Emperor Ferdinand I, 1556–64)

Maximilian (Emperor Maximilian II, 1564–76)

How did the 'brothers' quarrel' affect the balance of power within the empire?

For details of the **Peace of Augsburg**, see pages 26 to 27. 'The Peace rebalanced Germany after the turmoil of 1546–53, recognising the supremacy of the imperial constitution while writing into it the primacy of the states.' (Jean Berenger, *A history of the Habsburg Empire 1273–1700*, 1994)

In what ways, and with what consequences, did the German economy and society change during the period 1517–59?

At first sight, the German economy seems to have flourished from *c.*1460 to *c.*1540. Textile production, manufacturing and mining were vigorous. Natural resources were exploited as never before. Trade was booming all along the Rhine, the Danube and Germany's lesser rivers. The population was expanding and consumer demand with it. Towns saw spectacular expansion. In fact, general European economic changes had already inflicted damaging blows before 1500. The once matchless **Hanseatic League**, at the height of its power in the fifteenth century, was losing its market share of international trade in the Baltic and across northern Europe to Flemish, English and Swedish merchants, and its control of Baltic shipping to the Dutch (80 per cent of the grain sold in Amsterdam in the 1540s had been bought in the market at Danzig). The lack of a native German merchant fleet was a serious weakness and put Germany at a major disadvantage. Added to those commercial problems, north German dependence on large-scale herring fishing in the Baltic was almost destroyed when, for whatever natural cause, the summer herring shoals vanished in 1473. Once so powerful, the Baltic economy was in decline, its strength undermined yet further (and ever faster) by the rise of the so-called 'Atlantic economy' based on Antwerp and Seville.

One major exception was metallurgy. Silver was mined in the Hartz mountains and Saxony, as well as the Tyrol, Carinthia and Bohemia. Together, these supplied most of the bullion produced in Europe; in the period 1460–1530 production increased fivefold. Copper, lead and zinc came from the same areas, while iron ore mining was developing well in the Rhineland, Thuringia and the Upper Palatinate. Mining employed a total of 100,000 Germans in 1523. Productivity improved significantly as technical developments to pumps made deep mining possible, and improvements in the chemical processing of ores led to higher yields from mined rock. But external catastrophe struck with the Spanish discovery of vast silver deposits in America in 1545–48. This instantaneously undercut the European supply. German mines could not compete and from the 1550s silver imports from America outpaced European production. German mining fell into a long slump. In turn, that hit badly German banking houses such as the Fuggers and Welsers in Augsburg. The fifteenth-century expansion in silver mining had enabled German banking to develop and challenge the late-medieval Italian near monopoly in financial services. From *c.*1550, German banking was much weaker.

Population estimates put Germany at *c.*12 million people in 1500 and *c.*15 million in 1550. Growth was especially strong in the west and the south.

The **Hanseatic League** was an organisation of primarily Baltic trading towns (either ports or market centres on major overland trade routes). Led by Brunswick, Hamburg, Lübeck, Danzig, Riga and Reval, originally more than 120 towns were members. By 1557 the total had shrunk to 63.

Assess the impact of external forces on the German economy.

Complaints were frequently heard that 'Germany is overcrowded'. Almost all of Europe saw a rising population from *c*.1450 and the conviction that there was intolerable overcrowding was common. In fact, Germany lagged behind the most dynamic parts of Europe (the populations of England and the Netherlands grew by 50 per cent over the same period, the Scandinavian countries by 66 per cent). Some urban growth was spectacular. Manufacturing and trading centres in central and southern Germany flourished; Augsburg, Danzig and Munich, booming on the production of cheap textiles, are good examples. The mining towns of Saxony also saw rapid expansion. Yet German urban growth was limited – there were 19 towns with populations of over 10,000 people in 1500, and only 20 in 1600 (whereas in France the number rose from 32 to 44); more than 2,800 of Germany's 3,000 towns had fewer than 1,000 inhabitants in 1550. The same applied to rural Germany and all of central Europe, for reasons not understood by historians. Population growth was, however, the most significant fact about sixteenth-century Europe, and it occurred against a backdrop of major war, regular epidemics and all too frequent famine. Urban expansion reflected hardship in the countryside, but urban expansion caused social and political unrest. Housing could not cope and there was significant expansion of both suburbs and slums. There were not enough jobs. Begging and crime rose. There was a noticeable increase in **anti-Semitism**.

Against this **anti-Semitism**, Charles V confirmed and reinforced the legal status and privileges of the Empire's Jewish population at the diets of 1530, 1544 and 1546.

Sixteenth-century Europe was overwhelmingly rural. In 1500 about 75 per cent of the population of Europe lived in villages and worked in agriculture. Population pressures here caused 'land hunger'. In some parts of Germany it was possible to clear forest or plough mountain pasture, but opportunities to create new, high-quality farmland were limited. Many areas had no option but to subdivide existing farms and tenancies. Such action meant, however, lower yields and smaller incomes. No wonder then that many peasants left their villages, drawn to towns by dreams of a better tomorrow. Between 50 per cent and 80 per cent of early-sixteenth-century German peasants lived in one village for at most 10 to 20 years. Even if (as in most cases) they then travelled less than 20 miles, there were enormous numbers on the move at any moment. The towns could not cope with the flood of migrants, especially those with no craft skills. The towns suffered a disproportionate increase in the number of their poor. Augsburg in 1560 had doubled its population since 1490, but it had three times as many beggars.

Why did population growth cause problems for German towns?

Historians are careful to distinguish between those permanently poor (the 'structural poor') and those pushed temporarily into poverty (the 'occasional poor'). It was the latter that caused sixteenth-century authorities such anxiety; their numbers were so unpredictable, their appearance so sudden. They were regarded as a social danger, as carriers of disease and as criminals. By 1530

Germany in half and meant that both systems operated within the empire. Historians are uncertain how to explain this remarkable difference, but suspect that the primary answer lies in the much thinner populations east of the river. Labour there was in short supply so it was that, rather than money, which lords needed the most.

Whichever side of the Elbe, all such changes were deeply disturbing to the peasantry and, on top of falling real wages and rising prices, put them under growing strain. In the struggle to live, much peasant land had to be sold; on average, the proportion of land in German states owned by peasants fell from one-third in 1500 to one-sixth by 1550. In consequence, the number of peasants no longer self-sufficient in grain shot up, leaving them at the mercy of fluctuating market prices for basic food – guaranteeing yet higher rates of peasant debt and starvation. One consequence was peasant revolt. Peasant resistance became part of German politics. There were 18 significant revolts between 1500 and 1524, all of which used as their banner the **Bundschuh**. These tensions became crystal clear in 1524–26 with the uprisings known as the 'Peasants' War'. It is vital to understand their fragmentary character. The war was never one movement with one manifesto and one leader. In the beginning the uprisings were not even armed, but rather demonstrations and strikes. The complex story of risings is not relevant here, neither in themselves are the religious demands that some made, although any modern division between the secular and the **religious** is meaningless. One highly distinctive feature must, however, be noted. In some uprisings, notably those in Alsace and the Upper Rhineland, demands for social justice were seen by the peasants as part of the Christian gospel. Obedience to the laws of God required disobedience to earthly rulers who broke divine laws by enslaving God's children and stealing the riches of the earth for themselves. Religious principles were used to justify the peasants' grievances and provide the blueprints for the reforms needed. That was not merely radical. It was revolutionary.

Any clear pattern is hard to detect. There was only one rising east of the Elbe (in Samland, East Prussia), yet opposition to developing serfdom was an issue in Swabia and the Black Forest. The absence of serfdom in Bavaria would seem to explain why that duchy was untouched, but Franconia and Thuringia, where serfdom was equally absent, were badly affected. What is striking is that *Bundschuh* were often led by prosperous peasants and skilled craftsmen, and many spent a lot of time attacking landless peasants. The manifestos of such groups were designed to appeal to comfortably off farmers and artisans anxious to preserve the sources of their prosperity from the hordes of the unskilled poor (as much as from the encroachments of their lords). Peasant demands even show self-confident **peasants** trying to gain access to new sources of wealth in forests and rivers. To a significant degree,

A *Bundschuh* was a laced peasant boot and, for reasons still unclear, was the symbol adopted in the fifteenth and sixteenth centuries to represent peasant resistance.

For discussion of the **religious** dimension of the war, see pages 147 to 151. 'Once the Twelve Articles had set out the idea that the word of God in the Bible (God's law) should serve as a guide for judging the justice of many social and economic practices, a powerful link had been forged that made peasant rebellion a potential revolution.' (Peter Blickle, *Die Revolution von 1525*, 1993).

'There is a possible correlation between the outbreak of the revolt and areas of advanced economic activity. The **Peasants'** War should not be seen as a revolt of backward rural areas against economic progress.' (Richard Bonney, *The European dynastic states 1494–1660*, 1991)

some *Bundschuh* were conflicts between prosperous peasants and impoverished lords for control of the same resources.

One manifesto stands out: the Twelve Articles of Memmingen, which sold *c.*25,000 printed copies in the spring of 1525. Parts involved attacks on the clergy and were overtly Protestant (although the preamble denied any link with Protestantism), but much of what the articles demanded concerned traditional local peasant rights and labour services. Lords were reviving (or inventing) medieval rules restricting or banning access to forests for hunting and rivers for fishing. They were also invading common land and denying its use to everyone else. Economic resources for centuries available to all in the **community** were under threat. Universally, the peasants demanded a return to the 'old law and customs'.

Bundschuh were crushed mercilessly; about 75,000 peasants were killed. Most peasants lost the gains in economic position and legal status that their ancestors had won in the century and a half of labour shortages that followed the Black Death (1347–54). But some gains were made and some concessions won, most notably reductions in labour services in Swabia and the Tyrol. Of longer-term significance, fear of renewed rebellion moderated nobles' behaviour for several generations. Equally, many rural communities did not abandon collective action. Especially in south-west Germany, villages had understood that their lords depended on the law for what they were attempting. So, peasant communities funded appeals to the Imperial Chamber Court to fight their lords with the law. Hired lawyers became the (often successful) champions of peasant rights. In the words of Bob Scribner, 'the peasants were certainly not cowed in defeat'.

'The notion of **community** was central to everything. The peasants called for community ownership of woods, waters and meadows . . . [and] village self-government.' (Michael Hughes, *Early modern Germany 1477–1806*, 1992)

Why was Germany divided by the Protestant Reformation?

1521	Edict of Worms declares Luther an outlaw.
1526	First Diet of Speyer.
1529	Second Diet of Speyer; the Protest. Colloquy of Marburg.
1530	Diet of Augsburg.
1531	Schmalkaldic League formed.
1534	Schmalkaldic invasion of Württemberg.
1536	Wittenberg Concord.
1542	Schmalkaldic invasion of Brunswick.
1546–47	Schmalkaldic War.
1552	Princes' War; Peace of Passau.
1555	Peace of Augsburg.

This section focuses on the political impact of the Lutheran Reformation in Germany. Before you study it, read pages 123 to 137 for an explanation of the main religious teachings of Martin Luther and an analysis of the authorities' reactions to them from 1517 to 1521. Pages 137 to 156 then go on to consider their religious impact on Germany between 1517 and 1530.

The Reformation became the issue dominating German politics. Perpetually, it disrupted imperial plans. Every diet was taken up with threats and compromises as the Reformation ruptured the political framework of the empire. Exaggerating old rivalries and encouraging new feuds, it divided emperor from princes, cities from princes and princes from princes.

The German Reformation was sparked off at the end of October 1517 when Martin Luther, a friar and a professor of biblical theology at Wittenberg University, criticised both corrupt practices in the way indulgences were offered to the people and also distorted teaching about their effectiveness in the process of obtaining the forgiveness of sin and a place in heaven. Luther's attempt to correct a contemporary abuse was not welcomed and he himself became the object of attack. Forced into a corner by the religious authorities, he had little choice but to broaden the thrust of his complaints to include other aspects of church life. Most important of all, in 1519 he was pushed into denying the absolute authority of the pope. Compromise proved impossible and in 1521 he was expelled from the Catholic church and condemned to eternal punishment in hell when Pope Leo X excommunicated him. Simultaneously, Rome persuaded Charles V to declare Luther an outlaw (the Edict of Worms). That should have been the end of the matter. Luther should have been arrested and executed. But he had won too many powerful supporters.

Hopes that Luther's excommunication and the edict would be universally enforced were killed off in 1524 at the Diet of Nuremberg when the states declared themselves able to act 'in so far as they recognise themselves as bound to it'. How could that be when, by that time, just 4 princes and 15 imperial cities had committed themselves to the Protestant cause? Indeed, every diet during Charles V's reign contained a Catholic majority. On every occasion, most opponents of the Catholic emperor's religious policy were fellow Catholics. What was going on? Whatever many thought of Luther, most were united by longstanding concerns over church abuses. Every diet from 1456 compiled lists of grievances, known as **gravamina**, detailing failings in the clergy and calling for church reform. Whatever people thought of Luther's theology, he was seen across Germany as a reformer of abuses. To bear down on Luther before those reforms had been achieved would be (and would be seen to be) condoning the status quo.

Strength of feeling on the *gravamina* combined with suspicion of imperial intentions. Whatever Charles's actual view of the constitutional balance between himself and the states, most princes were convinced that he wanted to centralise power. Further, they presumed that the Reformation issue was being used to further that political end. Religious uniformity was a pretext. The emperor aimed to undermine princely sovereignty. None championed that view more forcefully than the count of Hesse. No German ruler was more

'*Gravamina* nourished anti-Roman and anticlerical feelings . . . The smouldering resentments they reflected and encouraged offered a fertile soil in which protestantism flourished in Germany.' (Gerald Strauss, *Nuremberg in the sixteenth century*, 1966)

anti-Habsburg than Philipp of Hesse, but his misgivings were widely shared and, together with the *gravamina*, created a bloc able to obstruct every diet. For the most part, a Catholic emperor was being blocked in his campaign against Protestantism by Catholic rulers. Whether or not some states struggled for religious truth, they certainly battled for political advantage and in defence of their sovereign autonomy.

Given the regent's constant need for money to fight the Turks and the French, he was always vulnerable to pressure. What is more, Charles's long absences limited imperial influence even further. These constraints became all too clear in 1526 at the Diet of Speyer, opened two months after the Turks invaded Hungary and one month after Pope Clement VII and the French king Francis I formed the anti-Habsburg League of Cognac. In response to imperial demands that the Edict of Worms be implemented at once, the states bargained the war taxation needed for a climb-down on religious controls. Known as 'territorialism', Ferdinand's concession left each state free to determine 'matters treated by the Edict [of Worms] as each hopes and trusts to answer for it before God and his Imperial Majesty'. It was as critical a victory for the Reformation as for the political interests of the states. From that ground the states would never move and, because neither emperor nor regent could drive them from it, the temporary working formula of the Recess of Speyer eventually became imperial law in the 1555 Peace of Augsburg. The Edict of Worms had become optional. Encouraged by the direction of events, some cities and princes used the Recess to promote (if not actually introduce) religious reform.

Three years later, it looked as if the emperor might be able to force his way through. Like the regent, many a prince was alarmed by the speed of the evangelical advance and the emergence of so many variant forms of Protestantism. Most sympathised with Ferdinand's call for an end to 'violence against ancient usages and customs'. Early in the 1529 Diet of Speyer, a clear majority endorsed the censorship of printing and a ban on further religious changes. Their primary anxieties lay, however, with the advance of varieties of Protestantism more radical than Luther's. Hence they demanded the suppression of all who denied the physical presence of Christ at communion (an idea known as **sacramentarianism**) and imposed the death penalty on all who rejected the validity of baptising babies.

The diet proposed the 1526 Recess be cancelled. Led by the count of Hesse, 5 princes and 14 free cities lodged the 'Protest', an action driven by 'our souls' salvation and good conscience'. They were a tiny group, and only five dared sign the defensive military alliance that Count Philipp created one week later. Philipp tried to strengthen their position by hosting at Marburg a round-table conference in which inter-evangelical theological divisions could be resolved.

Why was Ferdinand forced to compromise in 1526?

Those who supported **sacramentarianism** followed Zwingli in denying the bodily presence of Jesus in the bread and wine at communion. More than any other point of disagreement, this question was the focal issue of Protestant divisions – see pages 129 to 130.

'For the first time, protestant states came together in a **common act**. By their stance, they made plain the existence of a separate religious group in the Empire, different from the majority.' (Heinrich Bornkamm, *Luther in mid-career 1521–30*, 1983)

The **Tetrapolitan Confession** was written by Martin Bucer (reformer of Strasbourg and leader of the Protestant south German cities) and his lieutenant, Wolfgang Capito. The **Augsburg Confession** was primarily the work of Philipp Melanchthon, professor of Greek at Wittenberg and Luther's right-hand man. Because Luther was an outlaw (Edict of Worms, 1521) and thus could not set foot outside Protestant territory, Melanchthon acted as chief Lutheran spokesman at all imperial gatherings.

How effective was the emperor's strategy in 1530–31?

The Protestant world was seriously weakened by deep splits on theology, and the military power of the Swiss would be essential should the emperor seek to impose the Edict of Worms by force. Marburg failed. Agreement on communion (one of the central issues in dispute during the Reformation) proved impossible. There would be no united front binding the Wittenberg reformers with their co-religionists in southern Germany and Switzerland.

None the less, the 'Protest' was a **common act**. It gave the evangelicals their first corporate identity, which the military pact then turned into a political community. Yet the upper hand was definitely not theirs. The year 1529 had been a stupendous one for Charles V, with victories over the French and the Turks. He was at the height of his power. All the more intriguing then was his strategy at the diet summoned to Augsburg in 1530. There were no edicts or deadlines. Instead, Charles called for consultations to resolve divisions in the faith. The emperor wanted the Reformation dispute to be settled within his territories as a prelude to an all-out crusade against the Turks. That meant resolution must be amiable. It was a vain hope. While Clement VII did everything he could to block settlement of religious matters by politicians, the evangelicals remained incapable of presenting a united front. Charles therefore received two contradictory Protestant statements: the **Tetrapolitan Confession**, a sacramentarian text from Strasbourg and three other southern cities which followed the teachings of the Swiss reformer Ulrich Zwingli; and the **Augsburg Confession**, a Lutheran statement from five princes and two cities.

As the emperor realised that neither an inter-Christian accord nor a crusade would be possible, he changed tack, demanding the Protestants return to Catholicism. Not long afterwards, he adjourned the diet and used its recess to threaten legal and military action against any who did not obey. Charles had set out to achieve peaceful resolution but ended by fanning the flames of division. In response to the Recess of Augsburg, four Lutheran princes, five Lutheran free cities and six sacramentarian free cities followed Philipp of Hesse in assembling at Schmalkalden in 1531 to create a permanent military league for their mutual self-defence. As Euan Cameron puts it, 'thereafter the question was not whether the Protestants could be brought back into the fold, but for how long war between catholic and protestant states could be averted'.

The Schmalkaldic states would never themselves initiate war. As the minority, they had everything to lose. What happened next would depend on Charles, and war with Francis and Suleiman the Magnificent kept him perpetually on the back foot. The long stand-off was put to good use by Hesse. From an emperor desperate for assistance against the Ottomans in 1532, the league extracted the Peace of Nuremberg which suspended all religious lawsuits in the Imperial Chamber Court, thereby establishing immunity for Protestant disobedience. Emboldened, Philipp launched an indirect strike against the Habsburgs by organising the invasion of the duchy of Württemberg in 1534. Swift victory restored Philipp's Lutheran cousin Duke Ulrich, removed his lands from the Habsburg estates and allowed the introduction of the Reformation to that major southern territory. It was an audacious coup and, with a similar move into Brunswick in 1542, indicates just how far Charles was disarmed within Germany.

Almost as remarkable, Philipp pressed the league's Lutheran and sacramentarian wings into theological consensus, the 1536 **Wittenberg Concord**. His motive was simple. Religious differences did more than damage Protestant credibility. They threatened the political unity so vital to all Protestant dealings with the emperor. Although in truth the concord did little more than obscure differences within broad forms of words, the count continued to lead the way in fostering inter-Protestant harmony. Equally, he sought to strengthen their hand through alliance with Lutheran Denmark and negotiations with England. The evangelicals held the advantage.

'Everybody shouts: a Council! A Council!' reported the papal ambassador in Germany in 1521. Church councils were like parliaments for the Christian church and three had met during the fifteenth century. The Fifth Lateran Council ended six months before Luther wrote the Ninety-Five Theses. From 1523, the imperial diet regularly demanded 'a general, free Christian Council in the German lands'. Charles believed not merely that the Lutheran affair would best be settled by a **council**, but that the Lutheran affair *could* only be settled by a council. That is striking because it implied that Luther's excommunication was provisional and argued that there was an ultimate authority in the church above that of the pope. Long battles had been fought on that very proposition during the first half of the fifteenth century and, despite papal decrees forbidding appeals to a council over the head of Rome, the idea (known as 'conciliarism') was never suppressed.

In the strength of this conviction that the Lutheran problem could be settled only by a council, we see another reason why diets were so reluctant to enforce the Edict of Worms. From the moment Charles left Spain in 1529, he too focused on the need for a council and began pressing Rome to call one. Clement VII was, however, far from enthusiastic. Like his predecessors, he feared revived conciliarism and the downgrading of papal authority. Clement found a valuable ally in Francis I, for whom settlement of German difficulties must strengthen Charles V and perhaps tip the balance against France in the Habsburg–Valois conflict. Pope and emperor were at loggerheads over a conciliar solution.

Clement's successor took a very different view. Paul III (1534–49) understood the need for internal church reform and after a summit with the emperor in 1536 issued the long-desired summons. It was not to be, chiefly

Alarmed by ongoing Protestant divisions, Philipp of Hesse led political moves for inter-Protestant co-operation while Martin Bucer worked on the theological front. The **Wittenberg Concord**, written by Melanchthon, should have been the keystone of this double strategy, but the sacramentarian Swiss kept their distance. Lutheran–sacramentarian relations were often no more than lukewarm. Luther's comment of 1529 says it all: 'they cannot by us be considered as brothers and members of Christ'.

'Luther was in the church and remains there. He can only be excluded if he is condemned by a judicial sentence pronounced by a **council**.' (Konrad Peutinger, secretary to the city of Augsburg, 1522)

Why was the emperor unable to get the church council he needed?

At **colloquies** in Leipzig (1539), Hagenau (1540), Worms (1540–41) and Regensburg (1541), moderates from both sides sought to heal the Reformation breach. Prominent among the Protestants were those who from 1529 also sought the union of rival Protestantisms (Bucer and Melanchthon, backed by Philipp of Hesse). Luther and Paul III agreed to the talks, but probably hoped for failure.

Irenic means believing in and working for peace. The word implies that many issues in dispute are actually of secondary importance – hence the key irenic belief that unity is more important than purity. In the Reformation, irenic beliefs held that it was a far greater sin to split the Christian church than to squabble endlessly about exactly who was right on individual details of theology.

Melanchthon and Cardinal Contarini had agreed, at the Colloquy of **Regensburg**, a formula known as 'double justification' which (in their opinion) successfully united Lutheran and Catholic beliefs on the central theological debate of the Reformation: how does salvation work and, in particular, what are the respective roles of God and man in that process?

because of the resumption of Habsburg–Valois war. None the less, Charles had been shocked by Luther's refusal to send delegates and he began to develop a parallel line of advance. During 1539–41 he encouraged **colloquies**, round-table conferences that produced remarkable agreements on individual theological controversies. But negotiated reconciliation was not achieved, so Charles redoubled his campaign for a council. Rome published a new summons in 1542, but new problems surfaced. Paul could not accept Charles's belief that thorough institutional reform must be the council's top priority. Pope and emperor were now at loggerheads over the agenda.

War remained another obstacle, but seems to have given Charles new resolve. In 1544 he offered Francis long-cherished territory. Simultaneously, he negotiated a truce with Suleiman. No one had striven harder or more faithfully for a council than Charles V and, at Trent in December 1545, 28 years after the Ninety-Five Theses, it finally began. His commitment was remarkable. An unswerving Catholic, he never claimed to be a theologian and seems never to have shown much interest in (or understanding of) the theological controversies. Like most rulers, Charles appears to have viewed religious problems largely in terms of public order. Protestantism disturbed and divided his domains, prevented common defence against the Turks and suggested treasonable alliances with France. In the words of the Edict of Worms, Luther 'writes nothing which does not arouse and promote sedition, discord, war, murder, robbery and arson . . . for he teaches a loose, self-willed life, severed from all laws'.

Charles stood far from the **irenic** position of his brother, yet circumstances forced him to adopt pragmatic tactics. If talks offered the best way forward at one moment, force might be employed at another. Charles seized the chance offered by international peace in 1544–46 to break the Schmalkaldic League. His aim seems to have been to break the defensive shield around the Protestant states and so force them to Trent. With the carrot of church reform ahead of them and the stick of the emperor's army behind them, Charles believed the Protestants would have no option but to agree a settlement.

In the Schmalkaldic War, Charles was triumphant. At the Battle of Mühlberg, an army under his personal command inflicted a crushing defeat on the Schmalkaldic princes. The Saxon elector was captured and Wittenberg, the Lutheran capital, was occupied. With stage 1 completed, the emperor introduced a temporary religious settlement, the Interim of Augsburg (1548). This ordered all states to observe Catholic doctrine and practice. But it also ordered reform of the clergy and offered three concessions: clergy who had married could remain so; the people could receive wine at communion; and salvation theology was defined using the formula agreed in 1541 at **Regensburg**. Charles expected Trent to copy such changes.

Charles V at the Battle of Mühlberg, by Titian, 1547. Charles was present at the battle, but he was so crippled by gout that he could neither put on his armour nor mount his horse. Why then would he be painted in this way? Before answering, look at the equally unreal image of Francis I on page 88.

All around, however, events spun out of Charles's control. Trent pressed ahead with debates on Reformation theological controversies and, on each, rejected Protestant thinking. The hinge between emperor and pope, never properly joined, came apart. Just weeks before Mühlberg, with imperial victory in sight, Paul III had even withdrawn the 12,500 mercenaries lent to Charles lest the scale of his triumph inflate Habsburg power. The pope would not wait upon the emperor's political needs. The decrees of Trent and the Interim of Augsburg were incompatible. Reunion through a council had become impossible.

Meanwhile, Charles's all-conquering political coalition in Germany fell apart. Probably that was inevitable, given that it depended on the alliance Charles had made in 1546 with the mercurial Duke Maurice of Saxony, a Lutheran but an ambitious independent player in the tortuous politics of Reformation Germany. Emperor and duke agreed on no more than breaking John Frederick, elector of Saxony. During 1550–51, Maurice began to reassert his Lutheran credentials, obstructing the Interim in order to repair relations with the Lutheran states. Within months the duke had partially rebuilt the league and secured external funding by an alliance with the French (Treaty of Chambord, 1552). In the ensuing Princes' War of 1552, Maurice drove Charles from Austria and allowed Henry to seize the fortresses of Lorraine. Further humiliations then came with the Peace of Passau in which the Saxon duke forced the emperor to abandon the Interim and release the Schmalkaldic princes.

What motives underlay Maurice's behaviour in the period 1546–52?

The year 1552 was the turning point. On top of Charles's humiliation by Trent, Passau wrecked imperial strategy. Princely power had triumphed and, even though neither principal player was involved, that outcome shaped the final settlement (the Peace of Augsburg, 1555; for details see box below). Maurice died in 1553. The emperor, disillusioned by the treacheries and inconstancies of life, withdrew from imperial affairs and delegated responsibility to Ferdinand. None the less, Augsburg was the direct legacy of Maurice's decisive intervention in 1551–52. Without the Princes' War and the Peace of Passau, it is inconceivable that Lutheranism would have been legalised. Ferdinand's initial plan (to impose a single religious order) was overwhelmed by objections. He had no option but compromise.

- Catholicism and Lutheranism would hold equal legal standing across the empire (except in Burgundy, where Catholicism alone was recognised).
  This was a limited acceptance of Protestantism, using the definition of the 1530 Confession of Augsburg. It excluded all other forms: Zwinglianism, Calvinism, Anabaptism and other radical variants.
- Each ruler would decide the faith of his state.
  This is called 'territorialism' or 'particularism'. Equally it is known as cuius regio, eius religio *('whoever the Lord, his the religion').*
- If subjects could not accept that decision, they had the legal right to emigrate.
  Augsburg never granted religious toleration to the people.
- In imperial cities with mixed Catholic and Lutheran populations, both would enjoy legal protection. All Lutheran cities must allow Catholic worship if any wished it.
- No right to Protestant reform would be allowed, however, to ecclesiastical princes. Should they wish to become Lutheran, they must resign.
  This clause is known as the 'Reservation' and kept much of central and southern Germany Catholic.

The Peace of Augsburg, 25 September 1555.

The Peace of Augsburg legitimised the Confession of Augsburg and recognised the status quo. As such, it was a permanent version of the experiment permitted by the 1526 Recess of Speyer. Hitherto, every agreement had been no more than a truce in the ongoing struggle between emperor and princes. Charles's goal had always been religious uniformity. Augsburg represented Ferdinand's acceptance of the impossibility of that aim. Equally, it reflected his own need to create a good working relationship with the states (ready for the day when he would wear the imperial crown). Catholic and Lutheran would have to cohabit. Augsburg was the only practical politics.

Why, and with what results for the Holy Roman Empire, was Charles V at war for so much of his rule?

Habsburg–Valois rivalry 1519–59

1526	Treaty of Madrid.
1529	Treaty of Cambrai.
1534	Schmalkaldic invasion of Württemberg.
1543	Defeat of Duke William of Cleves.
1544	The *alternativa*.
1552	French capture of Metz, Toul and Verdun.
1552–53	Charles fails to recover Metz.
1554	Marriage of Philip to Mary I of England.
1557	Battle of St Quentin.
1558	Battle of Gravelines.
1559	Peace of Câteau-Cambrésis.

The empire, Burgundy and Aragon had for generations been rivals of France. Each had its own quarrels. Between 1506 and 1519, however, all were **inherited** or won by the same prince: Charles of Habsburg. Such an accumulation of territory had not been seen since the Roman Empire. Naturally, such a concentration alarmed many, for it upset the balance of power. But none feared it more than the French, who felt themselves surrounded and under grave threat. In 1536, Charles told the pope, 'Some say that I wish to be monarch of the world. My thoughts and deeds prove that the contrary is true.'

Medieval political and religious theory saw Europe as a single entity, referred to as Christendom, with the pope its spiritual and the emperor its secular leader. Even for popes this was never true, let alone for emperors. The many separate political states made nonsense of any notion that Europe's

For Charles's various **inheritances**, see the family tree on page 3. The Italian Wars are covered from Charles's perspective in Chapter 2, pages 57 to 59, while Chapter 3, pages 82 to 91, considers them from the French perspective.

kings would accept imperial sovereignty over them. Not everyone believed the famous statement by Count **Gattinara**, Charles's imperial chancellor. The chancellor regarded Charles's exceptional inheritance as making him the heir of great Christian Roman emperors like Constantine and Justinian. Gattinara and his circle saw Charles acting as a moral force to bring order and stability to Christendom. They even began to use Old Testament prophecy to cast Charles's monarchy as the great empire which, lasting until the end of the world, would unite everyone under a single law, faith and ruler.

Charles V did not believe in the count's delusions. He knew his own mind. Charles showed great confidence in his ministers but took advice only when he wanted it. Often he never consulted them – Gattinara complained of lack of **respect** for him. Charles's government was very personal, rather than bureaucratic. We can be confident that Charles's foreign policy was his own. In his regular wars against Francis I and Henry II, he struggled to recover ancestral land which (as he saw it) belonged to his family. Never did he make a move to seize other parts of France. Unlike Henry VIII, he never talked of conquering France and making himself king. When he told the Council of Castile in 1528, 'any prince who invades and takes what is not his is justly to be condemned as a tyrant', he meant what he said. Charles's objectives were, as he explained to the Venetian ambassador in 1530, 'to preserve what has been passed on in trust from my ancestors and to wage war on the infidel'.

In every case in which Charles disputed territorial ownership, the rival claimant (or occupant) was the king of France: parts of the Pyrenees (especially Navarre), Naples, Milan and a series of duchies and counties between Switzerland and the Channel associated with the duchy of Burgundy. The lands of Burgundy had been the focus of dispute since the death in 1477 of Duke Charles the Bold. His successor was his daughter Mary and both the French and the Habsburgs attempted to arrange a marriage with her. The contest was won by the imperial interest and Mary married the future Emperor Maximilian I (Charles V was their grandson). But the French had already invaded, claiming the lack of a male heir meant the Burgundian territories should pass back to their original owner, the French crown. By the time Charles inherited the duchy at the age of 6 in 1506, several wars and treaties had produced an uneasy stalemate.

As he did in Italy with Milan, when Charles went to war over the **Burgundian** lands he did so in the dynastic interest of the Habsburgs. As yet, nations barely counted. International affairs were directed by the 'rights' of each ruler's family. Claims had to be asserted and defended. International politics was driven by the interests of dynasties; their lands were the source of their power and wealth. For a long time the great rivalry between Charles V and Francis I was concentrated on their disputes over Milan and Naples. But

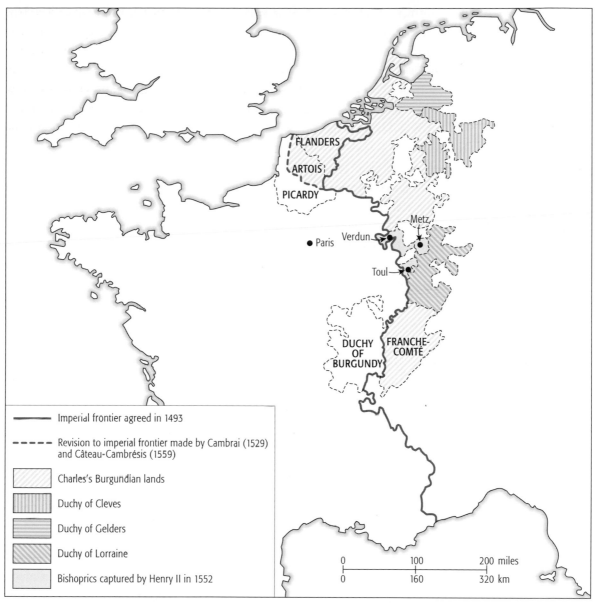

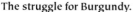

The struggle for Burgundy.

Charles had been born and brought up in the Netherlands. He was a Burgundian and his Burgundian inheritance was always close to his heart. It was Francis who struck the first blows in the region when in 1521 he paid a dissident Burgundian noble, Robert de la Marck, lord of Sedan and duke of Bouillon, to attack Charles's duchy of Luxembourg, and then himself sent French troops over the border to ravage the Burgundian county of Hainault. Since Charles was heavily committed in Italy, he drew the gullible and overambitious Henry VIII of England into the war in his place; English attacks on northern France would draw attention away from the Burgundian frontier. This strategy worked, allowing the emperor to remain focused on north Italy. The Netherlands might thus seem to have been marginal, a sideshow to the main event in Italy. That this was not so can be seen from the behaviour of both sides after the Battle of Pavia (1525), when Francis was taken prisoner while attempting to take Milan. The Treaty of Madrid which followed included an agreement by which Francis surrendered all rights to the Burgundian lands, as well as his Italian and Pyrenean claims. On his release, however, the Burgundian arrangements caused a fresh Habsburg–Valois rupture. Francis rejected the treaty, claiming it was invalid because he had been forced to sign against his will, and Charles **failed** to get what he wanted. The French king declared that it was 'contrary to all reason and equity' to give away his patrimonial lands. He could not give them up because his people would never allow it. The insoluble problem between Francis and Charles was as much Burgundy as Milan.

When after repeated failures Francis was forced back to the negotiating table in 1529, the emperor made sure that Burgundy was high on the agenda. In the Treaty of Cambrai, Francis surrendered all his rights as overlord of Artois and Flanders. This may not seem much of a concession; Charles was count of both and already held them both. But to think like that is to miss something crucial to the medieval mind. Lordship was central to feudal politics. Obedience to one's lord was the hinge of medieval society. For Charles to be the subject of the French king left him wide open to charges of treason whenever, as emperor or as king of Aragon, he was at war with Francis I. Such an anomalous situation would cause perpetual danger.

Cambrai took a more realistic approach to the **Burgundian problem**. Charles knew that he was in no position to take back Picardy or Burgundy by force. His treasury was empty and he needed peace with Francis to tackle German Lutheranism and the Ottomans in Hungary and the Mediterranean. In large measure, the Italian Wars were over and the French king spent much of the 1530s negotiating with Charles's enemies, German Lutheran princes and rebellious nobles in the Netherlands included. Such French interference was alarming. Germany was already seriously divided. For those German difficulties to become formally linked to the Habsburg–Valois struggle raised a nightmare scenario of a grand anti-imperial coalition. In fact, the idea of a Valois–Lutheran link probably originated with the Germans. The leading anti-Habsburg prince, Philipp of Hesse, was developing such a plan as early as 1528. Francis I was certainly a willing ally, eager as ever to stir up trouble. He it was who encouraged Catholic Bavaria to join the Schmalkaldic League, for some years largely funded this alliance and egged Philipp on to attack Württemberg.

'The emperor **failed** to obtain from his victory what he wanted above everything else – the recovery of the Burgundian territories lost to France after 1477 . . . Burgundy was the essential sticking point.' (Matthew Anderson, *The origins of the modern European state system 1494–1618*, 1998)

The Peace of Senlis (1493) created the **Burgundian problem** that Charles inherited: France held the original duchy of Burgundy itself, together with the county of Picardy. The empire had Franche-Comté (the alternative name for the county of Burgundy) and the counties of Artois, Charolais and Flanders. All were disputed during Charles's reign.

The loss of **Württemberg** (1534) had strategic implications, because the duchy was conveniently placed as a stepping stone for the emperor, between the Habsburg Tyrol and the Burgundian province of Franche-Comté. Without Württemberg, the successful defence of the Burgundian inheritance would be much harder, and the recovery of Burgundy itself very much more difficult. Why, therefore, Charles did not attempt its recovery seems mysterious. He fought endlessly for Milan, yet Württemberg was, arguably, far more important to Habsburg interests. The reason reveals just how medieval Charles was. We think in terms of strategic territory. He thought in terms of dynastic territory. Milan belonged to his family; Württemberg did not. The political or military advantages were not the key issue. Württemberg bound the Habsburg lands together; Milan did not. Württemberg made the defence of the Habsburg lands easier; Milan did not. But none of these points could outweigh Charles's bedrock fundamental: patrimonial land.

For **Württemberg**, see the map on page 7.

In your own words, explain why Charles abandoned Württemberg.

In 1540, Charles proposed the re-creation of the old Burgundian state in a Habsburg–Valois marriage between his eldest daughter and Francis's youngest son. Charles would give the couple all his Burgundian lands if Francis would give them his. Perhaps it would have worked, but the emperor added strings demanding concessions in Italy too. As ever, Milan was the stumbling block and the ingenious dynastic scheme came to nothing. After further inconclusive conflict, Charles proposed another dynastic solution. In the Truce of Crépy of 1544, attempting to enlist Francis's assistance to fight the Turks and bring the Lutherans back into the Catholic fold, the emperor proposed the *alternativa*: the same French prince should marry either Charles's daughter Mary or his niece Anne. If a marriage went ahead with Mary, Charles would make the Netherlands and Franche-Comté her dowry; if with Anne, Milan. Both were remarkable offers and, given how precious these territories were, only make sense when we recall the dynastic and religious cores to his foreign policy. They were practical attempts to solve the problem of the multiple monarchies Charles had inherited. At the same time, the lukewarm reception given to the proposal demonstrates firmly the depth of Francis I's loathing of the emperor.

What was the purpose of the *alternativa*?

Unsuccessful marriage propositions were not the only schemes of these years. In 1538–40, Francis worked strenuously to cultivate the **duke of Cleves** and open a corridor into the Netherlands and the Rhineland. After several years of talks, and despite the duke's defeat by Charles in 1540, the French king signed in 1541 a tripartite alliance with Duke William and the Lutheran King Christian III of Denmark. To some degree, Charles was able to turn the tables. The defeat of Cleves in 1540 weakened his value to Francis, and a second campaign in 1543 forced the duke not only to become a Catholic but to surrender his Dutch states. In 1543, the emperor won back the active support of England

William, **duke of Cleves**, claimed the duchy of Gelders and the county of Zutphen in the Netherlands. Temporarily, William became even more important when in 1540 his sister Anne was married to Henry VIII. 'Crushing Cleves was like touching the secret spring of a delicate lock: everything opened at once. The Netherlands were free of a pincer threat, the northern Protestant bloc fell apart, Charles was able to turn on France.' (Geoffrey Elton, *Reformation Europe 1517–1559*, 1963)

For the development in fortifications and guns that had such dramatic military and financial impact on offensive **warfare**, see Chapter 4, pages 96 to 105 and 110 to 112. Henry did, however, capture Boulogne.

The **Princes' War** was led by Maurice of Saxony and the mercenary Albert Alcibiades, margrave of Brandenburg-Kulmbach. In April 1552, Charles wrote to Ferdinand, 'I am without authority, driven from Germany without anyone to support me there. I have so many enemies and power is now in their hands. What a fine end I shall have in my old age!'

Why was 1552 such a bad year for Charles V?

and possible joint invasions of France were discussed. Brief war in 1544 yielded Charles little since his invasion of the Champagne ground to a halt when his troops were unable to capture two fortresses. The changes in contemporary **warfare** and the escalating costs of campaigning made military breakthrough by either side increasingly unlikely. Generals had lost the opportunity for grand offensives, while their masters could no longer afford lengthy operations. That was why Francis devoted such energy to diplomatic warfare, building alliances with the emperor's enemies and encouraging them to do him harm.

The year 1547 saw the death of Charles's arch-foe Francis I. Immediately reviving claims abandoned in the Treaty of Cambrai, the new king Henry II summoned Charles to Paris to kneel before him and acknowledge him as his lord. So overt a breach was an ominous sign. To begin with, French activity concentrated in Italy. In 1552, however, Charles was surprised by an offensive in Lorraine which took the strategic bishoprics of Metz, Toul and Verdun. French power had taken a significant step eastwards since all three lay well inside the empire. What is more, Henry took control of the child duke of Lorraine, gaining control of this major border state. The situation was even worse. Henry had allied with the Schmalkaldic princes who, as he invaded Lorraine, attacked the emperor in the '**Princes' War**', forcing him to flee into Austria.

Simultaneously, Henry stirred revolts in Italy and encouraged the Turks to launch new campaigns in Hungary and the Mediterranean. The year 1552 marked the nadir of Charles's fortunes, the opposite of 1529. But his enemies lacked unity, while the emperor was always at his best when in a corner. Charles bought off Margrave Albert while Ferdinand negotiated with Duke Maurice the Peace of Passau. Within a month, Maurice was in command of the imperial army on the Hungarian front. New loans were raised. Albert provided Charles with 15,000 troops, while 10,000 Spanish soldiers were moved to the Rhineland, and the German Catholic states offered yet more. With these, the emperor rushed into a counter-attack to recover Metz. It was winter and all his generals advised against it. The campaign was a disaster, judged by historians to have been a graver defeat than his failure at Algiers in 1541. In the new military climate dominated by impregnable fortifications and powerful artillery, sieges had taken the place of open battles. Failure at Metz in 1552–53 was, for Charles, the equivalent of the major defeats that Francis I suffered at Pavia or Landriano. Even so, the political manoeuvrings of 1552 led to a significant recovery of the imperial position.

The accession of Mary I in England in 1553 brought a Catholic restoration and the prospect of an anti-French coalition, cemented by a marriage bringing England within Habsburg influence and opening up the possibility that England might be added to the Habsburg territories. Unpopular in England

and Spain, the marriage in 1554 of Mary and Charles's son **Philip** was a great Habsburg coup. Vital trade and communications links between Spain and the Netherlands would be much safer. France would be more effectively surrounded; Henry II described the marriage as 'putting a noose round my neck'. The final Habsburg–Valois campaigns ran on until the 1559 Peace of Câteau-Cambrésis (three years after Charles's abdication) and so fell to Philip, now King Philip II of Spain, to complete. Some of the fighting centred on Naples but Henry II attacked Artois in 1554. There he suffered the same setback Charles had faced at Metz: the inability to capture towns defended by the new-style fortifications. The indecisive nature of the campaigns fought after 1529 is striking, vivid proof of the altered nature of war. In 1557, however, a Spanish force from the Netherlands took the French by surprise at St Quentin in Picardy and inflicted on them their most severe defeat since Pavia. Barely 70 miles from Paris, the capital was in danger. But Philip was crippled by his father's massive debts. The victory could not be exploited. Both sides needed peace. They were pushed to the negotiating table by their deficits, and intermittent talks began as early as 1555. After another lucky break when the Spanish caught the French offguard as they crossed a river attempting to invade Flanders, victory at the Battle of Gravelines (1558) kick-started serious discussions.

Negotiations centred on Spanish interests in Italy and the Pyrenees, but the French withdrawal from Savoy restored the route between Milan and Franche-Comté so vital to the defence of Burgundian interests. There was an exchange of towns along the French–Netherlands border, and the imperial frontier was itself moved south to incorporate Flanders and Artois into the empire at long last. At Câteau-Cambrésis, French promises made since 1482 were finally confirmed: the Burgundian lands would belong to the Habsburgs. Like those for Naples and Milan, the long contest for Artois and Flanders thus ended in Habsburg victory. The greatest prize had, however, eluded Charles: the original duchy of Burgundy remained in French hands.

Dynastic unions often proved fragile. The Anglo-Habsburg alliance collapsed in 1558 on Queen Mary's death. The empire of Charles V proved only a little less ephemeral. Charles split his territories, and arranged them so that Ferdinand did not inherit Milan or the Burgundian lands (which in 1548 the emperor had made only a nominal part of the empire) when he became emperor. The separation of the Netherlands from Germany was the most significant element in Charles's abdication arrangements. It marked the triumph of the Spanish over the German branches of the dynasty. Emperor Ferdinand was not involved in the negotiations of Câteau-Cambrésis and the Lorraine fortresses lost in 1552 were not even mentioned; despite his protests, the French were left in possession. Habsburg–Valois warring had come to an end,

To raise **Philip**'s status, Charles abdicated in Naples so his son entered the marriage as a king. The marriage treaty made Philip king of England (Philip I), and the emperor promised that a son of Philip and Mary would inherit all the Burgundian lands, including Franche-Comté. The marriage would also strengthen traditional Anglo-Burgundian and Anglo-Spanish alliances.

Had Charles V's struggle for the Burgundian inheritance proved a failure?

but Franco-Spanish rivalry continued for more than a century. The Habsburg family was now two distinct dynasties, with the Austrian the lesser branch. The empire did not have the political or military strength of Spain and, by transferring the Netherlands, guaranteed it could never match its cousin in financial resources either. Without the imperial title, Spain remained a great power whereas the Holy Roman Empire shrank, unable to dominate the affairs of Europe as in the age of Charles V.

The struggle against the Ottomans 1526–56

1526	Battle of Móhacs; Ferdinand becomes king of Bohemia and Hungary.
1529	Siege of Vienna.
1532	Siege of Güns.
1533	Ferdinand first pays tribute to the sultan (thus becoming an Ottoman vassal).
1538	Treaty of Oradea.
1541	Ottomans occupy eastern Hungary.
1551	Transylvanian campaign.

For Charles V's north African and Mediterranean campaigns, see Chapter 2, pages 53 to 57.

Charles had transferred the Habsburg patrimonial lands to his brother Ferdinand, and for most of the reign left imperial affairs in his hands. For 170 years the Ottoman Turks had been pushing into Europe. By the 1460s they held all the Balkans. From the 1470s they began long-distance raids into Hungary, Croatia and Austria. When they captured Belgrade in 1521, the Danube valley offered a highway into central Europe and, using it, they destroyed the Hungarian state in 1526. From that moment, Habsburg and Ottoman faced each other directly. The imperial frontier had become the border of Christendom, and Ferdinand its guardian.

Magyar is the native word for the Hungarians.

His position was not good. As king of Hungary his position was very weak. The kingdom lay shattered after its crushing defeat at Móhacs and few Hungarians accepted him. Most supported the nobleman János Zapolyai, governor of Transylvania, who had led the opposition to Louis II and who now organised resistance to a 'German' sovereign. In November 1526, the Hungarian diet almost unanimously elected him king. Ferdinand had himself proclaimed king the following month, and invaded and defeated Zapolyai in battle. But the **Magyar** nobility would not have a foreign king and offered obedience to the Ottoman sultan in exchange for military aid. Poland and France recognised János and, when Sultan Suleiman the Magnificent brought his army into Hungary again, he installed Zapolyai as his **vassal** king. Only the Croats accepted Ferdinand as king of Hungary.

A **vassal** was someone holding land and authority, but under the superior authority of another. The Turks already had two vassal states along their European frontier (Wallachia and Moldavia). Hungary and, in time, Transylvania continued this policy. So far from Constantinople, indirect rule was more practical and vassal territories acted as a buffer between the Christian and the Islamic worlds.

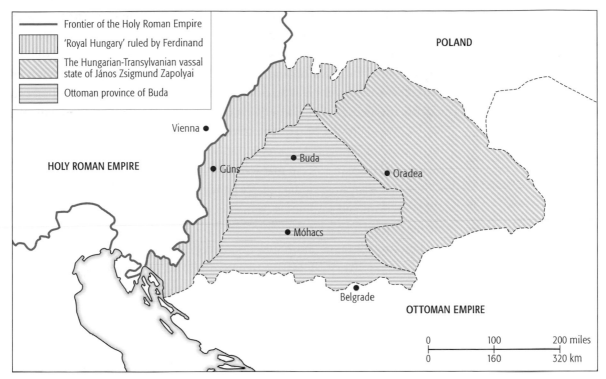

The legend of the map reads:

— Frontier of the Holy Roman Empire

'Royal Hungary' ruled by Ferdinand

The Hungarian-Transylvanian vassal state of János Zsigmund Zapolyai

Ottoman province of Buda

POLAND

HOLY ROMAN EMPIRE

Vienna ●

● Buda

Güns ●

● Oradea

● Móhacs

Belgrade ●

OTTOMAN EMPIRE

| 0 | 100 | 200 miles |
| 0 | 160 | 320 km |

The Hungarian front in 1541.

As imperial regent, Ferdinand's ability to act was also limited. Habsburg resources were already heavily committed to war against France and the emperor would rarely allow any diversion of funds or troops to Hungary; 1532 and 1541 were rare exceptions. The **imperial diet** exploited Ferdinand's vulnerability on every occasion, never allowing him sufficient money. In consequence, Ferdinand could usually raise an army of only 20,000–25,000 men. By contrast, Suleiman had a regular army of 65,000, plus 80,000 auxilliaries. Had they ever met head on, the outcome would never have been in doubt. Like Charles, however, the sultan had to divide his strength among the conflicting needs of his empire. Fortunately for Ferdinand, the Ottomans were regularly at war with the Persians, could not sustain major campaigns on both fronts and regarded the east as the more important. Offensives in Hungary were only ever launched during lulls in fighting Shah Tahmasp of Persia.

Suleiman had not exploited his victory of 1526. When he returned in 1529 to install Zapolyai, he crossed the imperial frontier and besieged Vienna; raiding parties pushed right through Austria and into Bavaria. Delayed by unusually heavy rains and then hit by unexpectedly early snow, the **Ottomans** had to abandon the siege after only a month. Throughout the crisis, Ferdinand stood alone. Absorbed in the affairs of Italy, the emperor sent virtually no assistance. Austria had a lucky escape and, when the Turks retreated for the

Diets always bargained mercilessly and Hungarian war was the real reason (not commitments against the French) why princely power and Protestant strength went unchecked in Germany. The Bohemian diet was little better. By contrast, the papacy regularly granted Charles and Ferdinand one-third of all Spanish, German and Austrian church revenues to fund war. Further, Pope Paul III tried twice to rally Christendom to a great crusade (1536, 1542).

Ottoman armies could campaign in Europe for only four months each year (June to September).

At least Charles saw the point this time and sent 18,000 Spanish troops for the attack on **Buda**. So did the imperial diet, which voted funds for 48,000 soldiers (in exchange, of course, for major religious concessions – the Peace of Nuremberg).

The **Treaty of Oradea** is also known by its Hungarian (Várad) and German (Grosswardein) names.

Why was Ferdinand unable to conquer his Hungarian kingdom?

winter, they retained the upper hand, leaving two-thirds of Hungary in Zapolyai's hands. The next year, Ferdinand tried unsuccessfully to take the capital, **Buda**. Suleiman's response was a massive counter-offensive. He planned to invade Austria and, in a repeat of Móhacs, bring Ferdinand to battle. For three weeks his forces were, however, held up by their inability to capture the fortress of Güns. Sensibly, Ferdinand retreated and refused to join battle. Eventually, the sultan ran out of time and had to pull back. His dominant position remained, however, indisputable. Even when it was he who requested a truce in 1533 so that war with Persia could be resumed, the terms were weighted against Ferdinand. He had no choice but to recognise Suleiman as his overlord and pay annual tribute, as well as to accept Zapolyai as king of all but 'Royal Hungary'.

Habsburg–Ottoman hostilities resumed briefly in 1538 when the Turkish vassal principality of Moldavia attempted to break free and recognise Ferdinand as its lord. More important, the rival Hungarian kings settled their long quarrel in the **Treaty of Oradea**. The 1533 truce was repeated so that each recognised the other but, crucially, they agreed that on Zapolyai's death his lands would pass to Ferdinand (because the former was unmarried). When Zapolyai died two years later, Ferdinand sent in troops to take possession. The sultan had not known about Oradea and would not accept its terms. Neither would the Magyar nobility, for Zapolyai had married since the treaty and had a son, János Zsigmund. Ottoman armies drove Ferdinand back and proclaimed János Zsigmund vassal king of Transylvania. The central triangle, however, they kept for themselves; eastern Hungary became the Ottoman province of Buda.

During 1542–47 Habsburg and Ottoman fought every season. Small gains and losses on both sides cannot conceal the stalemate that had developed. Each had spent 1533–42 building heavy defences. For 1,000 kilometres, Ferdinand had created a chain of fortified villages and fortresses manned by a permanent garrison of 10,000 troops. The conflict turned into a war of attrition (rather like the Western Front in 1915–17). Both sides made frequent raids; Ferdinand's Hungarian hussars were skilled commandos. Neither side could, however, break through and overwhelm the other. Skirmishing and truces took the place of epic battles and definitive treaties. None the less, Ferdinand was always the weaker contestant. When in 1547 he needed urgently to divert troops to crush rebellion in Bohemia, he had to renew the terms of the 1533 truce and increase his tribute to 30,000 gold florins.

New hope dawned in 1551 when Bishop Martinuzzi, chancellor of János Zsigmund, opened secret talks. All along, the anti-German Zapolyai party had acted to preserve the unity of Hungary. The three-way territorial split of 1541 made things far worse, so Ferdinand was now offered the Transylvanian lands (in exchange for suitable compensation). At once, Ferdinand sent an army to occupy Transylvania. Inevitably, of course, this provoked a mighty Ottoman reaction and the 7,000-strong Habsburg force was soon out of its depth. Even worse, Ferdinand's commander had the bishops assassinated, so the Hungarians turned against the Habsburgs. **Transylvania** was rapidly lost, and the broader war bogged down once each side was back behind its defensive lines. Things never improved on the battlefield and, because of that, deteriorated politically. By 1562, Ferdinand (himself emperor since 1556) had not only to renew the old humiliating truces but to accept János Zsigmund as king. Always too weak to launch major offensives, he was never able to make any headway; Hungary would not be recovered by defensive tactics. Although Ferdinand bore the title of king, he never ruled more than a quarter of Hungary.

'The assimilation of **Transylvania** into Habsburg Hungary would not have been easy because of the rapid progress of Calvinism in the principality. It was made impossible by the murder of Martinuzzi.' (Richard Bonney, *The European dynastic states 1494–1660*, 1991)

Was Ferdinand's payment of tribute from 1533 a betrayal of the true interests of Hungary, the empire and Christendom?

Summary questions

1 (a) Explain why Charles V faced problems with the German princes.

  (b) To what extent do you agree that Charles V was an effective emperor?

2 (a) Identify and explain *two* social and economic problems of Germany between 1517 and 1559.

  (b) How successfully did Charles V deal with the German Reformation?

3 (a) Explain *two* reasons for the success of the German Reformation by 1555.

  (b) Compare the importance of at least *three* factors causing war between Charles V and his enemies.

4 (a) Explain how population growth and price inflation affected Germany between 1517 and 1559.

  (b) Were religious or foreign affairs the more serious problem for Charles V throughout his reign? Explain your answer.

Spain 1504–56

Focus questions

◆ How united was Spain in 1516?

◆ How strong was Spain's economy by 1556?

◆ How successful was Spanish foreign policy between 1504 and 1556?

◆ How successful was Charles I as king of Spain?

Significant dates

1504	Queen Isabella of Castile dies.
1506	King Ferdinand of Aragon marries Germaine de Foix of Navarre.
1512	Ferdinand conquers Navarre.
1516	King Ferdinand of Aragon dies. Charles signs the Treaty of Noyon, recognising the French as the rulers of Milan.
1517	Charles arrives in Spain.
1519	Charles is elected Holy Roman emperor.
1520–22	The Revolt of the Comuneros.
1521	Charles captures Milan (lost again in 1524).
1522	Charles returns to Spain.
1523	The Council of Finance is established.
1525	Charles wins the Battle of Pavia, capturing Francis I and Milan. Barbarossa captures Algiers from the Spanish. Moors living in Aragon are ordered to convert to Christianity or emigrate.
1527	Charles's army sacks Rome.
1528	The Republic of Genoa allies with Charles against France.
1529	In the Peace of Cambrai, Francis I surrenders all claims to Italian territory. Charles leaves Spain for the empire. In his absence, persecution of Erasmians begins.
1534–35	Charles and Barbarossa struggle for control of Tunis.
1536	Barbarossa becomes grand admiral of the Ottoman navy.
1538	Charles's attempt to introduce the *sisa* fails. Barbarossa smashes the joint Spanish, papal and Venetian fleets at the Battle of Prevesa.

1540	Charles makes his son Philip duke of Milan, provoking a new round of Habsburg–Valois struggle in Italy.
1541	Charles's attempt to recover Algiers fails.
1546	Barbarossa dies and is succeeded by Dragut. Charles creates the Council of Italy.
1547	Charles's finance minister, Francisco de los Cobos, dies.
1551	Dragut captures Tripoli.
1556	Charles abdicates as king of Castile, Aragon and Navarre. The French attempt to invade Naples is defeated.

Overview

Except as a geographical description, the word 'Spain' meant nothing in the first half of the sixteenth century. The lands to the south of the Pyrenees were divided politically into four separate countries: Portugal, Castile, Navarre and Aragon. By 1516, the last three were, by accident of inheritance, ruled by the same man: Charles of Habsburg. But these states had not yet been united into the single country we know today as Spain. Variety and diversity were the hallmarks of what (for convenience) we shall call Spain. Charles was a foreigner and he succeeded to discontented kingdoms. His insensitive blunders only made things worse and major rebellion soon broke out. Charles survived the Revolt of the Comuneros more by luck than skill (and the skills were not his but his regent's). These years were a tough education, but from 1522 Charles learned to understand Spain and govern it effectively. The political calm (even contentedness) of Spain in the period 1522–56 contrasts sharply with the bitter mood of its people in 1516–21.

Economically and financially, Spain's state of health during Charles's long reign was less rosy. Despite the remarkable achievements of Francisco de los Cobos in raising revenue, the cost of Charles's endless wars bankrupted Castile. Spain's economy was also weak. Its agriculture was seriously distorted, concentrated too much on keeping sheep (for the high value of their wool) and too little on growing grain (to feed the rising population). Little interest was shown in using home-grown raw commodities like wool and silk to develop domestic industrial production. The fundamental problem was that Spain was looking for fast and easy profits. In consequence, it made itself heavily dependent on imports. The wealth produced by America could have been directed into strategic investment (commercial, industrial and agricultural). That unique opportunity was squandered.

Spanish foreign policy during these years involved a combination of crusading in north Africa and a long struggle with France for dominance in Italy. King Ferdinand seized a series of coastal fortress-ports from the sultanates of

Fez, Algiers and Tunis in 1505–10. The arrival of the Barbary corsairs under Barbarossa in 1518, however, set in motion a contest for command of the western Mediterranean – which Charles was not well placed to win. He had constant distractions elsewhere in his vast empire. His navy was weak and the Castilian way of crusading was not well suited to the sustained campaigning required. The offensive Charles himself led against Tunis in 1535 was a unique triumph. In the 20 subsequent years Spain's position was undermined relentlessly. In Italy, by contrast, King Ferdinand prevented a French takeover of the kingdom of Naples and ended up ruling it himself. The contest over Milan dragged on far longer, but a string of military victories in the 1520s left it firmly in Charles's hands – and made Charles the master of Italy. Thereafter, none could dislodge him. As he was Holy Roman emperor as well as sovereign of the Spanish kingdoms, it has often been suggested that Spain's interests regularly lost out to imperial needs. The evidence suggests the opposite. Even though he was often absent from Spain, Spanish needs seem to have remained at the front of Charles's mind. When he abdicated and split his territories in 1556, Spain gained by far the better part of the bargain.

Because of the Comuneros, Charles stayed in Spain for most of the 1520s. Thereafter (before his abdication and retirement), he was rarely there. That he could so neglect Spain indicates how stable it was. In stark contrast to his first years, good government became a hallmark of his reign. To some degree, administrative reforms helped. But Spanish equilibrium resulted essentially from the skills (administrative and financial) of Francisco de los Cobos and Charles's deliberate decision not to challenge either the power of the nobility or the traditions of Spanish government. Only in religious matters was the tranquillity of Spain disturbed. Protestantism was no problem but, building on powerful characteristics already present before 1500, Charles's Spain became increasingly intolerant of all views that differed from a very narrowly defined 'norm'. A fear that Spain was in danger from subversive forces began to grip both Charles and his subjects. On the surface, Spain under Charles I was strong and successful. Beneath the surface, however, all was not well in this developing superpower. The government was bankrupt. The economy was unstable. The people were narrow minded and paranoid (and therefore insecure). Reinforced by the resources of America, Spain in 1556 should have been formidable. In many ways it indeed was. But there was always something of an illusion about Spanish greatness.

How united was Spain in 1516?

Spain did not exist in 1516. Charles was king of three countries: Castile, **Aragon** and Navarre. Each was separate and determined to stay that way. As

As king of **Aragon**, Charles was also king of Naples (including Sicily and Sardinia).

King Philip was told in 1506, 'each is sufficient unto itself, so laws ought to be appropriate to the province, and not identical for all'. There was no government and *cortes* covering all of Spain. Rather, the governments, *cortes*, laws, officials, taxation, coinages, economies, armies and languages of each kingdom were distinct. The people of one were foreigners in the others. Customs barriers remained in force. Charles's Spanish subjects saw him as ruling what historians term a '**multiple monarchy**': a grouping of separate elements linked only by their individual obedience to one of the lordships which by accident of inheritance had fallen into the hands of one ruler.

Charles grew up in Burgundy in the Habsburg world of **his father** and succeeded to his Spanish crowns by chance. On the death of his maternal grandparents, their Spanish thrones should have passed to their son, but he had died. So too did the three people next in succession. Only in 1500 did Charles's mother become heir and she lived on until 1555. But when her husband died in 1506, she became (at least temporarily) insane. Relegated to the shadows, she lived in virtual imprisonment while others ruled in her place. Even then, Charles might never have succeeded in Aragon and Navarre. Ferdinand II worked to prevent his inheritance because he did not want a Habsburg takeover. When that had happened in the Netherlands after 1477, local interests were soon ignored, local taxes exported, local independence compromised – all to serve the Holy Roman Empire. Ferdinand did not want that to be Aragon's fate. He thus remarried, but his new son lived only a few hours. Even then, Ferdinand built plans around Charles's younger brother, who was being brought up in Castile. Dynastic roulette handed Charles his Spanish kingdoms.

A *cortes* was a parliament – there was one in Castile, and Aragon had one for each of its three provinces.

The Spanish term for **multiple monarchy** is *monarquia*.

His father was duke of Burgundy and heir to Maximilian I, lord of the Habsburg lands in central Europe (see the map in Chapter 1, page 7) and Holy Roman emperor.

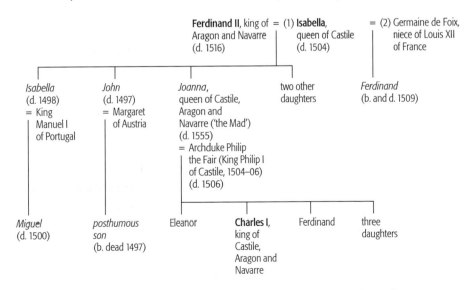

An unpredictable succession – the royal family of Spain. (Names in italics indicate a relative ahead of Charles in the line of succession. For Charles's Habsburg ancestry and inheritance, see the family tree in Chapter 1, page 3.)

Charles I (of Spain),
portrait by Bernard van Orley, 1516.

For the medieval idea of government as a **contract** between king and people, see Chapter 3, pages 76 to 77.

From the moment of Charles's accession there was political uncertainty. He was 16 years old, he was not in Spain, had never been to Spain, spoke none of the Spanish languages and had no Spanish advisers. By the time he arrived in October 1517, he was already mistrusted. Each *cortes* lectured him on their rights, making it clear that he was bound to them by a **contract** that required him to protect their laws, learn their language, live among them and appoint no foreigners. Those were warning shots. Charles had started with massive disadvantages beyond his control. Thereafter, however, he suffered from bad advice. A stranger far from home, the young Burgundian prince remained under the influence of the Burgundian councillors he had brought with him for comfort and security; chief among these was Guillaume de Croy, lord of Chièvres. Equally naturally, the Castilian and Aragonese nobility were annoyed and frustrated by these outsiders who treated them with contempt, who monopolised their king and who stole their rightful places in royal service.

Discontent grew. Rumours began to circulate that Charles was mad (like his mother) and the crown should pass to his brother Ferdinand, who had spent his entire life in Spain and was therefore regarded as a Spaniard. Others remembered Joanna and argued that she was the rightful queen and a regency could be arranged. Then in 1519 Charles's paternal grandfather, the Emperor Maximilian, died. Against the advice of all Spain, Charles stood as a candidate to succeed him. To the fury of all Spain he won the election and, as they had feared, prepared to go to Germany. Medieval monarchy was personal. In the Middle Ages the belief was that rulers had duties as well as powers. How could a prince abandon his people? As the contemporary thinker Erasmus put it: 'nothing so alienates the affections of his people as for a sovereign to take pleasure in living abroad, for they seem to be neglected by him'. Many believed Charles would never return. The Spanish felt orphaned.

What would have been achieved by making Ferdinand king or restoring Joanna?

Dissatisfaction was tangible. The belief that the Burgundians had siphoned off 7 million ducats was exaggerated, but illustrates the mood. Even as Charles left, he showed that he had understood nothing, appointing Adrian of Utrecht, another Burgundian, as regent. Rebellion broke out almost at once in Castile: the Revolt of the Comuneros (1520–22). In understanding its origins, historians take a broad view. Some hostility to Burgundian dominance was commercial. Prominent among the supporters of the revolt were Castilian textile producers alarmed by the growing imports of cheap Flemish cloth and fearful that too much raw wool would be exported to feed Flemish looms. Part of Castile's dissatisfaction lay in its centuries-old jealousy of Aragon. The regency for Joanna after her husband's death had been dominated by Aragonese officials. In the jaundiced eyes of many, Charles spent too much of 1518–20 in Aragon. We must also note the revolt's urban core. The growing numbers of merchants and lawyers (the most important among the residents of Castile's expanding towns) were increasingly resentful of the dominating influence of the nobility. This was a developing confrontation between urban and rural interests, but also the start of a contest for power between new and traditional social groups.

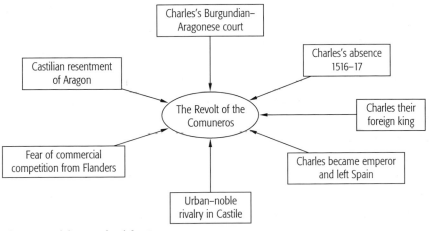

The roots of the Revolt of the Comuneros.

Comuneros means an alliance of towns.

Literally, **Santa Junta** means 'Holy Council'. It was the organisation in which the rebellious towns met together and decided tactics.

Explain what the towns really wanted.

List the reasons why the Comuneros was defeated. Divide the list into two columns, one headed 'luck', the other 'skill'.

The Revolt of the **Comuneros** was centred on Toledo and, to begin with, was very limited in scale. Only five towns with seats in the *cortes* sent representatives in August 1520 to the **Santa Junta**. The expansion of the revolt came only when the regent's army sacked Medina del Campo and massacred its inhabitants. The response was explosive. At once, the 13 other towns joined the junta, which took Queen Joanna from her monastic prison and used her as their figurehead. At this point they also revealed their hand, calling for the setting up in towns of autonomous republican governments like that in Venice. That was a blast against not only the regional power of the nobility but the central power of the monarchy. The towns were not merely defending antiquated medieval privileges. The Comuneros is a valuable reminder that early modern Europe experienced a major struggle between local power and central power. Almost everywhere, princely power won. The defeat of the Comuneros meant the defeat of their alternative image of the balance of power.

Up to that point, the nobility had made no move to uphold Charles's rule, which shows how broad resentments in Castile were. But the Comuneros began to fragment. During the autumn of 1520, one group sided openly with copycat peasant uprisings and directly attacked the nobility. Once the aristocracy saw their own position in danger, they moved swiftly to support the crown. Simultaneously, the king's position was strengthened instantly by the coincidental death of the hated Chièvres. A fresh start was possible and it was the regent who led the way. He suspended taxation and appointed two Castilian nobles as co-regents. Meanwhile, he negotiated with Portugal to ensure that, unlike in recent civil wars, there would be no foreign intervention. Once noble sympathies had been recovered and the frontiers secured, the regency moved. Nobles offered troops with enthusiasm and at the Battle of Villalar (April 1521) the towns were crushed. By early 1522, the last outposts of resistance had been overwhelmed. Through a lot of luck and a certain degree of skill, the Revolt of the Comuneros was defeated.

The regent's insights into Spanish sensitivities had been crucial and his last, most vital act was bringing Charles home. Once back (1522), the king at last began the task of learning to understand Spain. He did not set foot outside it again until 1529, even though urgent problems needed his attention elsewhere (especially in Germany). Most rebels were pardoned and, in fact, much of what they had demanded was granted during the 1520s. The crown trod cautiously, governing in the deep-rooted tradition of partnership. Charles might have returned with an army of foreign mercenaries to protect him and his throne but, although discontent never vanished, the army was soon redundant. Given the long-standing grievances that underlay the Comuneros, the subsequent peacefulness of Castile (at least on the surface) is remarkable. Although he taxed Spain heavily to fund wars in Italy and Hungary, Charles made no attempt on regional traditions, ignoring the repeated proposal of his imperial chancellor Count Gattinara for a common legal system, administration and currency throughout Spain. Charles was even sensitive enough never to use his imperial title when on Spanish soil. The years 1522–29 (the longest continuous period he ever spent in any of his many territories) changed Charles. He learnt Castilian and Catalan. He discovered a pride in his Spanish ancestry and had his own heir (the future Philip II) brought up in Spain as a Spanish prince. He himself chose Castile for his retirement and burial. Even when away from Spain, as he very often was after 1529, it was always near the forefront of his mind. Charles had fallen in love with Spain.

Despite the Battle of Villalar, was the Comuneros in fact a success?
(Before answering this question, you may want to read pages 60 and 62.)

How strong was Spain's economy by 1556?

Royal finances in Castile were not strong. Queen Isabella (1474–1504) had improved the efficiency of tax collection, but there had been no reform of taxation. The nobility and the church enjoyed major concessions, so the tax burden was totally unbalanced; about 90 per cent fell on the poorest in the kingdom. After Isabella's death, the crown's financial position declined and this was made worse by the enormous sums needed as bribes to win Charles the imperial throne (1519) and to crush the Comuneros (1520–22). Urgent action was needed.

In February 1523, the Council of Finance was created in Castile to control revenues and, for the first time, draw up an annual budget. Under its resourceful secretary **Francisco de los Cobos** (d. 1547), the council worked hard. Receipts from the most important tax, the *alcabala*, rose by 50 per cent. Yet such a rise failed to keep pace with inflation. Things would have been better had Charles not agreed in 1534 to convert the *alcabala* into a fixed lump sum. This was a serious mistake because inflation was soon eroding its real value. What might have been done is shown by the *servicio*, a personal tax that more than tripled its yield (even though, unlike the *alcabala*, the clergy and nobility were exempt from it). A further recurrent problem was that the budget was always inaccurate. In line with contemporary practice, debt repayments were not included under expenditure. By contemporary standards, however, the council was as efficient as could be found in Europe. The roots of los Cobos's problems lay beyond his control. For one thing, Charles seems to have inherited a double dose of personal extravagance, from Queen Isabella and Emperor Maximilian. He lived well beyond his means, keeping a luxurious court and constantly buying works of art and jewels. A king was expected to live grandly; a magnificent court displayed power. Nobody could ever persuade Charles, however, to cut back.

Charles came to rely heavily on **los Cobos**, who acted effectively as secretary of state.

The *alcabala* was a sales tax set at 4 per cent.

For the crippling **cost of war**, see Chapter 4, pages 110 to 112. For comparison of its effects on France, see Chapter 3, pages 72 to 74.

The major reason why Charles could not be kept 'out of the red' was the ever-mounting **cost of war**. In the early days, Charles's campaigns were funded primarily by the Netherlands and Naples. As they groaned under the impossible strain, and as fears of a repeat of the Comuneros receded, Castile began to bear the brunt instead. Charles increasingly used the Castilian Council of Finance to organise most of his loans, which he then guaranteed against Castilian revenues. When in 1540 Charles famously wrote 'I cannot be sustained except by my Spanish realms', this was what he had in mind. Unfortunately for Castile, Charles's military expenditure after 1540 escalated out of control.

1523	0.2 million ducats
1538	1.0 million ducats
1556	12.0 million ducats

Castilian crown debt.

Why were ordinary revenues inadequate?

The *cortes* would never allow significant tax increases, while exemptions prevented taxation from becoming the major source we understand today. Charles's one serious attempt to tax his noblemen (1538) collapsed in the face of their stern hostility to the *sisa*, his proposed tax on food that los Cobos estimated would raise 800,000 ducats a year. Since 'ordinary' revenues could not help, the council was forced to raise 'extraordinary' revenue. From 1529 it began to sell and mortgage crown land. Isabella had occasionally raised government loans called *juros*, selling bonds at a guaranteed 7 per cent rate of interest. Charles's council began issuing these regularly from the 1540s. But the escalating debt problem involved more than stockpiling financial obligations for the future. *Juros* worked by allocating a specified source of revenue to pay their interest and repay their capital. As more and more were issued, fewer and fewer revenues were therefore ending up in the treasury. By the 1550s servicing the *juros* used up 65 per cent of each year's total income from taxes.

Use the table below to work out the percentage rate of growth from one decade to another. Rearrange the ten-year periods in ascending order of growth rate.

1516–25	295,370
1526–35	704,431
1536–45	2,108,673
1546–55	5,221,178

Crown revenues from America (in ducats).

Things could have been worse. Unlike every other European monarch, Charles received revenues from the developing empire in America. In the period 1516–55, he received 8.3 million ducats from American taxes and the crown's one-fifth share of all bullion looted or mined. This sum must be seen in context. American revenues never made up more than 15 per cent of Charles's income. For much of his reign, his total annual receipts were worth about 1 million ducats (1.5 million after 1542). America never funded King Charles; Castilian peasants paid him more in tax every year than was received from America. Furthermore, American revenues were unpredictable. Whereas they averaged 252,000 ducats per year in 1534–43, they fell to an average of 118,000 ducats in 1544–50. Of course, los Cobos was grateful for all extras and America was a unique windfall. Yet los Cobos needed growth; campaigns in the 1540s were pushing the deficit to the limit. Three major wars, lasting in total less than five years, were fought during the 1540s. Each cost the equivalent of two to four years' total income. When in 1546 Charles instructed him to negotiate new *juros* to fund a war to crush the Lutheran princes, every future revenue source due from 1547 to mid-1550 was already signed away. As ever, **los Cobos** pleaded for peace, but was over-ruled. In desperation, the council was forced into the extreme step of confiscating all American bullion as it arrived. The emperor got his war and shattered the heretics. The king of Spain, however, bankrupted many of his merchants and created a terrible legacy of mistrust.

In the 1550s royal finances collapsed. In his last four years, Charles borrowed 10 million ducats against Castilian revenues (when his income was no more than 6 million). Not surprisingly, it was increasingly difficult to find new loans. When bankers were prepared to take the risk, the interest rates demanded ranged between 30 per cent and 52 per cent. Throughout his reign, Charles borrowed 30 million ducats (42 million with interest) on the revenues of Castile. Not even a superpower digging silver out of the ground in America could carry on like that. Philip II had no choice but to declare bankruptcy in 1557.

Against such a background, how did Spain's economy fare? The population numbered about 5 million in 1530, around 80 per cent of whom lived in Castile, and was growing fast. As everywhere in Europe, the Spanish kingdoms were overwhelmingly rural. Agriculture was the core of the economy and population growth created an agricultural boom. Even though most peasants did not own any land, the rise in food prices and thus in the profits of agriculture was good news for all but the poorest peasant labourer. Land was a good investment and in Charles's reign successful merchants and lawyers used urban profits to buy into the buoyant land market. Some land was cultivated more intensely, but much of this agricultural investment involved putting in irrigation systems or draining marshes to farm new land; large areas were totally **deserted**. No crop was more lucrative than grain; cereals dominated Spanish arable farming. Bread was the prime food of the Spanish and there were ever more mouths to feed but, in fact, none of the Spanish kingdoms could feed its people. The need to import grain was a constant drain on Spanish wealth. When harvests were poor, the risk of famine increased enormously – and after 1539 there was a series of weak harvests. Any grain surplus from Naples, which was part of Aragon's empire, was imported. The grain fields of Sicily were even more productive than those of Naples, but climate change in about 1531 produced poorer harvests while growing Mediterranean piracy intercepted many cargoes.

Spain suffered periodic crises of subsistence. In part, these resulted from the drought and scarcity that affected the Mediterranean world: low,

'Without relief, there cannot fail to be serious trouble. The need is extreme if we are to breathe. To tell the truth as I should, we are at the end of the rope.' (**Los Cobos** to King Charles, September 1546)

Los Cobos died in 1547. How successful had he been as Charles's finance minister?

In the famous seventeenth-century Spanish story of Don Quixote, most of his travels are through **deserted** countryside.

unpredictable rainfall and poor soils (half the land was low grade while barely 10 per cent was really fertile). To some degree, they were also caused by population growth as demand outstripped supply in regions already unable to feed themselves. But Castilian agriculture was out of balance. Spain seriously undervalued grain production and all arable farming. Crown and aristocracy were united in seeing sheep farming as the prime activity for Castile. Little investment was needed and the profits of wool far exceeded rewards from cereals. It is true that sheep suited a land of poor soils. But the scale of sheep farming reflected choice, not necessity. Easy profits suited landowners and the *mesta* always enjoyed royal support (providing reliable tax revenues and major loans). As population pressures drove up demand for bread, and the developing American colonies too began to call for grain, there should have been a shift in agricultural activity. The crown was, however, too much in the *mesta*'s pocket.

The golden age of the *mesta* ended *c.*1550 when inflation began to make Spanish wool uncompetitive. Throughout Charles's reign, however, the economy was straight-jacketed by the all-powerful *mesta*. The textile industry was stunted by *mesta* contracts with merchants selling Spanish wool in more lucrative export markets. Rising cloth prices and growing demand both at home and in America could have been used to establish a vibrant textile industry. That Spain, the great European producer of wool, had to satisfy most of its needs for cloth through imports was a scandal. But the *mesta* was too powerful a lobby and the crown, even allowing for its compromised position on wool, showed little interest in promoting new areas of economic activity. Raw silk production in Granada and Valencia was reasonably successful but, again, most was exported. The native silk-weaving industry struggled.

Far more successful were the industries of northern Spain: iron and shipbuilding. The early-sixteenth-century iron industry was transformed by the shift to water-powered forges and, as population growth and American settlement created rising demand, production expanded. The shipyards too turned out an ever-increasing tonnage. Shipping was an excellent investment, especially because of America, and by 1550 the Spanish had the second largest merchant fleet in Europe. Again, royal support was limited and inflationary pressures began to make yards uncompetitive. Wherever one looks, **Spanish industrial activity** did not flourish as it might have done. Several factors that held back the craft industries have already been noted. Levels of technology were, on the whole, well below those in northern Europe. Lack of investment was another weakness. Some of America's riches could have been diverted to great effect, but the *mesta* and the *juros* soaked up virtually all spare capital. Ongoing under-development locked Spain into an imports dependency and a

Merino sheep were kept for their high-quality wool. The complex organisation that oversaw their breeding, feeding and shearing was the ***mesta***, a very powerful institution with enormous legal privileges. In 1550, the *mesta* controlled about 3.5 million sheep.

Assess the advantages and disadvantages of the *mesta*.

'Spanish industrial activity became weaker as the sixteenth century went on. There was no equivalent to the mini industrial revolution which had such an impact on England.' (David Vassberg, *Land and society in golden age Castile*, 1984)

perpetual balance of trade deficit. The final adverse factor was contemporary **inflation** which, tragically, many thought was the result of excessive exporting of finished goods. In 1552, one royal edict banned the export of virtually all manufactured goods while another ordered the import of foreign cloth.

What of commerce? Aragon was a Mediterranean trading empire in decline. During Charles's reign, trade in the western Mediterranean was disrupted by rising Ottoman power. More important, the close links forged between Charles and the Republic of Genoa from 1528 gave their merchants significant privileges. Before long, almost all the cloth being bought in Naples and Sicily was Genoese. Aragon's trade was collapsing. By contrast, Castile's trade with northern Europe enjoyed some vitality; Burgos grew fat on the export of wool. But this was a narrow prosperity. As we have seen, Castile's products were raw materials and thus of low value (unlike those of France, the Netherlands and England). Its one chance would have been a textile industry, but we have already seen why that could not develop. As a result, Castile's imports in the 1540s were eight to ten times more valuable than its exports. The only way to sustain such an imbalance was to pay for all those foreign goods in cash. As most of the crown's share of American wealth went abroad to repay German and Italian bankers for their war loans, so the greater part of privately owned American bullion was exported to cover the balance of payments deficit.

The Atlantic trade itself was the one commercial success story. Based on the port of Seville, American trade rose in volume by 800 per cent between 1506 and 1550. Until the 1520s, the infant colonies operated at a loss, consuming far more from the motherland than they could send home in exchange. From the early 1530s, the balance in the flow of goods reversed and **bullion** (all looted) poured into Spain for about 20 years. By the mid 1550s, however, the easy plunder of Aztec and Inca riches was over. Thereafter, Spanish settlers had to create wealth from the raw materials around them. That took time to organise and so 1550–62 were lean years. The first half of the century had, however, been a time of extraordinary vitality that turned Seville into a boom town whose population jumped from about 60,000 in 1530 to about 150,000 by 1588. Thanks to America, Seville became the largest city in Spain and the third largest in Europe.

America itself stimulated general Spanish production: mostly wine and olive oil, cloth, horses and metal tools to sustain the settlers. Perversely, America failed to stimulate greater grain production back home in Spain. Rather, the colonists became yet another burden, requiring the purchase of even more foreign grain. This is odd, because Spain always saw America as a market for its own produce, and so forbade the manufacture in Mexico or Peru of anything produced in Spain. Of course, other goods were very welcome;

Prices in Spain rose by an average of 10 per cent between 1521 and 1550. The highest **inflation** occurred in the 1520s and 1540s. During the same period, the real value of wages fell by about 20 per cent.

Explain why it mattered that Spain imported far more than it exported.

Why were Spain's colonies uneconomic before c.1530?

Major silver deposits were discovered at Potosí (in Bolivia) in 1545, and at Guanajuato and Zacatecas (both in Mexico) in 1548. Once developed, they became the major sources of American **bullion**. Equally, however, they stifled other economic activity. Mining dominated the Spanish American economy in part because Potosí and Zacatecas were so rich – all other forms of wealth creation were, by comparison, too unpredictable and too hard. Silver made the Spanish colonists lazy.

colonists were expected to help the mother country. Thus the exporting to Spain of animal hides, timber and sugar developed from the 1530s (for Spanish consumption and for re-export). Nevertheless, another great opportunity for the economic development of Spain was missed. The colonies consumed all sorts of goods. Here was the perfect stimulus to kick-start arable farming and manufacturing capacity. Both were ignored. Instead, the colonists bought eagerly from Flemish, French and English merchants. Castile failed the great colonial test presented by America: the vision to use American wealth to create sustained economic development back home.

What were the structural weaknesses of the Spanish economy?

What Spain really wanted from America was gold and silver. Bullion more than paid for the empire, offered the dream of instant riches to colonists and merchants alike, and made Charles the richest monarch in Europe. But we must be careful not to exaggerate. For one thing, bullion flowed in far larger quantities during the reign of Philip II than in the time of his father. For another, as we have seen, much of that bullion did not stay long in Spain. Regularly, the *cortes* asked Charles to ban the re-export of American bullion. Neither Castile nor Charles would have survived if the *cortes* had got what it wanted.

If so much American silver drained away, could it have been responsible (as was once believed) for the inflation that began to trouble Spain? Between 1501 and 1550, prices doubled, rising on average by 2.2 per cent each year. Around the city of Valladolid, rents increased by over 80 per cent from 1530 to 1555. Links between bullion and inflation remain highly controversial. One problem with the theory is that inflation was more serious in the first half of the century (when the volume and value of bullion imports were relatively small) than in the days of Philip II (when bullion imports were far higher). Following this clue, some scholars now believe that population growth was the engine driving inflation – more people created rising levels of demand for food, clothing and other commodities which could not be met, thus forcing prices up.

In your own words, explain briefly the case against American bullion as the cause of inflation.

How successful was Spanish foreign policy between 1504 and 1556?

Medieval Castile was little involved with the rest of Europe and made little impact on it. By contrast, Aragon was a thrusting state that created a considerable trading empire across the western Mediterranean. Under Ferdinand and Isabella, Spanish foreign policy was therefore Aragonese foreign policy. Aragon had the long frontier with France and the Mediterranean territories. Any threat to either was a threat to Aragon, and the likely source of any such threat was France. Aragon and France were medieval rivals (whereas Castile and France were allies). Ferdinand negotiated a carefully crafted network of treaties with every anti-French state. When France invaded Italy in 1494 and occupied the kingdom of Naples, ruled by a branch of Aragon's royal family (until 1458 ruled directly by Aragon), Ferdinand was alarmed. Between 1495 and 1504, he succeeded in expelling the French and securing Naples for himself. In these Italian Wars, Aragon involved itself in high-level European politics. **Ferdinand's** formidable victories gave him an immense reputation. The diplomatic and military humiliation of France was judged to herald the birth of a new power.

In 1504, international acclaim was ringing in Ferdinand's ears. Italy continued to dominate his mind and he began to look northwards at French-controlled Milan. In 1512 he established a friendly regime in Florence to give him leverage in central Italy and an operational base for future campaigns; when its pro-Spanish Medici rulers were overthrown in 1527, Charles intervened to restore them. Ferdinand helped an Italian coalition expel Louis XII from Milan in 1512 and for the next 25 years Spain worked to keep the French out. By the end, Milan was under direct Spanish rule.

Ferdinand reinforced his intricate web of alliances with a series of dynastic marriages, some designed to tie Spain to Portugal, the rest to bind the anti-French coalition more tightly:

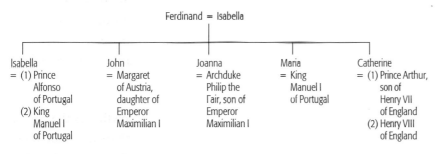

Ferdinand = Isabella

Isabella	John	Joanna	Maria	Catherine
= (1) Prince Alfonso of Portugal (2) King Manuel I of Portugal	= Margaret of Austria, daughter of Emperor Maximilian I	= Archduke Philip the Fair, son of Emperor Maximilian I	= King Manuel I of Portugal	= (1) Prince Arthur, son of Henry VII of England (2) Henry VIII of England

Ferdinand's marriage alliances.

But this strategy faltered early in the new century. Its pillar, the alliance with Maximilian I, foundered with the death of his heir, Philip, in 1506. Its associate link with England already hung in the balance after the death of Prince Arthur (1502). The death of Isabella (1504) unsettled things further. Ferdinand felt isolated and, in that very different climate, sought better relations with France – his diplomacy was always supple. This explains his marriage in 1506 to Germaine de Foix. (See family tree on page 41.)

In time these insecurities passed and Ferdinand's final years saw a resumption of anti-French hostility. Chief among his acts was his exploitation of the death in 1512 of King Gaston of Navarre. He seized the Pyrenean kingdom, an old source of friction between Aragon and France. Ferdinand's stepmother

For the success of **Ferdinand's** troops, see Chapter 4, pages 97 to 98. To the contemporary political thinker Machiavelli, Ferdinand was 'a new prince because from being a weak king he has risen to being, for fame and glory, the first king of Christendom'.

Summarise Ferdinand's attitude to France and Italy.

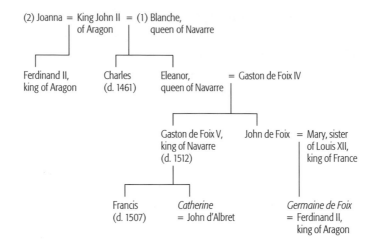

Ferdinand II and the disputed succession to the kingdom of Navarre. (Names in italic are those of rivals for the throne in 1512.)

Identify policies and actions in Ferdinand's foreign policy that would support his nickname of 'the cunning fox'.

The **Maghrib** is that part of north-west Africa covered today by Morocco, Algeria and Tunisia.

The word *presidio* implied a site that was a military base and a trading post. See the map on page 53.

had been its queen and now he took the opportunity to proclaim the rights of his wife, Germaine de Foix (see the diagram above). As ever, he prepared the ground well, persuading his son-in-law Henry VIII to invade France (thereby distracting Louis XII) and bribing Pope Julius II to excommunicate the rival claimant and her husband. Arguing that French invasion was imminent, Ferdinand then occupied Navarre in 'self-defence'. No wonder his contemporary Louis XII nicknamed him 'the cunning fox'.

The years after Isabella's death also saw campaigns against the Muslim states of the **Maghrib**. These fitted within Aragon's expansion in the western Mediterranean. Further, they represented continuity with Castile's resurgent tradition of crusade (the recent conquest of the emirate of Granada 1482–92) and its determination not to let Portugal monopolise the wealth of the decaying sultanate of Fez. Ferdinand portrayed this enterprise as a crusade, although his prime motive was probably financial. He could obtain large papal grants. And, since crusade was a Castilian passion, he could, by dressing the venture in a religious context, bring it about with Castilian troops and funds. We should not, however, dismiss the justification as purely cynical. Ferdinand was interested in crusade and, late in life, started to plan the conquest of Egypt and the liberation of Jerusalem. Whatever his motivation, the planning was (as ever) superb. The Maghrib sultanates were politically weak and Ferdinand conquered eight *presidios*.

No European ruler had controlled so much of north Africa since Roman times. Yet Ferdinand did not go on. When the sultanates could have been toppled with ease, why did he stop short? Trouble was brewing in Italy by 1510–12 and Ferdinand saw Milan as more important; his grandson Charles was to think the same way. He was content to secure a series of outposts that

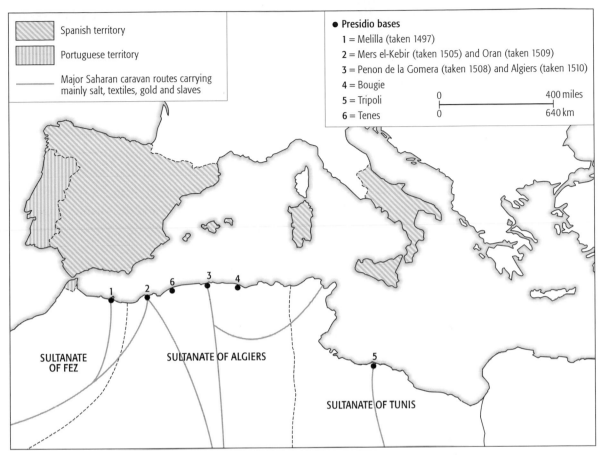

Legend:

- ▨ Spanish territory
- ▥ Portuguese territory
- —— Major Saharan caravan routes carrying mainly salt, textiles, gold and slaves

● Presidio bases
1 = Melilla (taken 1497)
2 = Mers el-Kebir (taken 1505) and Oran (taken 1509)
3 = Penon de la Gomera (taken 1508) and Algiers (taken 1510)
4 = Bougie
5 = Tripoli
6 = Tenes

0   400 miles
0   640 km

SULTANATE OF FEZ

SULTANATE OF ALGIERS

SULTANATE OF TUNIS

Ferdinand in north Africa.

would protect Spain from possible attack and give control of the trade of west Africa for which the *presidio* ports were outlets.

> Assess the political, military and economic value of the *presidios* taken between 1505 and 1510.

Charles I

Charles was emperor and duke of Burgundy as well as king of Castile, Aragon and Navarre. The overlap between some of his interests makes it difficult to define what was 'Spanish' about his foreign policy. We have already identified Aragonese needs (the wish to reduce the power of France and keep French influence out of Italy, the ambition to dominate western Mediterranean trade) and Castilian concern to reverse the power of Islam. When Charles fought the French he was, however, acting also in accordance with the Burgundian and imperial traditions. When he battled with the Turks, he was also fulfilling his duty as emperor. Charles actually split his crusading into 'imperial' and 'Spanish' arenas, giving his brother Ferdinand charge of combating the Ottomans in central Europe while himself taking responsibility for the Mediterranean. That division is reflected in this book, so the Hungarian front is considered in Chapter 1 (see pages 34 to 37). So neat a division is not possible for the struggle with France; the contest over Milan was as imperial as it was Spanish. On the other hand, no Spanish claims were involved in campaigns in the duchy of Lorraine or the county of Flanders (although most of the money to pay for them was extracted from Spain). Such elements are examined, together with the Italian Wars, in Chapter 1 (see pages 27 to 34).

Note that some historians deny Spain had a foreign policy under Charles. The leading exponent of this view is Henry Kamen, who argues that Spain was not a great power and did not act aggressively at this time. Its naval strength was negligible while the troops in Charles's armies were too cosmopolitan to be thought of as 'Spanish'. The wars fought in Italy and the Mediterranean (as elsewhere) were, he claims, imperial.

The Mediterranean

1525	Barbarossa captures Algiers.
1528	Genoa allies with Charles.
1530	Charles installs the Knights Hospitallers on Malta and in Tripoli.
1534	Barbarossa captures Tunis.
1535	Charles recaptures Tunis.
1536	First French–Ottoman treaty.
1541	Charles's attempt to recapture Algiers fails.
1551	Charles loses Tripoli.

Charles valued the 800-year-old Castilian legacy of crusading. As emperor, he was jointly responsible with the pope for the defence of Christendom. These traditions linked naturally in Charles's mind. In 1532, for example, he met Pope Clement VII 'as well to consider the state of religious matters as to co-ordinate resistance to the Turk, and also to secure peace in Italy'. Those are his words and they sum up his goals. But they also reveal his problem. By 'religious matters' he meant Protestantism in Germany, and by 'peace in Italy' he meant the expulsion of the French. His time and resources were limited. Charles had to prioritise and, if the Mediterranean seemed to end up as Cinderella among his activities, we must be careful not to dismiss his talk of crusade as propaganda or some meaningless medieval relic. We know he was influenced by Burgundian ideals of the Christian knight. Charles must be judged according to his own claim that he tried 'to follow the sign of the Holy Cross in true faith and conquer Infidels under the banner of Christ'.

Barbary is a name for the coastal area of north-west Africa. A corsair is a pirate operating under licence from a government (rather than privately on his own).

Charles inherited the Maghrib *presidios*. Their hinterlands remained in Moorish hands, but under puppet sultans obedient to Spanish wishes. From 1518, however, a new force appeared in the region: the **Barbary** corsairs (see

Charles's dream. Bronze medal,
c.1530. Supported by an angel (left),
Charles turns to confront the power
of Islam.

map on page 56). Led by the **Barbarossa** brothers, they moved fast and in 1525 overcame the Castilian garrison in Algiers. The corsairs were Charles's opponent in the region, not the Ottoman Turks. Ottoman power dominated the eastern Mediterranean, but the two halves of the Mediterranean were almost self-contained worlds. Sultan Suleiman I (1520–66) was a warrior who repeatedly led his armies in battle, but who detested the sea. Like Charles, he had major preoccupations, so there was no way he could push west of Egypt. When Barbarossa offered his services and accepted the sultan as his lord, the Ottomans acquired an agent they were happy to fund and equip. Ottoman rule in the Maghrib was indirect.

The tide of battle swung backwards and forwards; Algiers changed hands five times. The contest focused on the central Mediterranean, the frontier between the Spanish and Ottoman zones. The sea lanes around Sicily were the most critical area to Charles because they guaranteed the safety not only of his Neapolitan and Sicilian coasts, but of regular grain supplies to Spain. Charles reinforced the region in 1530 by handing Malta and Tripoli to the crusading Knights Hospitallers. He also put the Genoese fleet to sea under Andrea Dorea to patrol the shipping routes and raid the Greek coast. In 1534, however,

Barbarossa is a nickname meaning 'red beard'. Of Greek parentage, all four brothers used the name, but in this book it relates to Khair ad Din (c.1482–1546), known always in the west simply as Barbarossa. He was appointed by Sultan Selim I as *beylerbei* (governor) of Algeria in 1520, and in 1536 Sultan Suleiman I made him *kapudan* (grand admiral) of the Ottoman navy. His successor was Turgut Reis (called Dragut in the west), who took Tripoli in 1551.

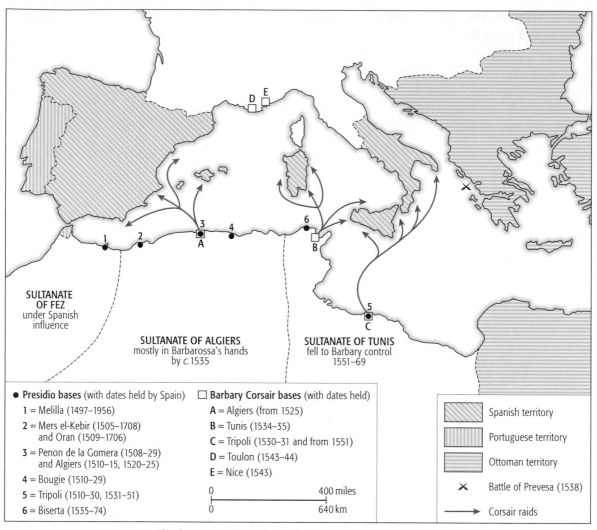

Charles's struggle with the Barbary corsairs.

'The Spanish were particularly interested in the position of **Tunis** for it allowed them to control the Sicilian channel, and seriously hamper communications between Istanbul and Algiers.' (R. Mantran, *The Cambridge history of Islam*, 1970)

Raids into Charles's territories were especially severe in 1534, 1535, 1537, 1540 and 1543.

Barbarossa upset the balance by seizing **Tunis** and, from there, raiding southern Italy. Charles had to act and the following season he led in person a successful armada to restore Tunis to his puppet sultan. But there were no follow-on land campaigns and, in the meantime, the French established contact with the sultan; in 1543–44 Barbarossa was even allowed to winter in Toulon.

Two things need to be made clear to understand the Mediterranean theatre. First, Barbarossa was a corsair chief, not a traditional king. His interest was in piracy and coastal **raiding**, not territorial conquest. The threat to Charles's territories and some of his subjects was real but limited, because Barbarossa's objectives were limited. Second, Charles's involvement was limited too, and not just because he was so busy elsewhere. Castilian crusades were not long wars of conquest. The tradition of the **Reconquista** was one of garrisons on frontiers and periodic raids. *Presidios* represented successful crusade: strong points giving dominion over puppet rulers. In Fez, Charles maintained his grip by exploiting successive sultans' fears of being squeezed between the ambitions of Portugal and the corsairs. Algiers and Tunis worked less well, and Barbarossa faced only occasional challenges as he established a wide dominion. Charles was not merely the prisoner of extensive obligations. He was the victim of the Castilian way of crusading.

Historians criticise Charles for not conquering the Maghrib. They argue that strategically and economically it was more important to whoever ruled Castile, Aragon and Naples than anywhere in northern Italy was. Charles's obsession with Milan allowed Barbarossa to grow strong, and weakened Spanish power in north Africa. The consequence is beyond dispute: the puppet sultanate of Algiers and much of Tunis were lost, along with several *presidios* (most crucially Tripoli in 1551). While the 1535 Tunis campaign made Charles a crusading hero in Europe, it did not reflect reality in north Africa. But the explanation of the cause of this ignores Castilian ideas of crusade and the problems plaguing a man who was emperor as well as king of Aragon and Naples. If Charles made a fundamental mistake, the same error was also made by King Ferdinand (and he was never emperor, so it cannot be said that Spanish interests lost out to imperial needs). What is more, it must be noted that Charles's naval power was limited, even after his alliance with maritime Genoa in 1528. As for allies, the papal fleet was small, and Venice usually avoided war to keep Middle Eastern trade flowing; France, of course, was pro-Ottoman. Christian naval power was weak and divided. On the one occasion when they did combine their fleets, at the **Battle of Prevesa** in 1538, Barbarossa smashed them.

Italy, 1516–29

1516	Treaty of Noyon.
1521	Charles captures Milan.
1525	Battle of Pavia.
1527	Sack of Rome.
1528	Genoa allies with Charles.
1529	Battle of Landriano.

Aragonese–French rivalry went back centuries and from 1495 focused on Italy. Ferdinand had won the contest for Naples and assisted France's expulsion from Milan. In 1515, however, the French returned and, after spectacular victory at the Battle of Marignano, took Milan. Then Ferdinand himself

The **Reconquista** was the medieval Christian quest to drive Islam out of Spain (the Arabs had conquered it 711–18). 'The word *conquista* to the Castilian implied essentially the establishing of the Spanish presence – the securing of strong points, the staking out of claims, the acquisition of dominion over a defeated population.' (John Elliott, *Imperial Spain 1469–1716*, 1963)

What factors explain the way Charles acted in the Mediterranean?

The **historian** Ferdinand Braudel calls this failure 'a tragedy for Spain' and 'one of the great missed opportunities of history'. (*The Mediterranean and the Mediterranean world in the age of Philip II*, 1972)

'**Prevesa** undid Charles's Tunisian triumph, revived Barbarossa's reputation and secured the Central Mediterranean to the Turkish navy.' (Geoffrey Elton, *Reformation Europe 1517–1559*, 1963)

What was the purpose of the Treaty of Noyon?

died. A breathing space was vital so in 1516 the Treaty of Noyon was signed, recognising Francis as duke of Milan. Further, was it possible that the Italian Wars might be over – that they were an old problem that had just died with the previous generation: Julius II (1513), Louis XII (1515) and Ferdinand (1516)? This is an intriguing might-have-been, but Charles's election as emperor (1519) destroyed any possibility of that, for it completed the encirclement of France. A trial of strength was as inevitable as its prime battleground. In alliance with the pope, Charles drove the French from Milan in 1521 and crushed their counter-offensive in 1522 at the Battle of Bicocca.

Charles was apparently the new master of Italy. His formidable position alarmed the Italian states and secretly they changed sides. Treachery was a feature of Italian politics and this was a story to be repeated over and over. In 1524 it produced a new French invasion. Milan was recovered and an army dispatched to Naples. A swift counter-stroke turned the tables, however, and in February 1525 Charles won a crushing victory at Pavia. The French were slaughtered and Francis I was taken prisoner. In the subsequent Treaty of Madrid (1526), France surrendered all claims to Navarre, Naples and the Burgundian lands. But the benefits of Pavia were lost because Charles made the mistake of trusting the French king's word, releasing him before the terms had been implemented. Once free, Francis repudiated the agreement and created the anti-imperial League of Cognac. When an imperial army raped and looted in Rome in 1527, Charles was widely criticised. But the Sack of Rome demonstrated his power in Italy and led on to fresh triumphs. Attempting again to recover Milan, the French suffered another humiliating defeat in 1529 at Landriano. More significant still was the defection to Charles of the hitherto pro-French Republic of **Genoa** in 1528. Genoese banks would now become a major source of imperial funds and her fleet would be used in operations against Barbarossa.

Why was Charles unable to achieve decisive victory in Italy in the 1520s?

'The movement of **Genoa** into the imperial camp . . . was the greatest single step in consolidating in the peninsula a dominant Spanish position.' (Matthew Anderson, *The origins of the modern European state system, 1494–1618*, 1998)

Financed by the first significant shipments of bullion from Mexico, Charles was the undisputed master of Italy and in the 1530s his dominance there took on an increasingly Spanish (rather than imperial) character. Spain already ruled the entire south. Florence was her poodle and Milan her pawn. Genoa inevitably looked more to the Mediterranean and became Charles's prime assistant (financially and militarily) in the campaigns against Barbarossa. The rise of Barbary power meant that the papacy too was forced to think in Mediterranean terms and look to Charles as king of Aragon and Naples to act. Of course, Genoa and Rome also saw Charles as the emperor; Genoese loans from 1528 were fundamental to wars in the Netherlands, Hungary and Germany. But Italy was being made to revolve around the interests of Spain.

Why was Italy so important to Spain?

After 1529, the Habsburg–Valois Wars took a decisive northwards shift. With most conflict focused primarily on eastern France and the Netherlands, Charles's Habsburg interests predominated rather than Spanish interests. None the less, Francis never gave up on Milan, or even on Naples. His search for alliances with anyone hostile to Charles was designed, as he put it in 1533, 'to recover that which plainly belongs to me and my children, and has been usurped by the Emperor'. Contact with the Turks formed a central strand in that strategy. Both sides had difficulties with so scandalous an association. Their interests did not always coincide and Franco-Ottoman alliance rarely got beyond discussions. But the danger to Charles was always there, as was demonstrated in 1541 by the information French agents sent to Barbarossa on Charles's preparations for the attack on Algiers. Even worse, a French fleet joined with Barbarossa in 1543, captured the imperial port of Nice and wintered on French soil.

The Italian Wars themselves resumed after Milan's duke died in 1535 without a son. Such an event could only reignite **Francis**'s claims, but both sides were in financial difficulties and truces were quickly signed; for some time, the Italian theatre was quiet. That changed with the accession of Henry II in 1547. The new French king was married to an Italian princess and Italian influences were strong at his court. By 1551 the corsairs were being pressed to raid Neapolitan coasts. Between 1552 and 1555 Henry supported revolt in Siena against Spanish rule. In 1553 French troops took Corsica from Genoa. Finally, France allied with the ferociously anti-Spanish Pope Paul IV and in 1556–57 attempted once more to take Naples. Everything went wrong and the victorious Spanish army of the new King Philip II advanced as far as Rome. The enterprise of Italy, begun back in 1495 by Ferdinand, had ended in triumph. Spain dominated **Italy**.

Beyond war in the Mediterranean and Italy, one further Spanish thread can be seen in Charles's foreign policy. Like all rulers then, Charles thought in terms of his dynasty. Dynastic alliances secured a throne and provided allies for the defence of territory. How a king used the opportunities available tells us much about the concerns closest to his heart. Charles himself wed the Portuguese princess Isabella in 1526. This was a marriage for Spain. It maintained close associations forged by Ferdinand and Isabella, guaranteed peace in Iberia and was very popular in Castile. That ongoing link was later reinforced by the marriage of his sister Catherine to Isabella's brother King John III of Portugal, his daughter Joanna to a Portuguese prince and, most telling of all, his heir Philip to another Portuguese princess. While most of Charles's sisters were married to Danes, Hungarians and other Habsburgs, two of his three children were married to Portuguese. That he used his

'**Francis** wanted nothing else, while Charles was as determined as ever to prevent it passing into French hands.' (Robert Knecht, *Renaissance warrior and patron: the reign of Francis I*, 1994)

'The Council of **Italy**, created in 1555, was a sign that Mediterranean policy was ceasing to be that of an empire and becoming part of Spanish foreign policy.' (John Lynch, *Spain 1516–1598: from nation state to world empire*, 1991)

Explain the importance of dynastic marriages. How were Charles's dynastic marriages of use to Spain?

Between 1516 and 1522 most Spaniards were convinced that Spain would be sacrificed to the Habsburg interests of King Charles. Judged from 1556, how far were they right?

trump cards in this way demonstrates that Charles's dynastic policy served the interests of Spain.

Charles had his only son brought up in Spain as a Spanish prince. In the way Charles arranged his inheritance, that commitment to Spain was underlined. When Charles abdicated and divided his vast territories, he did not merely return his lands to the Spanish and Habsburg halves he had inherited. The wealthy duchy of Burgundy was detached from the empire and allocated to Spain, to help fund future wars. The strategic duchy of Milan was passed to Spain as well. Though events after 1529 often suggested that the empire overshadowed Spain, it was Spain that was becoming ever more important. When he abdicated in 1556, he inaugurated not a revived Holy Roman Empire but a mighty Spanish empire.

How successful was Charles I as king of Spain?

Charles began to become Spanish from 1522. Spaniards were appointed in increasing numbers to senior posts at court and in the administration. Spain started to return to normal after the Comuneros. Fundamental to this was the king's determination not to challenge the traditions of his various kingdoms. He resisted suggestions from the imperial chancellor that a unified administration, legal system and coinage should be introduced. Instead, government continued in traditional ways. His grandparents had reorganised the administration into a series of advisory councils supported by their own bureaucracies. Charles adapted these and increased their number (see diagram below). But it was the old system that continued.

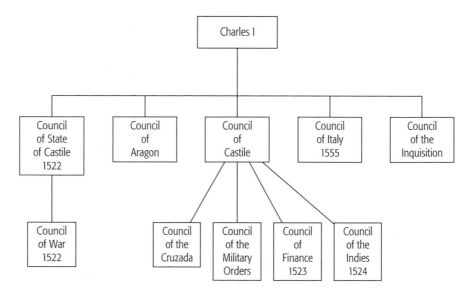

The conciliar system of administration (with dates of foundation).

The Council of State was unlike all the others because its function was to advise Charles generally on high politics. Set up in the wake of the Comuneros, it was designed to revive a sense of traditional Castilian government by Castilian magnates. After a few years, Charles called it less and less. Castile had settled down. The king was growing in confidence and increasingly taking decisions himself, after seeking advice from individual secretaries. Before long, the council was a political irrelevance, which indicates graphically the strength of Charles's monarchy by 1527–29. Government happened elsewhere, in the other councils. All but one had their responsibilities limited to a single kingdom. Each council was a smallish body which Charles halved in size to no more than nine officials, recruited increasingly from lawyers and the gentry (nobles became rare). Only the Council of the Inquisition operated across all borders, as if 'Spain' really existed.

In what ways did Charles change the conciliar system?

Opinion among scholars is that the conciliar system was clumsy. Councils had overlapping responsibilities, which caused endless inefficiencies. Snail-like procedures, combined with their odd mix of administrative and legal responsibilities, left them unable to cope with the flood of business. The system was saved by a group of officials – the secretaries – who in each kingdom linked the crown to a council. In most instances, Charles dealt directly with a **secretary** and, in consequence, their office rose enormously in status. The most prominent of these, **Francisco de los Cobos**, ended up secretary to most of the councils and thus a powerful co-ordinator, but remained primarily secretary of the Council of Finance. None of the secretaries was liked by the councils, which saw the independent role of the former as a challenge to their own authority. But los Cobos's paramount position from around 1527 made him the target of particular resentments and jealousies. The king was aware of los Cobos's perpetual search for influence and greedy eye for profit-making opportunities. But the secretary got things done like no other. His pre-eminent place was entirely a reflection of the king's trust.

'It was the **secretaries** who rescued the government from stagnation . . . they must be regarded as key agents in the Habsburg system of government.' (John Lynch, *Spain 1516–1598: from nation state to world empire*, 1991)

'The government of Spain ran so smoothly under the gentle guidance of **los Cobos** that it almost seems as if for twenty or thirty years the country had no internal history.' (John Elliott, *Imperial Spain 1469–1716*, 1963)

Charles was careful to preserve the *fueros* of his individual kingdoms. He never received significant taxation from any of the three *cortes* of Aragon, and they made it more than clear that new taxes were unacceptable. This unsatisfactory state of affairs Charles accepted because **Aragon**'s declining commercial prosperity meant too little wealth was at stake to justify provoking a crisis. At the same time, the office of the *justicia* was a perpetual check on any move to increase royal authority in Aragon; his very purpose was to uphold the *fueros*. By contrast, Castile was vulnerable to the growth of royal power. The crown regularly interfered in the elections to ensure 'suitable' men were chosen for the *cortes*. Once there, members were never allowed to discuss grievances before taxes had been approved. They met more frequently, the crown involved them in tax collection and in 1534 the king agreed to their

Fueros were regional rights and privileges, rooted in each *cortes*.

'Traditional liberties in **Aragon** survived because the kingdoms were too poor to challenge, rather than because their political liberties intimidated the king.' (Henry Kamen, *Spain 1469–1716: a society of conflict*, 1983)

proposal to change the *alcabala*. But if more active, the *cortes* gained no new power and, since the crown could (and did) make law without it, the one political check to Charles arose on the sensitive area of aristocratic tax exemptions. Twice Charles tried to erode their privilege (1527 and 1538). On each occasion they defeated him. What appears on the surface to be noble strength was, in fact, the flaw in the Castilian constitution. Because nobles were exempt from tax, they virtually never attended the *cortes* – its business was not relevant to them. Safe behind their own immunities, they had no reason to question royal expenditure and the increasingly expensive foreign policy that created ever larger debts. So weak did this leave the *cortes* that in 1544 it even asked Charles not to summon it more than once every three years. The one potential restraint on crown activity, and the one point around which parliamentary power could grow, did not exist. If in Aragon he had nothing to gain by provoking a political crisis, in Castile he had everything to lose.

Why didn't Charles face regular battles with the *cortes* over taxation and the costs of war?

Since Charles was usually an absentee ruler, he had to delegate even more authority than other contemporary rulers. In Castile, he appointed first his wife and later his son as regent. Elsewhere, he used the Aragonese system of viceroys, establishing them in Navarre, Sardinia, Sicily and Naples – and later in New Spain (Mexico) and New Castile (Peru). Devolution was the only practical politics. Most viceroys were Castilian nobles; this was one way he kept the aristocracy content. But Charles always charged his regent with keeping an eye on the viceroys and, on a day-to-day basis, they were regulated by the councils. Even though simultaneously he eased nobles out of the councils, the alliance of crown and nobility, forged during the Comuneros, underpinned the remarkable political stability after 1522.

To the sixteenth-century mind, the tranquillity of a state depended also on religious stability. In many ways, the church in the Spanish kingdoms could not have been in a better state. Isabella's reign had witnessed a raft of reforms to improve the quality of the clergy and monasteries. Spearheaded by the archbishop of Toledo, Cardinal Ximenez de Cisneros (d. 1517), much was accomplished. Effective reform would, however, be achieved only by long-term pressure and the religious renaissance continued through Charles's reign. The quality of that achievement has been seen as a major reason why Protestantism had such difficulty taking root in Spain and why **Spaniards** took such a prominent role in the Counter-Reformation.

Spanish theologians played a crucial part at the Council of Trent. **Spaniards** also took a leading role in the Dominican order and the new Jesuit order.

Yet Spain was troubled by three religious problems: the new fear of Protestantism and ongoing worries about former Jewish and Islamic groups. All three gave plenty of scope for the Inquisition, whose job it was to root out religious deviants. In fact, the Inquisition had since *c*.1510 been under mounting criticism for its ruthlessness after the conquest of Granada (1492). But Charles gave it wholehearted support and by 1523 the Inquisition was secure. From the moment Luther was excommunicated (1521), the Spanish authorities mounted a close watch. Books were sometimes discovered. Occasionally, individuals were convicted but by 1558 there had been only 105 prosecutions (63 per cent of which involved foreigners). The Inquisition had, however, little idea what Protestantism was and the **difficulty** was that it could not distinguish it from other religious movements. Most critically, they suffered from the near-universal inability to distinguish between Luther and Erasmus. This proved disastrous because Erasmian ideas on church reform were well established in Spain by the late 1520s. Cardinal Ximenez had been a staunch supporter. So was Charles himself. Tensions were, however, growing. The king's departure in 1529 removed crucial protection and the next four years saw a total reversal in the climate. Led by various inquisitors, panicked by the illusion of some great Protestant menace, Erasmian views were condemned as Lutheran and a great purge was launched; another panic set off a new round of interrogations in 1557. This irrational plunge into intolerance was tragic for Spain and the church. What is extraordinary (and so revealing of the power of individual inquisitors) is that, until his death in 1538, the Inquisitor-General, Archbishop Manrique of Seville, was himself a committed Erasmian. The truth is that separate schools of thought had emerged from Ximenez's reforms. One favoured a simple religious life of personal obedience to the Bible and strict moral behaviour; Erasmian ideas locked neatly with this. The other stressed the formal religious life of the organised church and was popular among conservatives. During the 1520s, the latter turned on the former and branded them as heretics. In other words, this was not a battle against Erasmus or Luther, but a struggle between rival visions for the soul of the Spanish church.

The shadows were equally long for two other religious groups and demonstrated that the once proud boast of *convivencia* was dead. Medieval Spain had one of the most vibrant Jewish communities in Europe, but persecution began in the fourteenth century; from 1391 this involved forcible conversions. The final such demand was made in 1492: convert or be expelled. Numbers are uncertain but perhaps 50,000 to 90,000 chose to remain and thus join the ranks of the *conversos*. The Inquisition was, in fact, established (1478) to monitor *conversos* because the authorities were convinced they practised Judaism in secret. Scholars are divided on this problem. Most suggest conversions were at best shallow. How could such a change, made under threat without instruction in the new religion, have any validity? Some historians have, however, started to question that, arguing that second- and third-generation *conversos* were good Catholics and, crucially, surviving Jewish communities regarded *conversos* as Christians. We may never know, but the Inquisition certainly thought them suspect. Of the 5,000 or so victims executed before 1530, 80–90 per cent were *conversos*. A further blow fell in 1547 when a second-

For similar **difficulties** in France, see Chapter 3, pages 80 to 82, where, in addition, Erasmus's ideas are briefly explained.

Why was Protestantism seen as so great a threat? (You should look at Chapter 5, pages 127 to 136, for further information.)

Convivencia was the happy co-existence of Christianity, Islam and Judaism in Spain. Medieval Aragonese kings prided themselves on this, using 'Lords of the Three Faiths' as an official title.

A *converso* was a Jew who converted, or someone descended from such a convert.

generation *converso* was rejected for a post in Toledo cathedral because of his ancestry. For a century, opinion had been growing that **limpieza de sangre** was an essential qualification for good Castilians. Now the prejudices burst out and the Toledo decision was copied all over Spain. Significantly, its key promoters were those same traditionalists who hounded the Erasmians.

An even bigger problem came to plague the third of Spain's faiths. The Moors of Granada, conquered in 1492, had been presented in 1502 with that same stark choice: convert or be deported. Those who stayed, and became *moriscos*, at once became subject to inquisitorial suspicions. The strong Islamic community in Aragon remained untouched until the 1520s; *convivencia* was stronger there. But in Valencia in 1521 and Aragon in 1525, Moors finally had to confront the terrible dilemma, even though the pope questioned the value of a forced conversion and converts were promised immunity from the Inquisition for 40 years. *Moriscos* faced an even more impossible struggle to survive. On top of the conviction that they still followed Islam, it was presumed that they were a security risk. The struggle against Barbarossa left *moriscos* suspected of being agents supplying information to the sultan and of constituting a secret army waiting for the command to draw the sword. Most Aragonese *moriscos* were agricultural labourers, forced to live in remote valleys in what were effectively ghettos. They continued to live as Moors and speak Arabic. The *morisco* problem was different from that of the *conversos*. Many had family in the Maghrib and travelled backwards and forwards. Some were indeed agents for the corsairs, or helped them when they came raiding. Above all, almost all really were still Islamic. Thus even though there were no more than 80,000 *moriscos* in Castile, this tiny minority was a target in the crusade against Islam.

Consider the three religious groups seen to be a problem. In separate columns, list the reasons why they were thought to be dangerous. How many of these reasons were genuine and how many the product of paranoia?

Summary questions

1 (a) Explain *two* problems facing Spain in 1520.

   (b) 'Charles I was unsuccessful in his foreign policy.' How far do you agree?

2 (a) Explain the financial problems of the Spanish crown during the first half of the sixteenth century.

   (b) To what extent had Charles I made Spain a stable country by 1556?

3 (a) Explain why the Revolt of the Comuneros broke out.

   (b) Was Charles I more successful in his wars against the French in Italy or against the Turks in the Mediterranean and north Africa?

4 (a) Explain the main aims of Charles I's foreign policy.

   (b) Assess Charles I's achievements in three major aspects of domestic policy.

3 France 1498–1559

Focus questions

◆ What political and financial problems faced French monarchs between 1515 and 1559?

◆ How absolute was Francis I?

◆ What religious issues and problems faced the French church from 1498 to 1547?

◆ How successful was France in the Habsburg–Valois Wars of 1499 to 1559?

Significant dates

1499	Louis XII captures Milan.
1500	Louis partitions Naples with Aragon.
1503–04	The French are driven from Naples.
1512	The Holy League expels the French from Milan.
1515	Bishop Briçonnet begins to reform his diocese and starts the Meaux Circle. Francis I wins the Battle of Marignano and recovers Milan. *The great French monarchy* by Bishop Seyssel explains how French monarchy worked.
1516	Francis negotiates the Concordat of Bologna, gaining greater control over the church in France.
1519	Francis fails to win election as Holy Roman emperor.
1521	The French are driven from Milan.
1523	Unsuccessful rebellion by the duke of Bourbon.
1524	Francis recaptures Milan.
1525	Francis I is defeated and captured by Charles V at the Battle of Pavia. Milan is lost again (and never recovered). Major Protestant persecution starts.
1529	In the Peace of Cambrai, Francis surrenders all claims to Burgundian and Italian territory.
1532	The duchy of Brittany becomes part of France.
1533	Francis starts to negotiate with the Ottoman Turks.
1534	The Affair of the Placards takes place and leads to a major escalation in the persecution of French Protestantism.

1535	Francis attempts (unsuccessfully) to join the Schmalkaldic League.
1536	Francis invades and occupies the duchy of Savoy.
1540	The Edict of Fontainebleau makes Protestant persecution much fiercer. The retirement of the constable of France (Anne de Montmorency) leads to a more aggressive foreign policy.
1541	An imperial invasion force comes within 65 kilometres of Paris.
1544–45	The massacre of Waldensian heretics in Provence.
1552	Henry II allies with the Schmalkaldic League (Treaty of Chambord), invades Lorraine and captures Metz, Toul and Verdun.
1553	The French capture Corsica.
1555	Henry introduces *le grand parti* to raise money for the crown.
1556	The French alliance with Pope Paul IV and attempt to invade Naples is a disaster.
1557	France suffers a crushing defeat by Philip II at the Battle of St Quentin.
1558	Calais is recaptured from the English. The Spanish inflict another massive defeat at the Battle of Gravelines.
1559	The Peace of Câteau-Cambrésis ends the Habsburg–Valois Wars.

Overview

French kings spent the secong half of the fifteenth century restoring a kingdom broken by the Hundred Years' War. This chapter assesses the strengths and weaknesses of France during the first half of the sixteenth century.

First, the state of France and French government are considered. France was politically stable but far from being a unified nation-state. There was no single legal system. Large areas were semi-independent and considerable power was held by provincial institutions. Throughout the period, the crown worked to increase its income and more than succeeded in covering the rising costs of domestic government. But most of these years were spent in war and the bills for that ruined everything.

The second section examines why historians do not now see Francis I as an absolute monarch. He was not the master of his realm. Large parts he did not even rule, while in those that he did rule he shared power with the nobility and the provincial *parlements*. New claims that kings were above the law just did not fit the facts. French government under Francis I was still medieval, and therefore a partnership under which restraints (constitutional and natural) were imposed on royal authority. It is important not to be taken in by royal propaganda.

Next, the chapter investigates religious problems, considering why Francis I betrayed traditional views on the independence of the French church to agree the Concordat of Bologna with Pope Leo X. It then looks briefly at the remarkably healthy state of the Catholic church *c.*1500 before plunging into the two great religious issues of early-sixteenth-century France: Christian Humanist reform and early French Protestantism. To both, the attitudes of the king and the *parlement* of Paris were crucial. Neither survived persecution.

Finally, the chapter examines the French side in the long Habsburg–Valois Wars. After establishing that these were a royal family struggle to secure its dynastic property (the kingdom of Naples, the duchy of Milan and the duchy of Burgundy), the efforts of Louis XII, Francis I and Henry II to achieve those goals are weighed. Louis held Naples only briefly, but was duke of Milan for 13 years of his 16-year reign. Francis and Henry both faced a harder task because, in the person of Charles V, all the disputed lands were held by a single enemy whose territories surrounded France and whose resources were considerable. Francis fared badly and ended his reign with nothing to show for the 9 million livres of debts he had built up. In Italy he was thrashed repeatedly and he lost the Habsburg–Valois Wars for France. By contrast, Henry II's much shorter reign saw a considerably more effective approach to struggle against Charles V. Even though massive debts pushed him into requesting the Treaty of Câteau-Cambrésis (1559), he had restored pride to France by recovering Calais and seizing the core of the duchy of Lorraine.

What political and financial problems faced French monarchs between 1515 and 1559?

France in 1500 was not the France we know today. The lands ruled by the king were substantially smaller. Part of the Pyrenees belonged to the kingdom of Navarre. Significant areas in northern and eastern France belonged to the duchy of Burgundy and were disputed with the Holy Roman emperor, and most of the long eastern frontier lay well short of its modern position. Brittany was effectively a separate state while massive areas of France were noble **fiefs** and semi-independent. In consequence, the French king was actually master of barely half the kingdom of France, which resembled a federation of states rather than a single country. On top of that, there were other vast areas over which control had only very recently been recovered. Some were provinces that the English had ruled, such as Normandy and Gascony. Others were fiefdoms whose ruling noble had died without a male heir, and thus returned to the king (e.g. the counties of Anjou and Provence in 1486). In all of these, old laws and customs were allowed to continue. In every sense, therefore, the French were not a united people living in a single political and legal unit, the kingdom of France. What is more, there was no such thing even as

A **fief** was land which a king gave to a noble in exchange for military service. Although the king remained the overlord of that noble, he gave up effective power over that land. The noble gained considerable independence, in effect becoming 'king' of his fief. French kings created fiefs for their younger sons and made many others during the Hundred Years' War as they searched for help to drive out the English.

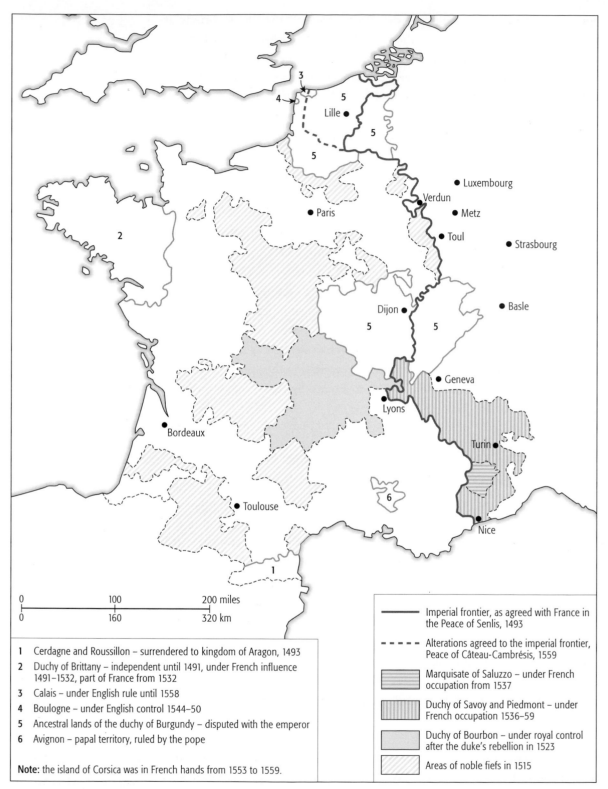

0   100   200 miles
0   160   320 km

	Imperial frontier, as agreed with France in the Peace of Senlis, 1493
- - - -	Alterations agreed to the imperial frontier, Peace of Câteau-Cambrésis, 1559
	Marquisate of Saluzzo – under French occupation from 1537
	Duchy of Savoy and Piedmont – under French occupation 1536–59
	Duchy of Bourbon – under royal control after the duke's rebellion in 1523
	Areas of noble fiefs in 1515

1   Cerdagne and Roussillon – surrendered to kingdom of Aragon, 1493
2   Duchy of Brittany – independent until 1491, under French influence 1491–1532, part of France from 1532
3   Calais – under English rule until 1558
4   Boulogne – under English control 1544–50
5   Ancestral lands of the duchy of Burgundy – disputed with the emperor
6   Avignon – papal territory, ruled by the pope

Note: the island of Corsica was in French hands from 1553 to 1559.

The small kingdom of France.

'the French people'. In the north-west, Breton was the only language spoken. In the western Pyrenees, the same was true of Basque, while at the eastern end the people spoke Catalan. Across most of southern France the *langue d'oc* would have been heard. It was very different from the *langue d'oïl*, the language of the north and the ancestor of modern French. Wherever we look, the primary characteristic that sums up France in 1500 is not unity but diversity.

None the less, France had great potential. Her population in 1500 stood at about 16.4 million, double that of Spain and four times that of England. During the next half-century, France's population was the fastest rising in western Europe and by 1550 the French numbered about 19 million. Agriculturally she was prosperous and commerce flourished. Ports like Dieppe and Marseilles were developing rapidly. Manufacturing was booming, notably the production of textiles, silk and iron. More than thirty French towns had at least one printing press in 1500. In resources as in population, France in 1500 was the strongest state in Europe. Yet that remarkable economic growth could not be sustained into the new century and began to fall behind population expansion. Unemployment rose and wages fell. The core weakness was the failure to step up agricultural production. When mixed with harsh weather, that produced a series of grain famines: 1528–32, 1538, 1543–46, 1551–52, 1556–57. The fast-developing towns were affected by food shortages even more severely than the countryside. Urban unrest became a real problem and the Grand Rebeine riots in Lyons in 1529 are a vivid reminder of the structural weakness beneath the surface.

> How strong was the French economy between 1500 and 1559?

French monarchy was strong because good foundations had been laid since the end of the Hundred Years' War in 1453. We think nothing of possible problems affecting succession to a throne but, when kings ruled as well as reigned, it was a matter of the utmost importance. Charles VIII (1483–98) and Louis XII (1498–1515) both died without a son, yet the succession was not disputed between rival claimants (see the diagram on page 70); that indicates political stability. Francis I (1515–47) and Henry II (1547–59) were strong and capable rulers, loved and feared by their people, as every effective ruler needed to be. Even so, that strength depended in part on sheer good luck. Neither was affected by the hereditary madness that cursed the royal house of Valois. Neither succeeded as a child to the throne – a fate France endured twice during the second half of the sixteenth century. Even though two of Francis I's sons died before him, he still had one son to inherit the crown, as an adult. To some degree, political stability in a system relying on hereditary rulers was always a matter of chance.

The other great proof of stability was that France suffered no major political crisis during the first half of the sixteenth century, not even when the king was a prisoner of war (1525–26). The only significant rebellion occurred in

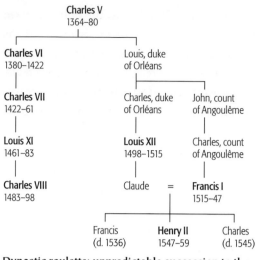

Dynastic roulette: unpredictable succession to the throne of France. (Kings are shown in bold type.)

1523, but it remained very much a personal quarrel between the duke of Bourbon and his cousin the king. Bourbon failed to draw the other royal dukes to his cause, let alone even a section of the nobility. In consequence, Francis I overcame his rebellious relative and confiscated his massive estates. In the process, Francis removed the greatest surviving fiefdom and added its revenues to his own. Bourbon's revolt was the great exception in the relationship between crown and nobility. French government was, as everywhere in Europe, still medieval, so authority was shared out between the nobility, the church, the towns and the monarchy. Medieval politics was a partnership in which considerable power and responsibility had to be entrusted to great men and institutions administering the localities. Without rapid communications, how could it be anything else? Devolution was as normal as it was inevitable in the Middle Ages.

That should not be interpreted to mean that France was without political tensions. No king would be so foolish as to attack directly the power of his noblemen. He would not have the resources or the capacity to govern without them; and their own military power would be more than sufficient to destroy him in the attempt. Sixteenth-century kings flexed their political muscles in more subtle directions. One area targeted was the size and scope of central government. A series of reforms by Francis I and Henry II restructured the bureaucracy to make it more efficient, and increased the number of civil servants to run it by about 50 per cent. They concentrated on finance, attempting to see that taxes were paid promptly and at the correct rate, and actually reached the royal treasury. In a kingdom as large and varied as France, power was well established at regional level in a series of seven *parlements* and seven estates. The *parlements* were supreme law courts while the estates were parliaments. Both were vital symbols of the laws unique to their province. At times, therefore, they came into conflict with the crown – usually over attempts by Paris to ignore local customs and collect the same taxes and enforce the same laws everywhere. Thus, Francis I clashed with the Estates of Languedoc in 1537–38 and the Estates of Normandy in 1546, demanding both agree to give up their ancient exemption from the salt tax (the *gabelle*). In both cases, the estates gave way.

Why might French kings see the regional *parlements* and estates as rivals to royal power?

The estates were always vulnerable to royal attack. While none was democratically elected, all had weak powers and met infrequently. By contrast, the regional *parlements* were active bodies with wide-ranging administrative and legal responsibilities. If any institution represented an alternative focus of power to the crown, it was the *parlements* because they held the ancient right to decide whether each royal decree could be enforced in their region. Francis I suspended the *parlement* of Rouen for four months in 1540 when it refused to register the Ordinance of Villers-Cotterets, on the grounds that its legal reforms undermined their local system of justice; in the end, both compromised. Most powerful of all was the *parlement* of Paris. While eventually (and with great reluctance) accepted the Concordat of Bologna (see page 78), it fought a running battle with Francis I during the 1520s over the persecution of Protestants, refused three attempts by Henry II in 1552 to introduce legal reforms and in 1555 prevented the introduction of the Inquisition.

Whereas political problems were occasional, financial difficulties were perpetual. Every medieval ruler was expected to 'live of his own', which meant that he must be self-sufficient financially, funded by his personal income drawn from his own lands (known as 'ordinary' revenue). Taxation was seen as 'extraordinary', to be collected only in emergency. This medieval theory did not fit the facts of sixteenth-century life. Traditional sources were no longer sufficient and the traditional methods of collection no longer adequate. Every ruler was in constant need of more money: even French kings who, uniquely, had the right to collect 'extraordinary' revenue regularly. Because of that, the French crown was the wealthiest, and the French people were the most heavily taxed, in Europe. The tax burden was spread, however, very unevenly. In consequence, **taxation** was an inefficient and limited source of royal funds. During the medieval centuries, the nobility and the towns had gained exemption from most taxes, while the clergy were taxed more lightly. Neither the slow rise in living standards nor the faster growth in total population was enough to lift the burden on the ordinary people, so heavily was it distorted. Between 1494 and 1559 the tax demand on the French peasantry increased by 80 per cent. No wonder that in the 1540s, the time of the greatest tax squeeze, tax revolts were frequent.

There were three major traditional **taxes**:
- the *gabelle* – a tax on salt,
- the *aides* – a sales tax (like VAT today),
- the *taille* – a tax on the value of land.
'The deep unfairness of so much taxation was the greatest of all obstacles in the way of governments which sought to ease their financial difficulties.' (Matthew Anderson, *The origins of the modern European state system, 1494–1618*, 1998)

Royal income needed to rise for various reasons. Inflation of about 2 per cent per year steadily eroded the value of all revenues – especially those from land, which were fixed and so could not be raised every year to compensate. As we have already noted, the size of the administration was growing and, as government expanded, it became more expensive. So too did the royal court which, following contemporary fashion, grew ever more magnificent because it was being used as an overt demonstration of the crown's power and status. Francis was addicted to building and spent lavishly, not only on upgrading existing palaces but on building new ones (as his châteaux at Fontainebleau and Chambord reveal).

Francis I's reign saw three phases of fiscal reform designed to increase royal revenues. In 1523, for example, he created the *Commission de la tour carrée* to hunt down corrupt tax officials. Over the following two years, he appointed first one and then two senior officials called *trésoriers* to take charge of all his income and report to him weekly on the state of what was becoming a central state treasury. Two-thirds of all the new jobs created in the royal bureaucracy during Francis's reign had financial responsibilities.

The net result was impressive. Total tax receipts rose from 2.5 million livres in 1515 to 7.4 million in 1547. Allowing for inflation, the real value of revenue collected from the *aides* and the *gabelle* each trebled, while that from the *taille* more than doubled. What made that all the more remarkable (and the cost in human suffering all the clearer) is that it was done by creating only one new **tax** and without reducing any of the tax privileges of the nobility. But one factor wrecked everything. Endless war condemned the crown to chronic financial weakness, as the following tables show.

Francis I introduced a **tax** on towns with fortified walls, the *solde des 50,000 hommes*, in 1543; Henry II the *taillon* (1549) and a tax on the clergy (1552). The first and the last did, therefore, erode the tax privileges of some. Significantly, neither king dared take on the nobility.

How had the ratio between royal income and royal debt changed between the accession of Francis I and the death of Henry II?

French financial weakness 1515–59 (in livres)		
	Total annual royal revenue	Total royal debt
1515	4.8 million	1.4 million
1517	5.0 million	4.0 million
1547	9.0 million	9.0 million
1559	12.0 million	43.0 million

French military expenditure 1515–53 (in livres)	
1515	7.5 million
1521–25	20.0 million
1536–37	5.5 million
1542–46	23.0 million
1553	13.0 million

How did the crown cope? We have already seen that no attempt was made to tax the whole population. In fact, only Henry II showed much imagination in searching out new sources of revenue. Francis relied on traditional methods of hand-to-mouth survival. In times of acute need, he forced towns and wealthy individuals to lend him money. In 1523 he took the treasures of Rheims Cathedral. In 1526 he had the senior finance officer Jacques de Semblançay executed for fraud. The man was guilty, but so were many others. The destruction of Semblançay removed the king's largest creditor and, at a critical moment in the Habsburg–Valois Wars, allowed Francis to cancel the biggest debt he owed. On a more regular basis, crown land, noble titles and jobs in government were all sold. This had been done before, but never on the scale now practised (especially under Henry II). In 1554, for instance, 80 posts of royal secretary were offered for sale at 6,000 livres each. Henry created a regional *parlement* for Brittany, simply to sell the jobs in it. Ingeniously, he even split in two every post in the government and forced each official to work alternate six-month periods, thereby doubling the offices he could sell.

Above all, both kings borrowed regularly and heavily. Conspicuous among their sources were the *rentes sur l'hôtel de ville*, adapted by Francis I in 1522 to pay the selected investors 8.33 per cent per year interest on the lump sum they lent the state. These became an important fund and by 1547 had produced 750,000 livres. Henry II was in even greater need; his short reign saw 6.8 million livres collected by this method. But the **costs of war** rose ever more steeply (see Chapter 4, pages 110 to 112), as did the bill for interest owed on the ever-expanding crown debts. During the last year of his reign, Francis had to find more than 1 million livres just to cover interest payments on previous loans. Ten years later, servicing royal debts was costing Henry II over 8 million livres. His finances were so desperate that in 1555 Europe's first ever government loan open for public subscription was launched. Paying 6 per cent annual interest and named *le grand parti*, it produced 16.5 million livres in four years. This was a triumph and indicated that, in one critical respect, financial affairs were in better shape under Henry than they were in his father's days. By the 1540s, Francis I experienced severe difficulty in obtaining new loans because bankers saw him as an unreliable borrower. Not so Henry II, who always repaid loans on time and was thus able to borrow significantly larger sums. The success of *le grand parti* was proof of his high credit rating.

In the end, however, even Henry was overwhelmed. The situation is summarised in the diagrams on page 74. In 1557 he ordered an inventory of every gold and silver object owned by the French church; these would be confiscated to fund the next season's campaigns. At the same time, the French state declared itself bankrupt. The Peace of Câteau-Cambrésis (1559) saved the treasures of France's churches, but it is significant that it was Henry II who

For the crippling effects of the **costs of war** on Charles V, see Chapter 2, pages 46 to 47.

Summarise the different ways in which Francis I and Henry II funded their domestic governments and foreign wars. Were their methods significantly different?

proposed peace talks to end the Habsburg–Valois Wars, not Charles V. The wars were as much a struggle between the economic as the military strength of superpowers; France lost in both respects.

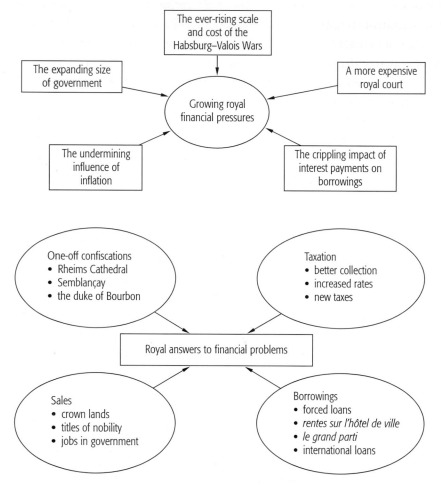

Royal finances: problems and solutions.

How absolute was Francis I?

For a long time, historians argued that Francis I laid the foundations of the all-powerful French state and monarchy that dominated Europe in the seventeenth and early eighteenth centuries (especially during the reign of Louis XIV). Building on the territorial unification achieved by fifteenth-century kings, Francis was seen as *le grand roi* who created a centralised government that united France properly and set it on the path to glory. In his achievements, no less than his ambitions, Francis was the first king of France to be the master of his realm. Not only did he create the right environment for the absolute monarchy of the future. He was himself the first absolute king of France.

The past 40 years have seen such claims questioned within a wider debate on the power that European kings possessed during the early modern centuries. Scholars have highlighted the many factors that, in practice, restricted royal authority. Equally, they have stressed the limited nature of many reforms to government, pointing out that most were in fact not innovations but restorations of systems used in earlier medieval centuries. Rather than speaking of a new-style, more powerful 'Renaissance monarchy', historians now emphasise the continuity of sixteenth-century government with the past and classify it as still essentially medieval.

Where does this leave an assessment of Francis I? Politically, his immediate predecessors had driven out the English and recovered substantial territory from great nobles. The French state in 1515 was larger and stronger than it had been since the days of King Charles V (1364–80). Francis himself continued that process, most notably by making the ancient duchy of Brittany part of France in 1532 (see the diagram below). At the same time, by occupying the duchy of Savoy in 1536, he pushed the imperial frontier in the south and secured control of Alpine passes giving access to Italy. Yet simultaneously he was unable to drive the English from Calais, and lost Boulogne to them in 1544. Further, the long wars against Emperor Charles V failed to restore any French ancestral territory in Italy. Naples remained beyond his grasp, while he was duke of Milan for barely six years (1515–21). Equally, the anti-Habsburg struggle did not recover any Valois family lands of the old duchy of Burgundy.

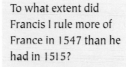

To what extent did Francis I rule more of France in 1547 than he had in 1515?

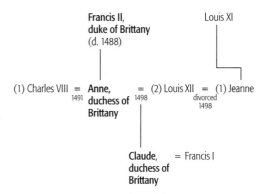

Francis II, duke of Brittany (d. 1488)

Louis XI

(1) Charles VIII = Anne, duchess of Brittany
1491

= (2) Louis XII =
1498

(1) Jeanne
divorced 1498

Claude, duchess of Brittany

= Francis I

The French takeover of Brittany. This was carried out with ruthless determination. As the diagram shows, two French kings in succession married the last duke's only daughter (in the case of Louis XII, only by means of a scandalous divorce, bought from the pope). In turn, Louis ensured Paris's grip on the duchy by arranging the marriage of his own heir to the next duchess.

The modern France did not exist by 1547. Indeed, Francis's kingdom remained full of territorial anomalies. Half his realm continued to be governed as noble fiefdoms, beyond effective royal control; the only significant reduction occurred not by royal policy, but through the accident of Bourbon's rebellion. The feudal independence of the nobility remained strong – as the armies they raised and the power they wielded during the long civil wars of the second half of the century (known as the French Wars of Religion) more than proved. In crucial respects, Francis was far from master of his realm.

That view is reinforced by the local *parlements* and estates, staunch champions of regional autonomy. We have already seen four royal contests with these institutions and, in every case, royal victory. It must also be noted that the king never summoned the national parliament, the Estates-General. On the other hand, Francis never tried to reduce, let alone abolish, these alternative sources of power. He left the duplication of authority between central and regional government intact. What is more, his own individual victories had no long-term effect on the balance of power between king and provinces. While each contest was a real battle, the defeat of one did not mean the defeat of all. Each triumph represented success for the crown on that single issue, at that moment. Henry II suffered a series of defeats at the hands of the *parlement* of Paris. Francis I had not altered the political balance because he had not fought a constitutional contest to determine whether the king alone made law, or whether he shared that responsibility with others.

Better than any other contemporary ruler, Francis I understood the importance of displaying the power of his monarchy and dynasty. He established the grandest European court of his day, glorifying the image of kingship. What historians term 'the cultivation of magnificence' and 'the theatre of kingship' were, however, a **confidence trick**. Crucial as they were, we must be careful not to fall under their spell and take at face value what was propaganda. Francis deliberately promoted the image of his authority, but we have only to look at the unfinished state of his château at Chambord to be reminded that we are being presented with an image, not reality.

The royal librarian Guillaume Budé published in 1518 *The instruction of the prince*. In this he argued that the king was God's direct representative and, as such, was owed the total obedience that his subjects owed to God himself. In such a position, the king stood above the law. The privileges of the nobility, the church, the estates and the *parlements* were exactly that – privileges granted by the king which equally could be removed again. No institution or individual had the legitimate right to share power that God had put directly into the king's hands. We have already examined enough of Francis's reign to see, however, that, while Budé might have been explaining how Francis I wished his monarchy worked, he was not describing reality. Interestingly, Budé's political theory itself admitted the danger inherent in the dream of absolute monarchy. To guard against a king behaving like a tyrant, he argued that a ruler would *choose* to subject himself to the laws and customs of his realm. He would, after all, wish to be loved and respected.

Francis was never an arbitrary monarch. He ruled according to the law and, unlike Henry VIII, respected the legal rights of his subjects. Again in contrast to England, judges held their positions for life (not just for the length of the

'The state appeared to become stronger during this period. Much of this development was an illusion, a **confidence trick** consciously perpetrated by rulers on their subjects.' (Richard Bonney, *The European dynastic states 1494–1660*, 1991)

king's favour) and rarely did Francis ever attempt to influence their decisions. Limitations did restrain sixteenth-century monarchy. For a description of political reality, we need to look at *The great French monarchy*, written in 1515 by Claude de Seyssel, bishop of Marseilles. De Seyssel offered a traditional, medieval image of the king as the father of his people, voluntarily sharing power with his nobility, the church and the law courts. Both sides had duties and responsibilities, to which they were bound by a **contract**. A king was not absolute but, with the nobles of his realm, first among equals. Political power was balanced and the contractual constraints that underpinned that equilibrium were necessary to preserve social harmony. Revealingly, the limitations on royal actions were described by the bishop as 'brakes'.

Francis's propaganda promoted the idea that he brought 'good government' to his people. This was a traditional virtue to claim, but a very necessary one. In the way he governed, he followed the traditional path of partnership explained by de Seyssel. The sheer size of France made royal control difficult. With a bureaucracy of at most 10,000 officials, how could Paris govern 16 million people when most lived at **distances** from the capital that in the sixteenth century meant a journey of between one week and one month to send a message just one way? In the Middle Ages kings were described as 'absolute', but that could not mean anything like the same thing as it must to anyone familiar with the impact of the telegraph and the railway on nineteenth-century government, let alone with twentieth-century dictators. There were too many limitations on his **power** for Francis (or any ruler contemporary with him) to be seen as an absolute monarch. We must question even how far he wanted to live the life of the king imagined by Budé. The expansion of royal government was modest, much more the product of financial desperation than of the desire to extend royal power. To the extent that royal government did grow and France did become more coherent, more controlled by the crown, such developments were not the responsibility or achievement of Francis I. Even more than Henry VIII of England, he devoted himself to hunting, women and war. Rather, it was the bureaucrats themselves who, like Budé, developed elaborate theories of all-powerful monarchy modelled on Roman emperors. All ambitious rulers try to master as much of their domain as possible; the desire to control seems to be inseparable from the desire to govern. In that the physical power of kings was growing, that growth was the restoration of something lost during the Hundred Years' War, not the invention of something new. 'Restoration' is the key word and we need to look backwards into the Middle Ages, not forwards to Louis XIV. The differences between the power and position of Francis I and those of his great-great-grandfather Charles V (1364–80) were minimal.

Summarise in your own words the different views of monarchy set out by Budé and de Seyssel. (You might find it helpful to set them out as a table, in separate columns.)

See page 42 for a Spanish view of **contractual** monarchy.

'**Distance** and bad roads did more to save men from the burden of government than constitutional safeguards or the debates of parliaments.' (Geoffrey Elton, *Reformation Europe 1517–1559*, 1963)

A small example of the reality of **power** for Francis I concerns the royal library. In 1537, a royal edict ordered printers to send the library one copy of every new book they published. Seven years later, barely a hundred had arrived out of the nine hundred or more titles produced in France between 1537 and 1544.

What religious issues and problems faced the French church from 1498 to 1547?

1515–25	Meaux Circle.
1516	Concordat of Bologna.
1525	The first sustained persecution of Protestantism.
1534	Affair of the Placards.
1535	Edict of Coucy; Francis attempts to join the Schmalkaldic League.
1540	Edict of Fontainebleau.
1544–45	Massacre of Waldensians in Provence.

The idea of an independent French **national church** is known as 'Gallicanism'.

Relations between the French church and the papacy had been poor since the early fifteenth century. Anti-papal traditions were strong in France, as were ideas of a **national church** linked to the crown and free from the 'foreign' leverage of Rome. Charles VII (1422–61) supported moves to limit the power of the pope, and in 1438 agreed the Pragmatic Sanction of Bourges which asserted that popes did not have ultimate authority. As long as the Pragmatic Sanction governed the French church, popes and French kings co-existed uncomfortably. Relations reached their lowest point under Louis XII, who, in pursuit of his ambition to be duke of Milan, attempted in 1511–12 to depose his arch-opponent in Italy, Pope Julius II. Francis I followed the opposite policy, seeking papal alliance to assist his quest. After his spectacular victory on the battlefield of Marignano, Francis judged papal support to be more critical than ever. Having seized Milan, he faced the harder task of holding on to it (as well as moving on to recover Naples). Louis XII was successful in Italy only while he enjoyed the backing of a pope (Alexander VI, 1492–1503). With Pope Leo X, Francis therefore agreed in the 1516 Concordat of Bologna to abandon French hostility to papal supremacy and to give up the Gallican claim that the French church was independent of Rome.

Why did Francis I want to sign the Concordat?

To many French clergy, the Concordat was a betrayal of ancient national rights. The politically active lawyers of the *parlement* of Paris backed them and for three years refused to register the Concordat in French law. But the treaty antagonised the clergy for another reason. Under its terms, Leo had extended the crown's entitlement to nominate candidates for the 900 most senior posts in the French church. In practice, French kings had chosen most bishops for more than a century and the independent right of the clergy to select their superiors had become very theoretical. None the less, the Concordat blessed and enlarged the practice. In liberating the church from much direct papal influence, the Concordat decisively subordinated it to the French crown. The real winner was neither papal authority nor Gallican freedom, but the power of kings.

St Jerome in his study, woodcut by Albrecht Dürer, c.1492. Jerome translated the Bible into Latin in the fourth century. Here he is depicted as a Christian Humanist scholar using biblical texts in Greek and Hebrew as well as Latin.

Aside from ecclesiastical politics, the point to note is the state of the French church *c*.1500. Contrary to what has long been said, church and clergy were not rotten to the core – quite the opposite: the French church was (like so much of the Catholic church across Europe) in the middle of a religious revival. Things were very different from the unsatisfactory and atypical state of affairs in Germany. In France there is strong evidence of religious vitality. Most bishops worked hard to see that the clergy offered good service to their parishes. Preaching was frequent and popular. Monks and friars were being reformed, and enjoying high recruitment levels. Most indicative of all, the French **people** were deeply attached to their local churches, participating eagerly in the frequent ceremonies and giving large sums to decorate and rebuild parish churches.

'A burgeoning religiosity stirred the **people**.' (Marc Vernard, 'France', *The Oxford encyclopedia of the Reformation*, vol. II 1996)

One notable church reformer was Guillaume Briçonnet, bishop of Meaux. In particular, he aimed to improve preaching and to that end gathered young scholars to train the parish clergy and spearhead missions to the people. They were known as the 'Meaux Circle' and their work turned out to be highly controversial. For one thing, they threatened the traditional interests of the friars who largely monopolised the late-medieval market in preaching (and the fees that came with it). It was no accident that those who accused the bishop and

Desiderius Erasmus (1467?–1536) was a wandering scholar and committed Catholic who wrote highly influential books in the fields of the ancient classical world and of Christianity. He was deeply critical of contemporary academic theology and popular religious practice, proposing an alternative view summed up in his phrase 'the philosophy of Christ'. This he rooted in the New Testament which, he argued, must be studied in its original Greek and Hebrew texts to peel back medieval corruptions and misunderstandings in order to find the pure original teaching of Jesus. When Luther launched his protest in 1517, many thought that he and Erasmus were arguing for the same things. This was a fatal misunderstanding that was not even swept away by a bitter dispute between the two in 1524–25 over whether man had free will. By the time of Erasmus's death, he was mistrusted by both Protestants and Catholics. (For the fate of Erasmianism in Spain, see page 63.)

The **Sorbonne** was the theology department of the University of Paris.

The authorities never understood the differences between the **early Protestants** and even in the 1550s still described all Protestants as *luthérien*.

his circle of heresy were indignant friars. Behind that petty jealousy, however, lay a more serious problem: the debate over the validity of Christian Humanism. This was a loose, international trend (never an organised movement) among some European scholars. Inspired by **Erasmus**, it aimed to recover the original form of Christianity through study of the original texts of the New Testament. So academic a programme, requiring sophisticated scholarship in Greek and Hebrew, could never become a popular movement. None the less, Christian Humanism in France attracted powerful backers, notably at court through Marguerite of Angoulême, Francis I's sister.

But the Christian Humanists made powerful enemies too. Although they respected the church, their proposed internal reforms tended to question the value of the monastic way of life and to despise the extravagant and often superstitious nature of much contemporary religious practice (especially that associated with the cults of saints). Chief among those scandalised by such ideas was the **Sorbonne**. With the friars, these Paris theologians led a sustained campaign in the *parlement* of Paris against the Meaux Circle, accusing it from 1520 of promoting the ideas of Martin Luther. Royal support for Briçonnet guaranteed protection, but his critics would not be silenced, especially after one of the circle became a Protestant. Seizing the opportunity of the king's captivity after Pavia, the *parlement* forced the circle to disband.

Meanwhile, genuine Protestantism crept into France from *c*.1519. Translations of Luther's pamphlets came in from presses across the imperial frontier; by 1530 there were four secret presses within France. Surreptitiously, Protestant ideas spread, by word of mouth as much as via the printed page. Small congregations sprang up in towns across northern and eastern France. The Sorbonne had, however, endorsed Luther's papal excommunication (1521), so Protestant cells had to operate in secret. We therefore know little about them, but many were not Lutheran. Even **early Protestantism** involved a broad range of ideas and groupings. In France, some looked to Zürich and the teachings of its reformer, Ulrich Zwingli. Others followed the lead of Martin Bucer in Strasbourg, while yet more were inspired by the more radical enthusiasts known today under the general label of 'anabaptists'. Early French Protestantism thus lacked unity and could not speak with one voice. This was an important defect that contributed to its sluggish beginnings in France.

French Protestantism was fragile. Trade links with Germany were poor so, unlike the Netherlands or Scandinavia, the constant transfusion of Protestant ideas along the lines of commerce was almost impossible. There were no large communities of German merchants – a critical propagator of Protestantism in other states. Also missing was the influence of that other midwife of Protestantism: a vigorous printing industry. Equally, the generally healthy condition of the French church denied to the Protestant cause the nourishing seedbed of

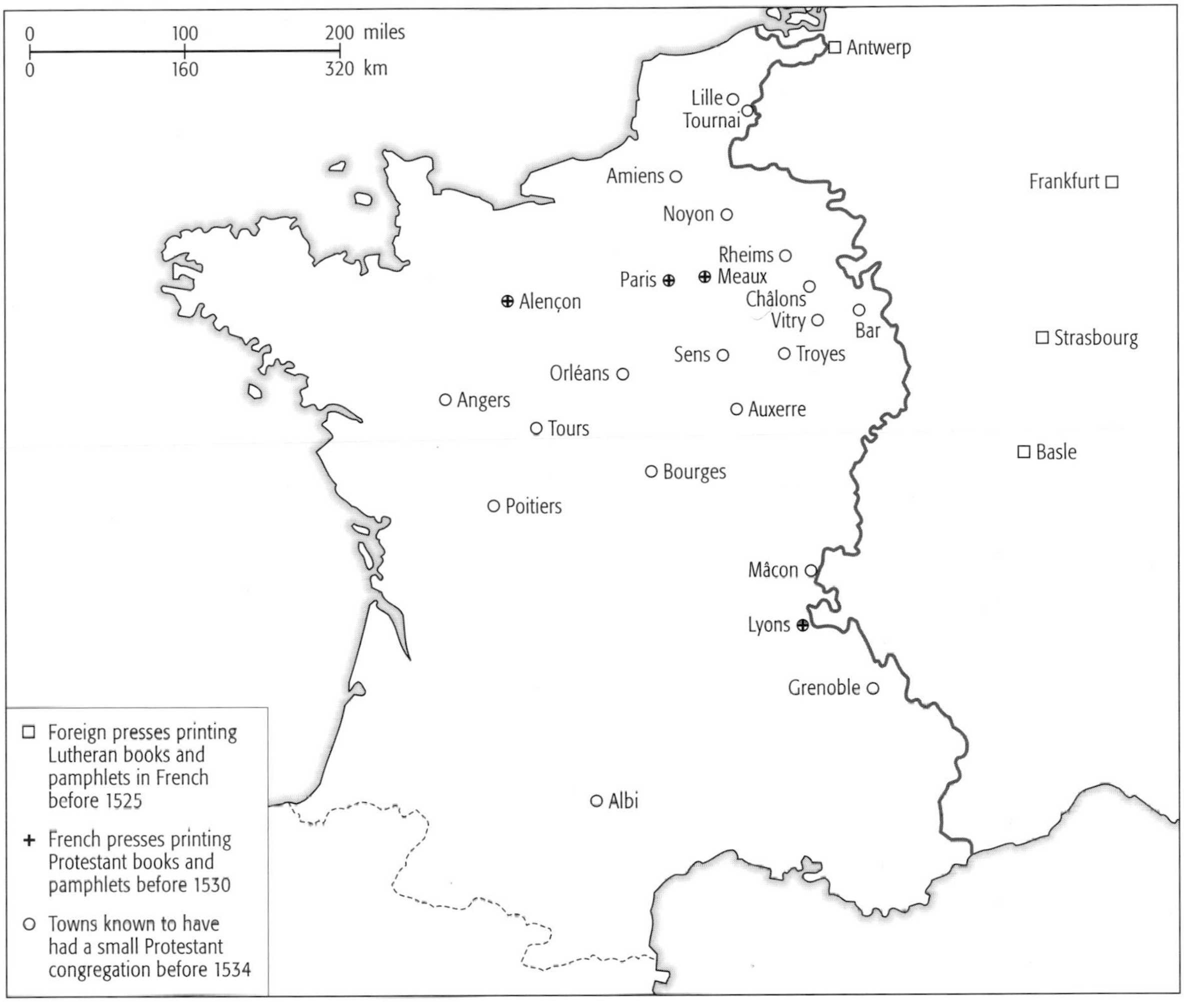
0
100
200 miles
0
160
320 km
Antwerp
Lille
Tournai
Amiens
Frankfurt
Noyon
Rheims
Paris
Meaux
Châlons
Alençon
Vitry
Bar
Strasbourg
Sens
Troyes
Orléans
Angers
Auxerre
Tours
Basle
Bourges
Poitiers
Mâcon
Lyons
Grenoble
Albi
□ Foreign presses printing Lutheran books and pamphlets in French before 1525
+ French presses printing Protestant books and pamphlets before 1530
○ Towns known to have had a small Protestant congregation before 1534

Early Protestantism in France.

anti-clericalism. When forced to live in such unfavourable conditions, it is no wonder that its growth was unspectacular.

The Sorbonne organised censorship of books from 1521. The first Protestants were burnt in 1525. Initially, however, the confusion over Christian Humanism and Protestantism gave the latter a fair degree of shelter. Royal support for the Humanists – and, in particular, Francis's repeated interventions to protect individual **scholars** and preachers he favoured – gave infant French Protestantism a vital protective shield. The king was no Protestant, but he was determined to deny the *parlement* of Paris control of the religious agenda and to keep definitions of heresy as narrow as possible (in order to exclude Christian Humanism); he did not want repression to stifle intellectual debate. Nevertheless, there were limits to his tolerance. By the late 1520s, some of his Protestant subjects were asserting their views in an aggressive manner.

Notable among the Christian Humanist **scholars** supported was Louis de Berquin (*c.* 1490–1529), who translated Erasmus into French. The Sorbonne had him imprisoned in 1523 and 1526. Arrested again in 1528, he was condemned for heresy and burnt.

Things boiled over in Paris in 1528 when a street statue of Mary was decapitated. The king in person led the ceremony of atonement and he personally paid for a replacement. He would not tolerate anything that disturbed public order.

For some years, the king's delicate policy kept France on a knife edge. Into the 1530s, the bishop of Paris encouraged his master to believe that reunion between Catholic and Protestant was possible. From 1532, Francis was exploring a possible alliance against the emperor with the **Schmalkaldic League**. An ambiguity thus served Francis rather well. French **Protestants** mistook this for genuine sympathy and prayers were repeatedly offered up for his conversion. But he never showed any sign of adopting the reformed faith or of following Henry VIII in displacing the pope as head of the national church. Instead, the position he took in 1528 over that act of religious vandalism was reinforced in 1533 by a sermon of Nicholas Cop, the new rector of the Sorbonne, which criticised the mass. Francis was away from Paris at the time, but shared wholeheartedly the disgust of his people at this outrage; Cop had to flee. One further event convinced Francis of the need to harden his line: the Affair of the **Placards** in October 1534. In this, printed leaflets abusing the clergy and attacking the mass were distributed across a number of French cities; one was found pinned to the king's bedroom door at Amboise. Francis was horrified, perhaps as much at the thought of his own vulnerability to assassination as at the subversive ideas the *placard* promoted. In the royal mind, Protestantism was now identified with criminal activity. The king endorsed the crackdown unleashed by the *parlement* of Paris.

At times thereafter, persecution was moderated if Francis needed to woo the Schmalkaldic princes – the 1535 Edict of Coucy is a good example, for, while on the one hand it offered an amnesty to religious exiles, all radicals who did not even accept Lutheran teachings on the mass were excluded. Most of the time, however, the pace of persecution was unrelenting. In 1540, the Edict of Fontainebleau gave the *parlements* overall control of heresy trials. Two years later, the Sorbonne began to produce regularly updated lists of banned books. Persecution rose steeply, and culminated in 1544–45 in the wholesale massacre of more than 3,000 Waldensians in Provence. Under such pressure, French Protestantism shattered. When Calvinism began to infiltrate France in the 1550s, it found most Protestant congregations derelict.

How successful was France in the Habsburg–Valois Wars of 1499 to 1559?

During the first half of the sixteenth century, France was the most aggressive European state. French foreign policy was dominated by an all-consuming

The **Schmalkaldic League** was the military alliance of German Lutheran princes.

It was in that spirit that major **Protestant** reformers dedicated important books to Francis: Zwingli in 1525 with his *Commentary on the true and false religion*, John Calvin in 1535 with the first edition of his *The institutes of the Christian religion*.

The incident gets its name from the word for a printed leaflet: *un placard*.

Explain Francis I's attitude to Protestantism. How did it change between 1521 and 1547?

struggle against its Spanish and imperial neighbours. Much of it centred on the attempt to gain control of the kingdom of Naples and the duchy of Milan, but also involved were territories between Switzerland and the North Sea in what would today be Belgium, Luxembourg and eastern France. The bitter struggle dragged on for 60 years. Why was this? Before examining the epic Habsburg–Valois Wars, it is essential to grasp what they were. The key to understanding them is the fact that they were not a modern conflict between modern governments. The Habsburg–Valois Wars were a great feud between two rival families, locked in an ancient dispute over their **rightful inheritance**. Naples, Milan and Burgundy were personal property that family honour demanded they preserve at all costs. When Charles of Habsburg inherited Burgundy and the Spanish kingdoms, and was then elected emperor, all the dynastic claims that challenged Valois interests were combined in the hands of one arch-enemy who ruled virtually every kilometre of territory on the other side of France's long borders. All the family lands the Valois were convinced had been stolen were now held by the same man: Charles of Habsburg. No wonder France felt so encircled and threatened, and struck out with such determination.

'The all-important theme underlying the events of this period was the pursuit of a ruler's **inherited rights** which may have had no practical application but which were ideologically sacrosanct.' (Richard Bonney, *The European dynastic states 1494–1660*, 1991)

Louis XII (1498–1515)

	Duchy of Milan	Kingdom of Naples
1499	Capture of Milan.	
1500		Partition of Naples with Aragon.
1503–04		Expulsion from Naples by Aragon.
1512	Formation of Holy League against Louis; expulsion from Milan.	
1513	Abortive attempt to recover Milan.	

Charles VIII had invaded Italy in 1494 to recover for the Anjou part of his family the crown of Naples. In under a year, he won and then lost that prize, driven out by a coalition of powers led by the pope and the king of Aragon. Both had major interests in southern Italy and neither was prepared to see it under French control. Louis XII then added his own **Orléans** family assertion that it was the ruler of Milan. This belief obsessed him. Although he plunged into Italy within months of his accession, Louis was no rash adventurer. He prepared the ground well, drawing Pope Alexander VI (1492–1503) away from the anti-French League of Venice. He was not to be disappointed, for a brief campaign put Milan in his hands. He none the less understood that

Louis's grandfather had married Valentina Visconti, daughter of the duke of Milan. When the last Visconti died without a son in 1447, the duke of **Orléans** claimed that, through Valentina, he was the closest living relative and therefore the rightful new duke. Orléans' rivals were the Italian Sforza family, also related to the Visconti by marriage.

he could never keep Milan and take on the might of Aragon to win Naples. He thus took a pragmatic line, negotiating with King Ferdinand of Aragon in the 1500 Treaty of Granada a joint invasion to conquer and partition the southern kingdom. This too was successful and gave Louis the city of Naples itself. Despite his caution, he had overstretched himself. Disputes with the Aragonese soon arose and, since Ferdinand could easily supply his forces from his island of Sicily with the large Aragonese fleet, the French were overcome.

Pitched against the military and naval might of Aragon, Louis could never hold Naples. **France** had only a tiny navy and was too remote to sustain such an outpost. The bid for Naples was doomed and, although the claim was not abandoned, it never again figured high among the priorities of Louis XII or his successors. Not so Milan, which the French held until 1512. Given the quicksands of Italian politics, that was a considerable achievement. From the moment Louis's alliance with the Swiss collapsed in 1509, the duchy was vulnerable; recruiting Swiss elite mercenaries had become impossible. The instrument of his own downfall was, however, Pope Julius II (1503–13), who strenuously opposed French interests in Italy. In 1512 he created a grand anti-French coalition, the Holy League, which threw Louis out of Italy and pursued him to Dijon. French humiliation in 1512–13 was far greater than in 1503–04 or 1495. It says a lot that, for all the royal emphasis on the rightful ownership of land, most Frenchmen were relieved, seeing Milan as an unnecessary burden (and Naples as a wild dream). But, as has been pointed out, this was not a French war, but a Valois war.

The changing fortunes of **France** in the Habsburg–Valois Wars are summarised in the diagram on page 91.

Explain why Louis XII lost Milan in 1512.

Francis I (1515–47)

To the family quest for its rightful property, Francis added a rivalry with Charles V. The vanity of the new French king was exceeded only by that of Henry VIII. He longed for personal glory in war and was driven to furious jealousy by the accumulated strength of the emperor. Far more than Louis XII, he bent everything to Valois triumph. For years he blocked any meeting of a general council of the Catholic church to tackle the Reformation because a solution to the religious rift in Europe would make life easier for Charles in Germany. From 1532 he repeatedly sought an alliance against the emperor with the Lutheran Schmalkaldic League; whenever necessary, he relaxed or even suspended domestic persecution of French Protestants to win their favour. Even though he bore the hereditary title 'The Most Christian King', he negotiated regularly with the Ottoman sultan, encouraging Turkish attacks on Charles's territories. Any enemy of the emperor was a friend to Francis I.

1515	Invasion of Italy; victory at the Battle of Marignano; capture of Milan.
1519	Failure in the imperial election.
1521	Loss of Milan.
1522–23	Unsuccessful attempts to recover Milan.
1524	Recovery of Milan.
1525	Defeat at the Battle of Pavia; capture of Francis I and loss of Milan.
1528–29	Unsuccessful attempts to recover Milan.

These Italian campaigns were usually accompanied by a strike (by one side or the other) across the Pyrenees, and/or a campaign in Flanders or Luxembourg.

Like Louis XII, Francis began his reign in war with a swift descent on north Italy. In one move, the hard-fought Battle of Marignano made him duke of Milan. Francis's glorious position then set the context for his outlandish attempt to become Holy Roman emperor on the death of Maximilian I in 1519. He was wasting his time and his money. The seven electoral princes had nothing to gain by selecting so powerful a ruler as the victor of Marignano; the German states were semi-independent and relied upon having a weak emperor to keep the constitutional imbalance intact. Equally, he lost the battle to bribe the electors. The contest was a once-in-a-lifetime opportunity for them to fill their own family treasuries. They all therefore quite unscrupulously encouraged all comers to think they had a chance. But Francis could not outspend Charles of Habsburg. Against his own 360,000 florins, the young Spanish king distributed about 850,000 florins. The great contest thus turned out to be no contest. Charles was unanimously elected as the Emperor Charles V in June 1519.

From that moment, the struggle took on a pan-European dimension. Francis's territorial disputes with Aragon, the empire and Burgundy were henceforth rolled into one epic dispute with the man who now ruled them all: Charles V. Throughout the 1520s, the focus remained Milan. The decade opened badly for Francis with expulsion from the duchy. Defeat at Bicocca in 1522 totally reversed the glory of Marignano. As so often in Italian politics, however, the triumph of one side set off a reaction against the victor. Pope Clement VII (1523–34) organised an anti-imperial coalition and, for a while, Francis seemed to ride a new triumphant wave. Milan was soon back in his hands and his troops advanced close to Naples. Hopes of honour redeemed were, however, dashed in February 1525 on the battlefield of **Pavia**, where the French were shattered and their king taken prisoner. Charles was now the master of Italy. In the humiliating 1526 Treaty of Madrid, he forced his prisoner to sign away all Valois claims in Italy and abandon all rights to the ancestral Burgundian territories.

Francis I lost **Pavia** for the same reason he had lost Bicocca: his army was out of date. See Chapter 4, pages 99 to 100.

A more comprehensive settlement could not be imagined but, although Francis exchanged his captivity with his two eldest sons (left as hostages for the implementation of Madrid), he renounced the treaty as an agreement made under duress. With papal support, he constructed the League of Cognac and for two years seemed to have turned Pavia into an empty defeat. Everything fell apart, however, in 1528–29. Francis lost to the emperor his crucial naval ally, the Republic of Genoa. That was followed by a disastrous attempt to seize Naples. Finally, in June 1529, the French suffered another humiliating defeat on the plains near Milan at the Battle of Landriano.

The so-called 'Ladies' Peace' of Cambrai which followed brought one phase of the Habsburg–Valois Wars to an end, decisively against French interests. Graciously, Charles confirmed Francis as the ruler of the Burgundian heartland around Dijon. That was a reversal of Madrid, but it gave Francis nothing he did not already hold. In exchange, the defeated Valois had to recognise that Milan and Naples, signed away in Madrid, really were lost. An unshakable Habsburg supremacy in Italy had been established. Despite glimpses of triumph, the campaigns waged in Italy since 1494 had come to nothing. Naples had been under French rule for less than 6 years, Milan for 21. Marignano was a distant memory.

Francis I had failed – not that he was prepared to concede defeat. The intense rivalry he felt with the emperor, and the voices of his ancestors summoning him once more to the defence of the Valois inheritance, made it impossible for him to understand the new international situation.

Compile a list of the reasons why Francis I failed in Italy between 1521 and 1529.

1532	Talks with the Schmalkaldic League.
1533	Talks with the Ottomans.
1535	Death of Francesco Sforza, duke of Milan; Francis reasserts his claim to be duke.
	Unsuccessful attempt to join the Schmalkaldic League.
1536	Treaty with the Ottomans.
1536–37	Invasion and occupation of duchy of Savoy.
	Unsuccessful attempts to recover Milan.
	Imperial invasion of Provence.
1538	Truce of Nice.
1541	Treaty with the Ottomans.
1543–44	Unsuccessful attempts to recover Milan.
1544	Imperial–English invasions of northern France (Boulogne taken); Truce of Crépy.

Francis I's desperation after Cambrai is shown by his persistent efforts to negotiate alliances with Protestant heretics and Turkish infidels. The

Habsburg–Valois Wars were broadening; Italy would no longer be the sole focus of battle. Francis might continue to launch offensives to recover Milan, but Charles thrust counter-strokes into France. Milan returned to centre stage only when the death of the last Sforza duke in November 1535 reopened the issue. Francis proposed his second son, Henry, as the successor, but the emperor, as feudal overlord of the duchy, objected that the prince was too close to the French throne (an assertion borne out just months later when Henry became heir to the throne). Inevitably, Francis was not to be dismissed so easily. In 1536 he invaded the duchy of Savoy, ruled by Charles's brother-in-law, with the intention of swapping it for Milan. Savoy remained under French control for 23 years, but the larger war **bogged down**. Imperial armies invaded Picardy and Provence; both were forced to withdraw. Both sides ran out of money and a truce was signed in 1538.

For an explanation of why the Habsburg–Valois Wars **bogged down** during the 1530s and 1540s, see Chapter 4, pages 102 to 105 and 110 to 112.

War resumed in 1541 when the emperor broke the truce by making his son Philip duke of Milan. Francis invaded the Netherlands and, activating his Ottoman alliance, helped the sultan raid Charles's Mediterranean coastlines. This time, the military tide turned more sharply against Francis. While the emperor drew the English into a cross-Channel invasion that led to their capturing Boulogne, Charles himself knocked out the duchy of Cleves, Francis's chief ally among the German states and the hinge of his position in the Netherlands. Isolated, the French had no option but to withdraw, and then found an imperial army just 40 miles from Paris. France had not faced so grave a threat since the Battle of Agincourt (1415). Humiliation loomed. But Francis was spared, saved by sheer good luck – the emperor was running short of money to pay his largely mercenary forces and, unable to guarantee their discipline, dared not press on. Another **truce** was agreed, but Charles in 1544 was anxious to neutralise French intervention in the decisive blow he planned to strike against the Schmalkaldic princes. He thus offered Francis an extraordinary bargain: a royal marriage between a Valois prince and a Habsburg princess, with either the duchy of Milan or the duchy of Burgundy as her dowry. Francis agreed to the truce, only to see the dream offer evaporate when his youngest son, the intended bridegroom, died.

For the **Truce of Crépy**, see Chapter 1, page 31.

Factional struggle over the direction of French foreign policy plagued Francis's court from 1538. Until 1540, the power behind the throne was the constable of France, Anne de Montmorency. Long experience in the endless wars encouraged Montmorency to hope that peace between his king and the emperor would be made. The desperate financial state strengthened his position and talks began about Milan. As a gesture of friendship, the constable even persuaded Francis to allow Charles V to march troops across France to crush a rebellion in the Netherlands. The creation of Philip as duke, not surprisingly, brought this détente to an end and the constable retired from court.

Look at the image of Francis I on this page. Consider the assessment of the Habsburg–Valois Wars after 1524 and pages 74 to 77 on the extent of his absolute monarchy. Explain why the king would have been portrayed like this.

In the short term there was chaos as two ministers in rapid succession were arrested for treason – both victims of intense factional plotting. By 1543 Francis was ill and barely on speaking terms with his heir. That only intensified the struggle between the rival court groupings, each of which crystallised around a royal mistress: the duchess of Etampes (favourite of the king and advocate of war) and Diane de Poitiers (favourite of the Dauphin Henry, ally of Montmorency and champion of peace). War in 1542–44 indicated the ascendancy of the duchess and the eclipse of the dauphin. By 1545, however, the crown was bankrupt; the previous campaign alone had cost 23 million livres, the equivalent of the crown's total income for two and a half years.

Francis I (painted *c.*1540 by François Clouet, official court artist). By this date, the king was ill and his campaigning days were over.

At the end, Francis could not afford to go to war. Since 1529 he had managed to take Savoy (1536), but all his objectives still eluded him. Milan remained beyond his grasp. Over and over he had, however, frustrated the emperor's plans. He had prevented a possible settlement of the Reformation and had stopped any concerted attempt to push back the Ottoman Empire. But he had never defeated the emperor and, indeed, had forced Charles to devote most of his energies to opposing French ambitions. In the quest for dynastic and personal honour, Francis I failed.

What were the foreign policy aims of Francis I? Why had he been so unsuccessful?

Henry II (1547–59)

1552	Treaty of Chambord with the Schmalkaldic League; capture of Metz, Toul and Verdun.
1553	Occupation of Corsica (held until 1559).
1556	Abdication of Charles V; disastrous alliance with Pope Paul IV against Philip II; abortive attempt to recover Naples.
1557	Defeat by the Spanish at the Battle of St Quentin.
1558	Capture of Calais; defeat by the Spanish at the Battle of Gravelines.
1559	Treaty of Câteau-Cambrésis.

Henry II was more cautious, more intelligent than his father. The year 1547 saw no repeat of 1515, when Francis had plunged into Italy, thirsting for honour and glory. If anything, Henry bore an even deeper hatred of the emperor – the legacy of his three years in captivity after the Treaty of Madrid. He seems to have been determined to avenge himself on his former jailer. But he was a realist who understood the perilous state of French finances. Even more than Francis, he devoted his energies to harming the emperor's interests through diplomatic contact with Charles's enemies. To that end, he established even closer links with the Ottomans and the German princes. Apart from one foolish venture into Italy, he did not repeat the old mistake of locking up precious troops and money south of the Alps. Rather, he pursued a more flexible strategy, aiming not to hit the same predictable targets, but to strike the emperor wherever he seemed weakest or whenever he was most distracted.

To what extent were there significant differences between the anti-Habsburg strategies of Francis I and Henry II?

Guided by Constable Montmorency as his chief minister, for five years Henry made no military move against Charles V. During that time he reinforced French dominance in Scotland and made peace with England, buying back Boulogne. Both were highly satisfactory outcomes, achieved at little cost, and necessary preliminaries to any resumption of the struggle against the Habsburgs. During 1551 his opportunity came as the Schmalkaldic League re-formed. For the first time, they approached the French

How significant was the influence of Constable Montmorency in French foreign affairs between 1538 and 1559?

crown and they admitted the Catholic king to associate membership. Under the 1552 Treaty of Chambord, **Henry II** agreed to fund their activities in exchange for their assistance in seizing the great fortress of Lorraine, the key to the Franco-imperial frontier. In a lightning war, Metz, Toul and Verdun fell into French hands. Francis I had never achieved anything so easily or so decisively.

Victory was followed by consolidation. Skilful as he was at raising new funds, Henry had the sense to take only calculated steps – here was another sharp contrast between father and son. The controlled policy of 1547–52 began to unravel, however, during 1552–56. For one thing, Dianne de Poitiers was becoming ever more powerful and fanatically anti-Habsburg. She also came to resent what she saw as the constable's cautious approach. To counterbalance Montmorency, she brought the ambitious Guise family to court. Their chance came with the election in 1555 of Pope Paul IV. A Neapolitan, he detested Spanish rule of his homeland and determined to use the French to expel them. Henry hesitated, but gave way in 1557. He should have stood firm. A Guise-led army marched on Naples, but was routed. Meanwhile, a second army under the command of Montmorency was smashed in the Netherlands at St Quentin in a disaster as crushing as Pavia. In 1558, Guise attempted to save the situation in Flanders, but was defeated at Gravelines. All Henry II had to show for his war of 1557–58 was the recovery of the small but highly symbolic county of **Calais**.

This final round of Habsburg–Valois conflict had, in fact, proved one war too many for both sides. Both were exhausted and bankrupt. Reinforcing Henry's rediscovered pragmatism was the restored influence of Montmorency and a growing awareness of the need to tackle the fast-developing strength of Calvinism within France. France did not come out of the Treaty of Câteau-Cambrésis well. This was a reflection not just of the defeats of the immediate past, but of the decisive failures of Francis I. Henry abandoned Valois claims to Navarre. In a **mood of brutal realism**, he also handed Corsica back to Genoa, restored Savoy to its duke and confirmed his father's abdication of rights to Milan and Naples. The crux of the Habsburg–Valois struggle had always been to determine who would be master of Italy. At Câteau-Cambrésis, Henry II could do nothing but acknowledge French failure. There were, however, other possibilities. The treaty left the Valois in occupation of the Lorraine fortresses and Calais – all solid gains. Charles V's abdication in 1556 was good news for the French since the division of his territories between his son and his brother broke the Habsburg encirclement and reduced any future Habsburg threat. France had more than sheer survival to celebrate.

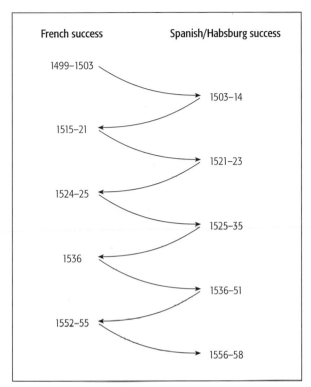

French success	Spanish/Habsburg success
1499–1503	
	1503–14
1515–21	
	1521–23
1524–25	
	1525–35
1536	
	1536–51
1552–55	
	1556–58

The Habsburg–Valois Wars: the swing of the pendulum.

Summary questions

1 (a) Why did Francis I face financial problems?

   (b) 'Francis I lost the Habsburg–Valois Wars.' How far do you agree?

2 (a) Explain the aims of Henry II's foreign policy.

   (b) Assess the strength of the French monarchy under Francis I.

3 (a) Identify and explain *two* reasons why the power of Francis I was limited.

   (b) How successful was France in the Habsburg–Valois Wars between 1525 and 1529?

4 (a) Explain the reasons why Protestantism had only limited success in France during the reign of Francis I.

   (b) How justified is the claim that Henry II was more successful than Francis I?

Warfare 1499–1560

Significant dates

1476 The defeat of the Burgundians by the Swiss at the Battle of Morat reveals the power of the infantry pike phalanx.

c.1490 The arquebus (the first accurate and reliable hand-held gun) is developed.

1496 The first-known attempt at 'ballistic shaping': an angled bastion is built (to counter the force of artillery fire) on the Boulevard d'Auvergne, a fortress on Rhodes.

1501–02 Alonso da Cordoba reorganises the Spanish army into *coronelias*.

1503 At the Battle of Cerignola, da Cordoba demonstrates the co-ordinated power of the *coronelia*, the arquebus and field fortifications. His victory wins control of the kingdom of Naples for Aragon.

1513 At the Battle of Novara, Spanish pikemen defeat the French. (Although they suffered heavy casualties from French artillery fire, the Spanish infantry were more disciplined than their French counterparts. In addition, the French had not dug field fortifications so the Spanish were able to over-run the French positions and capture the French artillery.)

1515 Alonso da Cordoba ('the Great Captain') dies.
The French win the two-day Battle of Marignano and so capture Milan.
The first-known complete set of *trace italienne* fortifications is constructed (at Civitavecchia).

1520 The first known use of the pistol.

1522 The French defeat at the Battle of Bicocca guarantees their loss of Milan. (Victory went to the empire/the Spanish because of their sophisticated field fortifications, defended by artillery and four lines of pikemen and arquebusiers. The French and their Swiss mercenaries hurled themselves in vain against these strong positions, suffering massive casualties.)

1525 At the Battle of Pavia, the French suffer their most humiliating defeat of the Italian Wars. (Imperial /Spanish victory was due once again to their co-ordinated use of arquebusiers and pikemen. French cavalry and Swiss pikemen were broken by the *coronelias* of the marquis of Pescara.)

1534 The Spanish army is reorganised, turning *coronelias* into *tercios*.

1540s Ravelins and the double Pisan rampart are both developed, making *trace italienne* fortifications even more formidable.

1549 The imperial army standardises the barrel sizes of its field guns (and thus also its cannon balls); France copies in 1552.

1552–53 Charles V fails to retake Metz. (He was foolish to attempt a siege in winter, especially with as large a force as 59,000 men. He ran short of supplies to feed and money to pay the troops. The power of fortifications was now such that successful attack was almost impossible.)

1557 The Spanish defeat the French at the Battle of St Quentin. (Henry II had invaded the Netherlands and was besieging the fortress town of St Quentin. A Spanish relief column attacked and defeated the French besiegers. In the age of *trace italienne* fortifications, this scenario of a contest between a besieging army and a relief column offered almost the only opportunity for open battle and victory on the battlefield.)

Overview

Historians of the fifteenth and sixteenth centuries talk of the rise of a new warfare. Early modern Europe was unusually violent, with war a permanent feature of life. There were only eight years during the sixteenth century when the continent was totally at peace. War was a natural activity of kings and the wars were fought to suit their needs and ambitions. Battle was judged to offer the greatest test of honour and the greatest opportunity for glory. Through war, a monarch defended not just his kingdom but the family ancestral lands held and/or claimed by his dynasty. The defence of family inheritance was paramount and, in an age when foreign policy was still controlled by kings, almost all wars were caused by breaches of agreements (real or supposed) between sovereigns. The Italian Wars began in 1494 when Charles VIII of France revived his family claim to Naples. They began again in 1499 when Louis XII added in his claim to Milan. Throughout the Habsburg–Valois Wars, most of the fighting along the Franco-imperial frontier similarly resulted from inherited claims to rights over (if not the possession of) the many counties and duchies between Lorraine and Flanders. Further, endless disputes were created simply because of the absence of clear borders defining and dividing states. Frontiers were often only vague zones, rather than precise lines. No wonder war was endemic.

This chapter investigates aspects of warfare during the first half of the sixteenth century and assesses changes that took place. Examples are drawn from the **Habsburg–Valois Wars** (1494–1559), and the concentration is wherever possible on one set of campaigns within those wars – the struggles to determine control of the kingdom of Naples and the duchy of Milan, known as the Italian Wars.

The first section considers the rise of infantry power and the dominance footsoldiers came to exercise on battlefields. This began in the 1470s with the creation of the disciplined infantry formation called a 'phalanx'. Two commanders of genius, Cordoba and Pescara, took up that idea and by 1525 had developed infantry capabilities dramatically. So critical were their innovations in the way infantry fought that they allowed the armies of Charles V to dominate the Habsburg–Valois Wars until *c.*1530.

Next, the chapter examines the simultaneous emergence of artillery and its impact on fortification design. Medieval war was dominated by sieges. The power of new cannons, however, made all defensive walls redundant. For the first time in centuries, the military advantage was held by generals to fight offensive campaigns. In consequence, the Habsburg–Valois Wars (until *c.*1530) saw bold offensives and spectacular battles. But meanwhile, engineers were developing new-style impregnable defences to neutralise artillery power. Called *trace italienne* fortifications, their creation ended open warfare abruptly. From *c.*1530, commanders were again locked into a static warfare, dominated by sieges and counter-sieges. The brief era of wars of movement was over.

These changes increased the size of armies and the next section looks at not only why that was so but investigates the controversy over the scale of that growth. Since no state could afford large, permanent forces, there was a major debate over the desirability of using mercenaries or citizen militias. The third section ends with an overview of the issues involved in that argument. Large armies using lots of guns cost money. So too did *trace italienne*. Kings struggled to find the necessary funds and the Habsburg–Valois campaigns of the 1540s and 1550s pushed both sides into bankruptcy. For all the military innovations of the period, the new fortifications prevented decisive victory. The wars were ended by the debts neither government could sustain any longer. But there was a silver lining in this cloud for kings. The financial burden on noblemen was even greater than that on monarchs. The expense of war helped destroy the independent military (and thus political) power of Europe's

For the political side of the **Habsburg–Valois Wars**, see Chapter 1, pages 27 to 34 (for the imperial perspective), and Chapter 3, pages 82 to 91 (for the French viewpoint).

aristocracies, thus strengthening royal authority. The chapter moves on to consider the noble cult of chivalry. The rise of the infantry and the dominance of guns threatened the traditional position of armoured cavalry. Knights condemned guns, moaning about the end of honourable warfare. How valid their complaints were and what chivalry was really about are investigated.

Finally comes a review of the great debate over the concept of 'the military revolution'. Each element of the argument is considered in the light of the Habsburg–Valois Wars. The chapter ends with a summary exercise testing the validity of the hypothesis.

The key issues are set out in the following table.

The rise of the infantry (pages 96 to 100)

- How and why did infantry c. 1470–c. 1510 come to dominate the European battlefield?
- In that dominance, what was the role of the Swiss pike phalanx?
- What difference did the advent of viable handguns make?

The rise of the artillery and developments in fortifications (pages 100 to 105)

- What impact did the development of effective siege artillery c. 1440–50 have on warfare?
- How did fortification designers cope with the power of these new siege guns?
- How did the new-style fortifications themselves then change the nature of warfare?

The size of armies and recruiting (pages 105 to 110)

- To what extent did the changes in warfare outlined above cause armies to become larger?
- Why were mercenaries used so widely?

The costs of war (pages 110 to 112)

- How expensive was war during the first half of the sixteenth century?
- Why did the costs of war help to crush the independent political and military power of the European nobility?

The cult of chivalry (pages 112 to 115)

- What was late-medieval chivalry?
- How did chivalric codes of honour cope with the arrival of the gun?

A military revolution? (pages 115 to 119)

- Overview of the 'military revolution' thesis.
- How did the Habsburg–Valois Wars impact on society?
- Summary exercise testing the validity of the military revolution thesis for the years 1499–1560.

All depended on the gun. Warfare in the late fifteenth century and the first half of the sixteenth century was twice transformed by the power of guns. Guns were the driving engine of the major military developments of the Habsburg–Valois conflict and explain why, for all the dynastic claims and dreams, the actual gains were so modest.

What were the main developments in military technology between 1499 and 1560?

The age of the armoured and mounted knight died slowly but, between 1450 and 1550, the role of cavalry was transformed. Where once knights had been the core of an army and its hammer-head in battle, that role passed to the infantry. So profound a change as this did not happen overnight. Individual battles in which infantry routed knights can be found across the medieval centuries (notable examples being Stirling in 1297, Bannockburn in 1314, Crécy in 1346 and Tannenberg in 1410). Some of these were unusual cases; William Wallace's spearmen were victorious only because the English knights at Stirling were trapped in a confined area. Yet from the fourteenth century, more infantry were being used on the battlefield; after all, they were far cheaper and easier to recruit (and replace) than aristocratic knights. But the lessons of these battles were not learned. The problem for infantry was how to survive the force of a cavalry charge. The solution, perfected during the second half of the fifteenth century by the Swiss, was to combine discipline with a 5-metre long **pike**.

The Swiss invention was the gathering of soldiers into a square, or **phalanx**. This was a highly trained mass of infantry, up to 6,000 strong, which could operate on the open battlefield with speed and mobility, changing direction easily and operating as effectively in offence as in defence. Phalanxes represented a revolution in training and tactics. Companies of footsoldiers armed with spears had been used for centuries, but they had always been vulnerable to cavalry. The bristling ranks of the Swiss pike phalanx, first deployed in 1475–77, revealed a new phenomenon in warfare: the invincible infantry.

Not only could they stand firm against a charge by cavalry or by infantry; they could mount their own offensive charge which delivered a blow almost equal to that of mounted knights. The Swiss innovation was most clearly revealed in 1476 at the Battle of Morat, where three phalanxes slaughtered a traditional army of 4,000 heavily armoured Burgundian knights. Medieval wisdom held that one knight was worth ten footsoldiers. Morat proved that was no longer necessarily true. At the Battle of Novara in 1513, the Swiss pulled off an even more remarkable feat that underscored the new infantry discipline. Even though under attack by cavalry from the flank and the rear,

Pike is a general term used for various 'staff weapons'.

A typical Swiss-style **phalanx** had 85 men shoulder to shoulder down each side and was 70 ranks deep, so its faces were each more than 110 metres long.

What was new about the Swiss pike phalanx? Why was it able to beat armoured cavalry?

Various types of fifteenth- and sixteenth-century pikes (with an axe second from right). On the extreme left and right are halberds. In the centre is a partisan and on either side of it are bills. The hook on the bill was designed to catch onto edges on a knight's armour, enabling the pikeman to pull him off his horse.

phalanxes were able to maintain formation and continue their advance, break the French lines and save Milan from Louis XII.

If properly armed and trained, infantry could now beat any opponent. But how many could match the Swiss? Morat showed only what might be. To most, the knight still seemed invincible and Morat a freak outcome representative of nothing. Improvements to armour continued to be made throughout the Italian Wars. Half of the 18,000-strong French army that invaded Italy in 1494 was composed of knights. But the pace of infantry development was speeding up, as became clear in the clash between French and Spanish armies at the Battle of Cerignola in 1503. Cerignola is instructive for several reasons. First, it revealed that a phalanx could maintain formation only on good terrain. The ground across which the French had to advance was a steep hillside. They were unable to keep together and so lost both their collective protection and combined force. Second, the battle showed that the phalanx worked only on an open battlefield. Like the English archers at Agincourt (1415), the Spanish under their commander **Alonso da Cordoba** had dug in behind a

Alonso (or Gonzalvo) da Cordoba
(1453–1515) was a Spanish general, known as 'the Great Captain' and one of Europe's soldiers of genius. He gained experience during the Castillian conquest of Granada (1481–92), and conquered the kingdom of Naples for Aragon (1495–1504). Cordoba reorganised the Spanish army and developed infantry tactics – as seen at Cerignola. A brilliant strategist, he was the first to understand the need for flexible infantry formations, co-operating with artillery and cavalry. Equally, he was the first to recognise the value of the arquebus. Grafting it onto Swiss pike tactics, he laid the foundations for more than a century of Spanish military supremacy.

The **arquebus** was the first effective portable firearm and was developed *c.*1490. Its range was up to 100 metres (but for real effect it needed to be used at less than 60 metres) and it could fire one metal ball every one to two minutes. By contrast, the effective range of a crossbow was 150 metres, firing 1 aimed shaft per minute, while a longbow could shoot 6 to 10 shafts per minute, all deadly at up to 200 metres. Although significantly slower than either bow, the arquebus alone could penetrate the solid sheets of metal (plate armour) that knights wore.

Summarise the innovations of Alonso da Cordoba:
- in the way he organised his troops;
- in the way his troops fought.

'Where a few days and a good drill sergeant might suffice to train a reasonably good **arquebusier**, many years and a whole way of life were needed to produce a competent archer.' (John Guilmartin, *Gunpowder and galleys: changing technology and Mediterranean warfare at sea in the sixteenth century*, 1974)

protective wall of ditches and stakes. These obstacles stopped the French in their tracks, well out of pike range of the Spanish. To that point in the battle, therefore, Cerignola might suggest the Swiss style was already out of date.

Cerignola is important, however, because it revealed further evolutionary changes in infantry warfare. Whereas the French that day were fighting with tactics unaltered from 1476, Cordoba had made a series of critical innovations. The first was his adoption of a fixed defensive position: a protective rampart in front of his infantry, much favoured by Italian armies. Charging opponents were thus stopped by a physical barrier and held in limbo, unable to strike yet vulnerable themselves to assault. Second, he introduced an extra infantry weapon: the **arquebus**. Halted and confused less than 30 metres from the Spanish, the numerically stronger all-pike French phalanx was a sitting target for Cordoba's arquebusiers. Fired at close range into a mass of troops, arquebuses caused more casualties than any other weapon then known. With field fortifications and guns, Cordoba had routed a larger enemy force and, in the process, changed infantry warfare. Cerignola left redundant the pure pike phalanx of Morat. Henceforth, pikes and arquebuses must be combined. In Cordoba's improved arrangements, arquebus detachments were trained to fight from within or in front of the spear wall. One weapon supported the other (on their own, the arquebusiers' slow rate of fire left them easy prey to attack by pike or by knight).

Cordoba's reforms did not stop there. He had taken the Swiss phalanx apart, breaking it into smaller formation called *coronelias*. Each of these comprised 250 footsoldiers (roughly 60 per cent pikemen, 20 per cent troops with javelins, 20 per cent arquebusiers) with its own supporting cavalry and field artillery. Operating in groups, *coronelias* could combine into a single phalanx or operate in smaller formations. That versatility was itself an important innovation only adding to infantry power.

Firearms had been slow to develop. They had been experimented with from the 1350s; the Burgundian army had 1,500 handguns in 1471. Italians favoured them throughout the fifteenth century, as did Yorkists during the Wars of the Roses (1455–87). But only with the emergence of the arquebus *c.*1490, and its improved successor the musket *c.*1512, did the era of the handgun finally dawn. It had psychological power. Machiavelli asserted in *The art of war* (1521) that just one volley was often enough to make the other side break, and that ordinary soldiers were more afraid of a single arquebusier than of 20 men armed with swords or pikes. Equally, firearms dramatically increased the killing power of the infantry; Venice spotted this immediately and in 1491 replaced all its crossbows with arquebuses. Further, it was far quicker and cheaper to train **arquebusiers** than bowmen. Even so, armies tend to be conservative organisations. France did not follow Venice until 1567, even though it had by then been on the receiving end of the arquebus for more than half a century. Most in France argued that at Cerignola it was no more than a supporting weapon, and continued to explain away the heavy casualties regularly inflicted on their troops by Spanish and imperial arquebuses. France continued to rely on the armoured knight. By contrast, the Spanish and German armies of Charles V were decades ahead in their wholehearted adoption of handguns – a major factor in the emperor's spectacular successes of the 1520s.

Cordoba's new way was then refined by Fernando de Avalos, marquis of **Pescara**. He removed the javelins and raised the proportion of arquebusiers to one-third of each *coronelia*, thereby demonstrating that he regarded it as a core weapon. At the same time, he enhanced the role of field artillery. Guns were the backbone of Pescara's way of war and their awesome power against knights and pikemen was, if further proof were needed, amply demonstrated in the victory he won over the French at Pavia (1525). Pescara's army was a

Known as 'the father of modern infantry', **Pescara** (1490–1525) was a Neapolitan and thus a subject of Charles V's Spanish crowns. A mercenary in imperial service, he captured Padua (1514), Milan (1521) and Genoa (1521). In command of the imperial forces in Italy from 1523, he won the spectacular victory over the French at Pavia (1525), but was mortally wounded in the battle.

The Battle on the Issus, by Albrecht Altdorfer, 1529 (detail). This shows a *coronelia* clearly and gives a vivid idea of the sheer power the infantry now exercised on a battlefield.

In what ways did the marquis of Pescara develop da Cordoba's reforms?

little smaller than that of Francis I but, whereas imperial losses numbered 700–1,500 men, French deaths totalled 8,000–14,000 (reliable battle statistics are rare for this period). The effectiveness of Pescara's arquebuses is seen most dramatically by looking at casualties among French knights. At the core of their 6,000 cavalry at Pavia were 1,400 noblemen. By the end of the battle, fewer than 400 were left alive, and most of the survivors were prisoners (including Francis himself).

Cordoba's and Pescara's *coronelias*, packed with arquebuses and supported by field artillery, gave Charles V's armies the military advantage. Further developments came in 1534 when Charles's Spanish forces were again restructured, this time into phalanxes of around 3,000 men called *tercios*. The reduced size gave a *tercio* greater cohesion while the increase in the proportion of arquebusiers (to 50 per cent) strengthened its striking power. Rapidly copied, the *tercio* became the standard European battlefield formation because it was designed for warfare in the age of the gun. Cavalry no longer dared to charge infantry, so the dense, shock-absorbing mass of a Swiss phalanx was no longer required. What was now needed was the firepower of each arquebusier, and the shallower *tercio* increased his opportunities to use his weapon; the phalanx locked too many men inside the square.

Why was a *tercio* thought to be better than a *coronelia* or a Swiss phalanx?

Charles V's commanders gave him the upper hand, but the Habsburg advantage could not last. After the humiliation of Pavia, France finally began to catch up and by the later 1530s had adopted Pescara's reforms and the *tercio*. Once both sides were rebalanced, the course of **war** could again go either way; superior weapons and tactics only have impact when they are new and possessed by just one side. The firepower of the arquebus, revealed at Cerignola and rammed home at Pavia, made commanders think more than twice about risking their troops in an open battle. Unless part of a siege, deliberate attacks became rare after 1530. The power of the gun had made the risk of defeat sufficient reason to avoid battle. Ironically, the emergence of a powerful infantry encouraged commanders to abandon offensive strategies. For the rest of the century, pitched battles usually occurred only when armies encountered each other by accident.

Geoffrey Parker argues European success 'in creating the first truly global empires between 1500 and 1750 depended upon precisely those improvements in the ability to wage **war**.' (*The military revolution: military innovation and the rise of the west, 1500–1800*, 1988) Outside Europe, the gun continued to give Europeans a massive military advantage. When Pizarro conquered the Inca Empire in 1531–34, he did so with only 168 men.

How did changes in tactics influence the course of the Habsburg–Valois Wars?

Siege artillery caught on far sooner and developed much faster than handguns. In use from the 1320s, cannons were weapons of significance by 1400. While their precise value is open to dispute (for example, there was difficulty in moving them and they had a habit of exploding), they played the pivotal role in the French reconquest of Normandy (1449–50) and the Ottoman

How far did pikes and arquebuses change the way battles were fought between 1476 and 1525?

capture of Byzantium (1453). Great guns would be concentrated to fire at the same small area of wall and literally batter it down. **Siege cannons** transformed fifteenth-century siege warfare because there was no defensive wall they could not smash. A massive advantage had been given to the besieger and, not surprisingly, kings rushed to expand their stocks. In the Spanish armies, the number of cannons grew from 16 in 1480 to 162 in 1508.

By contrast, the development of effective field guns for open battle lagged behind. Their limited accuracy, their slow rates of fire and (above all) their relative immobility combined to restrict their use severely, except for a preliminary bombardment. The first battle where artillery determined the outcome was Castillon (1453) at the end of the Hundred Years' War. But this was accidental. The advancing English passed in front of positions where French siege guns were dug in and, imaginatively, the gunners turned from bombarding the walls to mowing down infantry. More than half a century was to pass before the lesson of Castillon had been grasped: an army with mobile field guns on a battlefield would enjoy an enormous advantage. That truth was grasped by the French, who took batteries of guns (called culverins) into Italy in 1494. During their victory at Ravenna (1512), they bombarded the Spanish lines for more than two hours. But the true worth of field artillery was not proven until 1515 during the two-day Battle of Marignano. As Spanish and Swiss phalanxes moved across the battlefield, the French kept them under near constant fire from more than 70 culverins. With an effective range of up to 2,250 metres, these guns were manoeuvred to maintain an **enfilading fire** that annihilated imperial forces and gave Francis I control of Milan.

After Marignano, field guns became ever more important. Illustrated technical manuals were published. By the 1540s, mass-produced cast iron cannons and shot were being exported from Germany, the Netherlands and Sweden. Before long, the powers had so many guns of different size and type that they standardised their ordnance (the empire its 50 types in 1549, France her 17 types in 1552; curiously, Spain did not follow suit until 1614). We must, however, be careful not to exaggerate the importance of field artillery during the first half of the sixteenth century. Examples of guns being moved about during battle were rare, even for the French. In the Italian Wars, Marignano was unique. The real impact was made by siege guns, which sparked off a revolution in fortification design.

Across the medieval centuries, improved methods of attack continually forced engineers to find new ways to construct durable protective fortifications. In consequence, the castle became redundant. Castles were already obsolete before 1400. By the time guns affected siege warfare, **castles** were no longer being built; the gun did not make the castle extinct. For our period, 'fortifications' meant sets of defences built around towns. Medieval threats to

A fine example of the massive late-medieval **siege cannons**, known as bombards, is the weapon called Mons Meg which can be seen today at Edinburgh Castle. Cast in the 1440s for the duke of Burgundy, it weighs 8.5 tonnes and could fire one stone cannon ball about every six minutes.

Enfilading fire is overlapping cross-fire from weapons sited in different positions but shooting into the same area.

What was significant about the French use of field artillery at Marignano in 1515? Why did field artillery have little impact on European war between 1499 and 1560?

Sham **castles** were built by nobles in the fifteenth and sixteenth centuries, but none could be defended. They were designed to impress, to display the status and power of the owner. Good English examples of this are Tattershall Castle, Lincolnshire, and Thornbury Castle, Gloucestershire.

defensive walls, such as scaling ladders and catapults, had forced them to be built higher and higher. High and relatively thin walls were, however, no match for the horizontal fire of siege guns. Against these, defensive walls needed to be lowered, thickened and reinforced.

Until the outbreak of the Italian Wars, little was actually done to modernise existing defences. The change in fortification design began only in the 1490s, and until the 1530s it was confined almost exclusively to Italy. Perhaps the earliest example was the defences begun at Sarzanello in 1495, but this is a rare case. The general opinion in Italy was that guns had made fortifications useless. As late as 1519, Machiavelli could write that 'there is no wall, whatever its thickness, that artillery will not destroy in only a few days'. But there was an answer and, at the very moment when Machiavelli was despairing, a complete gun-proof system was being constructed at the papal port of Civitavecchia.

The first key change was the lowering and thickening of walls; and, because stone shattered easily under bombardment, they were increasingly made of brick. To absorb the impact and minimise the damage of cannon balls, walls were then back-filled with mounds of earth (this was effective because cannon balls then were solid, not explosive). Most medieval walls were about 2 metres thick at their base, but the new earth-reinforced ramparts were anything up to 12 metres thick. By the early sixteenth century, many engineers were saving time and money by leaving out the brick and simply piling up mounds of earth, reinforced with stakes.

It was also necessary to widen and deepen the ditch outside the walls, to create a more effective barrier to frontal assault and mining. Engineers from the 1520s were also building massive, gently sloping banks of earth (called 'glacis') in front of ditches so that the walls were almost totally hidden from horizontal (i.e. close) artillery fire. Together, these various changes made to protect fortifications from artillery are known as 'ballistic shaping'. That term does not, however, only mean the creation of anti-artillery fortifications. It also covers the design changes made to bring guns inside **fortifications** for use by defenders. Gunports were being added to existing defences from the 1380s, but most changes began with the Italian Wars; the finest surviving example is the defences built around Verona. In the employment of artillery in fortification defence, the great architectural change concerned towers (in their new squat form called 'bastions'). Bastion design became the subject of intense debate. Medieval towers were usually round, but that shape left substantial areas of 'dead ground' (blind spots) in front of every tower that fell outside all lines of fire by the defenders. Enemy troops there were safe.

Since artillery could now pound walls to create a breach, into which attacking forces would pour, the need to eliminate dead ground was urgent. Flanking fire along the walls was needed so that defenders could shoot enemy

Use the illustrations on page 103 to explain:
- why traditional medieval defences were of little use against the new siege artillery;
- how new-style fortifications were designed to meet the threat of the new siege artillery.

The new-style **fortifications** created by all these developments are known as *trace italienne*.

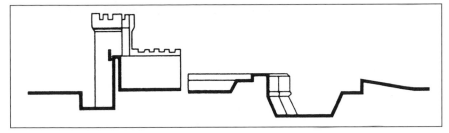

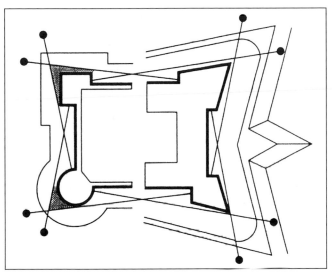

Above: Sections across traditional medieval (left) and *trace italienne* (right) fortifications.

Left: Plans of traditional medieval (left) and *trace italienne* (right) fortifications. Lines ending in a dark spot show lines of fire from towers and bastions. The shaded areas (left) illustrate the problem of 'dead ground' associated with medieval towers.

troops in the ditch. The solution was to draw out the bastion's shape to fill the blind spot and give defenders excellent all-round fields of fire. This created a triangular structure called an 'angled bastion', probably first used in 1496 on Rhodes against the Turks. For the next three hundred years, squat angled bastions projecting from squat earth-reinforced ramparts were used by all European military engineers, all over the world. Such **fortifications** were, however, very expensive and few entirely new sets were constructed before the major wars of the second half of the sixteenth century.

Angled bastions needed to be placed every 250–300 metres for effective coverage of walls and ditch. But there was one problem. If attacking troops managed to enter the ditch and reach the base of the walls, the defenders could not easily fire on them without shooting at their own walls. About 1550, this difficulty was overcome by

Outstanding examples of ballistic shaping from the Italian Wars can still be seen at the following sites:

Civita Castellana	fortress	begun 1494
Civitavecchia	fortress and walls	begun 1496
Nettuno	fortress	1501–03
Florence	Fortezza da Basso	from 1534
L'Aquila	fortress	c. 1535
Venice	San Andrea fortress (in the Lagoon)	from 1535

The last mentioned, and the changes to Verona, were the work of the architect Michele Sanmichele (c. 1484–1559), regarded as the finest military engineer of the period. He was a pupil of Bramante. His military building was all for the Venetian Republic, so his **fortifications** can be found across their overseas empire (his work at Iraklion on Crete in the 1540s is particularly well preserved). The first *trace italienne* fortifications in England were constructed in the reign of Elizabeth I. Of those that survive, the best examples are the ramparts at Berwick-upon-Tweed (Northumberland) and Pendennis Castle (Cornwall).

Use the illustrations on page 103 to explain:
- the problem of 'dead ground';
- how the angled bastion removed that problem.

Use the illustration on this page to explain:
- the function of an *orellion*;
- the role of a half moon;
- why the besiegers are shown bombarding three points along the walls.

refining the bastion's shape from a triangle into an arrow head. Into the notch created at the base of each bastion (called an *orellion*), guns could be placed to fire along walls, rather than directly at them. Two further significant amendments to *trace italienne* developed late in the Habsburg–Valois Wars. One was to site free-standing bastions (called 'ravelins') within ditches so that troops in a ditch were always under fire. The other, which sometimes includes ravelins, was the 'double Pisan rampart'. Here, the outer wall of a ditch was fortified so that besiegers in the moat came under fire from guns behind them and ahead of them.

Enfilading fire meant that an attacker needed to make not one breach but three: one in the wall and one in each of the neighbouring bastions (to silence the flanking guns). Yet to make just one breach in ballistically shaped defences, contemporaries calculated that 30 guns needed to fire 700–1,200 cannon balls (daily rates of siege artillery fire were 60–100 shots per day). Getting through the breach would be even harder. First, assault troops had to pass through a hail of fire in the ditch. More formidable, however, was the earthwork barrier that defenders would dig behind a breach. Known from its shape as a 'half moon', it halted a rush of troops inside the fortification.

Around its elevated rim would be sited small field guns and arquebuses, aiming at point-blank range down into the confined space created by the half moon in which the attackers were marooned. Meanwhile, in the wings were companies of pikemen waiting to strike those who survived the storm of shot.

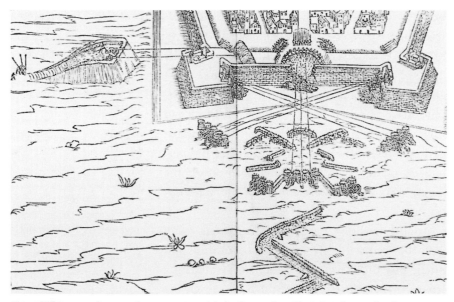

Trace italienne under attack, 1571. Note (a) the lines of artillery fire drawn for the besiegers; (b) the defences built by the besiegers for protection; (c) the earth rampart (left) built by the besiegers so that their artillery can fire inside the walls; (d) the half moon created behind the breach in the walls; (e) the *orellions* in the bastions.

As long as there was space within the walls to dig a half moon, towns could successfully survive breaches in their walls. Successful assaults against *trace italienne* fortifications were rare. When the defenders held the advantage at every stage, towns surrendered only if they ran out of food or ammunition.

Siege artillery held the upper hand then only until the 1520s. After that, as the successful defence of Milan against French attack in 1521 revealed, the advantage passed decisively again to defensive warfare. The emergence of stone castles in the eleventh and twelfth centuries had shifted the balance of war to defence and, until the fourteenth century, medieval warfare became essentially a matter of sieges, known as 'positional warfare'. Siege guns in the fifteenth century broke that stalemate and from *c.*1440 to *c.*1530 liberated commanders, allowing great movement of armies, decisive pitched battles and glorious rapid conquests. ***Trace italienne***, however, curtailed dynamic war and, in restoring the advantage to the defence, returned warfare to the checkmate of positional warfare. As direct contests like Pavia became increasingly rare, failure in a major siege became as important as victory on the open battlefield had been; Charles V discovered this following his inability to recapture Metz in 1552–53. Only in regions as yet unaffected by ballistic shaping could war continue to be a matter of rapid, aggressive action (e.g. the Ottoman invasion of Hungary in 1526).

Elsewhere, war had become a wearisome matter of manoeuvre and, as on the Western Front in 1915–17, of attrition. Even when commanders won battlefield victories, they became increasingly reluctant to follow them up because the size of forces, the time and the resources needed to occupy enemy territory were beyond them. Charles V invaded Provence in 1536, but did not have the troops or money for the sieges necessary to take it. Similarly, French victory at Ceresole (1544) was not followed through so, unlike Marignano, did not restore control of Milan to Francis I. The effect of *trace italienne* explains why the Italian Wars fall into two distinct parts: up to the 1520s, full of action and lots of battles; after *c.*1530, when nothing seemed to happen. The military consequence of the positional warfare dictated by *trace italienne* was that victory for Habsburg or Valois became impossible. The political consequence of that stalemate was that, at long last, the disputed frontiers had to be settled.

How far did an increase in the size of armies affect the role of mercenaries and the development of standing armies during this period?

Until quite recently, historians argued that early modern armies grew markedly larger. Estimates put rates of growth at prodigious levels, usually using supporting statistics from the empire. Granada was conquered by

Trace italienne 'created strategic problems to which there was no early solution. A heavily defended fortress or town, sheltering perhaps 10,000 men and supported by lesser strongholds in the vicinity, was far too dangerous to be left in the wake of an advancing army: it had to be taken, whatever the cost. And yet there was no short-cut to capture, however powerful the besieging army might be. This simple paradox rendered battles more or less irrelevant in all areas where the new fortifications were built, except (as often occurred), when they were fought between a besieging army and a relief column, so that the result decided the outcome of the siege, as at St Quentin (1557).' (Geoffrey Parker, *The military revolution: military innovation and the rise of the west, 1500–1800*, 1988)

Ferdinand and Isabella in 1492 with an army about 14,000–16,000 strong. Their grandson Charles V fought Pavia (1525) with 20,000–25,000 troops. By 1532 he could muster 100,000 forces and in 1552 some 150,000. Part of the explanation for this can be attributed to the sheer scale of the Habsburg–Valois Wars. For more than six decades, the two dynasties fought each other in Italy, in the Pyrenees and along the Franco-German frontier. The major cause of such phenomenal growth is said, however, to have been *trace italienne*. Before ramparts and bastions brought wars of movement to an end, successful campaigns could be fought with small armies. After *trace italienne*, the siege warfare that dominated the final three decades of the struggle demanded large garrisons tied down in numerous fortresses, and equally massive forces to give commanders any hope of mounting the total long-term blockade necessary to give the chance of a successful siege.

Certainly no state seems to have had any difficulty in raising whatever troops it needed. The army was always seen as an attractive alternative to a civilian life in which regular work and good pay were never easy to find. Today, however, scholars urge that such figures be treated with caution. They are official statistics, drawn from the papers of administrators sometimes talking of hoped-for numbers and always generalising without reference to the situation on the ground. In reality, the strength of an army in the field was much lower than official estimates; modern calculations suggest real numbers were never less than one-third (often up to one-half) lower than government figures claimed. Army sizes were notional for a number of reasons. Disease and desertion were constant problems – wastage rates of around 25 per cent each year were common. Simultaneously, numbers were deliberately inflated by fraudulent senior officers exploiting a system that handed to them (for onward distribution) the pay of all the troops declared to be under their command.

Taking all these factors into account, scholars now suggest that growth in armies was limited. The figures for Charles V used in the first paragraph of this section mix two very different categories: real numbers put into the field at Pavia on the one hand and the official musters of 1532 and 1552 on the other. If we compare like with like, and confine our view to the forces actually deployed in battle, we still see growth, but on a much more modest scale. In contrast to the 20,000–25,000 men Charles had at Pavia in 1525, he besieged Metz in 1552 with *c*.40,000 troops (about the same number his son Philip II fielded in 1557 at the Battle of St Quentin). On the other side, whereas Charles VIII invaded Italy in 1494 with about 18,000 men, Francis I fought Pavia with 25,000–30,000 while Henry II captured Metz in 1552 with around 38,000.

Note that these figures still place the significant rate of growth after Pavia. So the rise of the infantry and the growing importance of artillery did force

What factors led to expansion in the size of armies between 1499 and 1560?

Why was growth more marked after c.1525 than before?

What factors limited the growth of armies in the sixteenth century?

Why are historians today fairly cautious about calculating the size of armies?

armies to grow. So too did *trace italienne*. Siege warfare was extravagant in its demand for men. This can be demonstrated by comparing the forces deployed by the emperor at Pavia and at the Battle of Landrécis (1543) on the one hand, and at Landrécis and at Metz (1552–53) on the other. At Landrécis, Charles had barely 12,000 men. Why was this? There was no crisis of recruitment in the mid 1540s. The answer lies in the changing nature of Habsburg–Valois warfare after Pavia. Against the vigorous days of the 1520s, the emperor could no longer afford to field the large army that might have won him victory that day in 1543. Landrécis was in the southern Netherlands, close to the French–imperial border. In such a hotly disputed zone, neither side after *c.*1530 dared move most of its troops away from **garrison** duty. In consequence, open battles of the 1540s and 1550s tended to be indecisive, low-key affairs.

As armies advanced, garrisons had to be planted regularly. Sixteenth-century commanders were obsessed by the control of land. They needed to have substantial territory under their sway for practical as well as military reasons. From it they drew provisions to feed their soldiers. From it they collected taxes to pay their soldiers. As you will see later in this chapter, kings were unable to fund their wars and supply their armies; the early modern state was too small, too inefficient to be able to cope. To a large degree, sixteenth-century forces thus had to fend for themselves. The development of *trace italienne* and the reversion to siege warfare caused growth in the size of armies. Yet here too there were limits. Occupied territories could all too easily be bled dry by such parasitic forces. After the growth of the 1520s to 1550s, European armies remained remarkably static in size for more than a century. Forces beyond 40,000–60,000 were too large to supply and pay, and too difficult to move, in any era before Louis XIV. As for mass armies, they lay far in the future with Napoleon.

One further point about size is also now stressed by historians: the figures for the first half of the sixteenth century need to be seen in their medieval context. Most medieval battles were fought between armies of 4,000–6,000 men on each side; few exceeded 10,000. Yet some did. Edward I marched into Scotland in 1298 with 28,000 soldiers, the same number King Matthias Corvinus of Hungary moved against Vienna in 1486. In 1340, the French put 44,000 troops into the field against the English. Like so many aspects of the sixteenth century, is this an indication that the age of Charles V was still in essence medieval?

The use of mercenaries had long been a standard feature of medieval warfare. Usually foreign, they were primarily Swiss, German or Italian. Contemporary opinion judged the Swiss to be the best quality, but Germans (called *landsknechts*) were the most numerous – Francis I hired 23,000 for his attack on Milan in 1515. In times when permanent, professional armies did not exist,

'If a commander gathered the forces necessary to capture the enemy's strong places he risked losing his own. Providing **garrisons** on the scale necessary to secure the Netherlands consumed a sizeable percentage of imperial revenues, which in turn left less money available for offensive operations.' (David Eltis, *The military revolution in sixteenth-century Europe*, 1998)

The first significant battle of the long French civil wars known as the Wars of Religion, **Dreux** was a Catholic victory and a classic case of armoured cavalry unable to break the disciplined infantry *coronelia*.

mercenaries seemed the next best thing: professional troops who came fully equipped and ready for battle, and were always available for hire. Both sides used them extensively throughout the Italian Wars. Three-quarters of the armies of Francis I were hired (mostly German and Italian, together with English, Greeks, Irish, Poles and Scots; the core of his cavalry was Albanian). Almost always they were better trained than any domestic militia or conscript force hastily raised. Normally, they would fight for anybody against anybody – except for the Swiss, who refused to fight each other. At the Battle of **Dreux** (1562), Swiss mercenaries employed by both sides unexpectedly found themselves in direct confrontation and lowered their pikes, refusing to strike.

Small steps had been taken in the fifteenth century to create national, permanent (or 'standing') armies, under the control of the crown and funded from national taxation. France led the way with units of armoured cavalry set up in the 1440s, the *compagnies d'ordonnance*. Burgundy followed in 1473, as did Castile in 1481. Milan and Venice had small, full-time forces by 1500. The attraction was trained troops whose loyalty and discipline was assured on permanent standby. But such forces remained tiny. No further steps could be taken in this direction in the first half of the sixteenth century because, unlike Ottoman sultans, European kings could not afford large standing armies; Louis XII tried and failed in 1513–14 to create a large standing body of infantry, the *francs archers*. Because of that brutal financial fact, rulers were forced to rely on mercenaries, a highly developed system of private enterprise.

That dependence left monarchs vulnerable. Mercenaries were expensive and, ultimately, unreliable. Too great a reliance on them could prove disastrous. If they were not paid they would not fight, and they might well desert in large numbers, quite possibly joining the opposition. The chance of their going on the rampage was high, especially if they were owed wages; the two major sixteenth-century military atrocities, the Sack of Rome (1527) and the Sack of Antwerp (1576), were committed by mercenary forces with pay seriously overdue. The Reformation added a new uncertainty: religious loyalties. Medieval mercenaries were all Catholics and there seem to have been no ideological issues that complicated their loyalty to their paymaster. The emergence of Protestantism, however, shattered that safe presumption. For his campaign of 1545–47 against the Lutheran Schmalkaldic League, Charles V was careful to bring in good Catholic mercenaries from Spain and Italy. But things were not always so carefully organised, as Dreux also revealed. German Lutheran arquebusiers were quite happy to take employment on the Catholic side but, when it came to battle, refused to shoot fellow Protestants.

If mercenaries could not ultimately be relied upon, did that encourage a greater use of domestic militias? Some would have agreed with the German Lutheran reformer Andreas Osiander that the arming and training of willing

Draw up a balance sheet identifying (in separate columns) the advantages and disadvantages of employing mercenaries.

volunteers from the local population would work to the benefit of the state, the community and the individual. Only a tyrant had cause to fear a militia. Native soldiers would fight with greater loyalty because they fought for their own cause. They would also, Osiander argued, be more obedient and less likely to plunder or mutiny. In the uncertain atmosphere of a divided Holy Roman Empire, we can see why the preacher of Nuremberg was keen to protect his city state. Machiavelli agreed with such a view. As a convinced republican, he saw mercenaries as the tools of despotic rulers and militias as the guarantee of liberty. 'It is more difficult,' he argued, 'to bring a people, armed with its own arms, under the sway of their ruler than it is to bring one armed with foreign arms.' Yet Osiander and Machiavelli held the minority view. Most judged the French bishop and political thinker Claude de Seyssel (see Chapter 3, page 77) to be correct when in 1519 he stated that to arm the civilian population was to encourage rebellion. Under no circumstances should the people be given crossbows or arquebuses. Every wise ruler should keep on standby a force of foreign mercenaries, ready to strike down popular disturbances.

Several Italian states, like Venice, did establish reliable militias. France's own experience of militias was, however, more typical. Brought to prominence by Louis XI during the 1460s, they committed so many murders and robberies that Louis XII suppressed them and employed Swiss mercenaries in their place. Francis I tried again in 1534, as did Henry II in 1556. Both needed large armies but were keen to cut their spiralling costs. Again, however, they were found to be the cause of disorder. Early modern militias were unreliable. Rarely were they turned into effective fighting forces. Local levies were usually not well trained and invariably underfunded, so their equipment was inadequate and out of date. Furthermore, orders to proceed abroad on campaign led to mass desertion. Townsmen and peasants were content to supplement their wages by militia service, but few were willing to trade their occupations, animals and harvests for the real military life and (in a world without pensions) the significant chance of injury or death.

Even if rulers had wanted home-grown forces, the odds were stacked against the creation and maintenance of large domestic armies able to win on the battlefield. No militia force ever beat a **mercenary** army. Practical political and military considerations determined that, the potential dangers notwithstanding, sixteenth-century rulers had to hire Swiss or German pikemen and Spanish or Italian arquebusiers. They were specialists, and they were politically safe and virtually guaranteed the failure of all sixteenth-century rebellions. In that context, we should remember that nobles as well as peasants could revolt. Artillery was needed by kings as much to smash the strongholds of their own feudal barons as those encountered on foreign campaigns. At the same time, handguns ensured the defeat of peasant rebels. Guns in the hands

Why were attempts in the first half of the sixteenth century to raise militia armies largely unsuccessful?

'Since as a rule only the king could afford to hire **mercenaries** in bulk, they strengthened him against his nobles; they strengthened both king and nobles against the people, with whom they had no ties of sympathy.' (Kiernan, 'Foreign mercenaries and absolute monarchy', *Past and Present* II, 1957)

Contemporary estimates calculated each **soldier** needed 700 grams of bread, 450 grams of meat/cheese/fish and 3.5 litres of beer every day. An army of 30,000 men thus required more food each day than all but the largest towns. For an army of that size, the daily requirement for rations included 1,500 sheep or 150 cows, plus 45,000 kilograms of flour to make bread. Those needs themselves created further problems. Could they find such quantities each day or must they take supplies with them? If the latter, a notional army of 30,000 men would need a herd of about 20,000 animals (which would require 400 acres for grazing or 90 tons of fodder each day).

For further detail of problems of inadequate state **revenues**, see Chapter 2, pages 46 to 47, for Charles V; and Chapter 3, pages 72 to 74, for the Valois.

Henry VIII's **campaign** of 1544–45 against the French was expected to cost £250,000 but actually cost £650,000 (one year's total royal revenue in England was then c.£200,000). When the German city of Nuremberg went to war against the margrave of Brandenburg in 1550, it calculated the cost would total about 340,000 guilders. In fact, it cost 1.5 million guilders (their annual income was 170,000 guilders).

of foreigners were essential to the sixteenth-century state. Thus it was that Charles V stationed German troops in Spain, Spanish troops in Italy, Croat and Hungarian troops in Austria.

The costs of war

Princes spent money on many things. In the Renaissance, palaces and royal courts consumed larger sums than ever before. So too did the growing number of officials employed in royal administration. Yet the costs of war far outstripped everything else. As Louis XII prepared to invade Italy in 1499, he was advised that three things were needed if victory was to be his: 'money, more money and yet more money'. War has never been cheap, but the costs increased significantly during the fifteenth and sixteenth centuries. Armies cost more because they grew larger, because positional warfare demanded larger forces, because wars lasted longer and because ever more arquebuses and siege guns were required. While individually an infantryman was far cheaper than a mounted knight, there were many more footsoldiers in 1500 than in 1460, and in 1560 than in 1500. Every **soldier** needed regular supplies of equipment, food and pay. Then there were the mounting costs of the new style of fortifications and artillery. When Pope Paul III built a series of *trace italienne* bastions around Rome in the 1540s, each cost 44,000 ducats (about £10,000 in the values of Henry VIII's England). At the same time, Charles V re-fortified Antwerp and constructed 15 new fortresses, packed with 1,012 guns, along the southern border of the Netherlands. The total cost was more than 4.5 million florins (about £500,000).

War cost an exorbitant amount. The attack on Milan by Francis I in 1515 consumed 36 per cent of the French crown's annual revenue. When he re-invaded in 1524, the first season's campaign used 50 per cent of his annual income. Both figures seem good value, however, when compared to the French campaign against Charles V in 1554, which devoured the state's entire **revenues** for that year. That was no atypical example. The Florentine Republic spent its total revenues for 18 months on resisting French troops in 1526.

No sixteenth-century state could afford war, especially the protracted wars encouraged by *trace italienne*. No early modern government knew how to pay for its wars. State finances were always designed to fund peace-time government, and domestic revenues were almost always fully committed. Consolidated national debts barely existed. Administration was so crude that forecasts invariably under-estimated by a large margin the total cost of **campaigns**. Contemporary inflation meant that rulers had to increase revenues simply to stand still and afford ordinary domestic expenditure. The costs of war also outstripped the general economic expansion of the time. Governments were, therefore, obliged to adopt a range of desperate devices. They raised taxes, devalued their currency, sold jobs to the highest bidder and took out loans at excessive rates of interest. For immediate advantage, they mortgaged the future.

Financial difficulties also had direct impact on the way campaigns were fought, especially during the final two decades of the Habsburg–Valois Wars. Even if the battle were won, lack of cash meant that it was rarely followed up. As early as Pavia that was true. Charles V's triumphant victory evaporated because he could not afford the follow-on invasion of France. Indeed, Pavia had only been fought in the first place because the imperial army's pay was so overdue that Pescara feared it would disintegrate if not promised the imminent prospect of plunder in Milan. For exactly the same reason, Philip II's spectacular victory over the French at St Quentin (1557) could not deliver lasting political result. *Trace italienne* only made matters worse because it played havoc with all calculations for pay and supply. When the emperor's forces took five weeks (rather than the estimated one) to capture Peronne in 1536, the intended march on Paris had to be abandoned because the siege had used up too much of the commander's finely balanced war chest.

Warfare bankrupted governments, large and small. The Republic of Siena finally lost its independence, and was absorbed by its long-hated neighbour the Republic of Florence, because of the unsustainable cost of new *trace italienne* fortifications constructed in 1554–55 in the hope that they would protect Sienese liberty. When the Florentines attacked, the bastions lay incomplete and there was no money left to hire sufficient mercenaries. During the latter stages of the Habsburg–Valois Wars, both sides were crippled by the need to borrow ever greater sums (to fund new campaigns and to meet the rising interest payments due on all the earlier loans). At the abdication of Charles V (1555–56) and the death of Henry II (1559), both were literally bankrupt. In total, Charles V borrowed about 30 million ducats to fund his wars – loans incurring interest payments of at least another 12 million ducats. When his son Philip II became king of Spain, he discovered his entire income from Spanish taxation had been mortgaged for the next five years to cover just some of those debts. The Habsburg–Valois Wars were ended not by glorious success or humiliating failure in battle but by the crushing burden of debt on treasuries. War had become more a test of **financial** strength than of military power.

What of the political balance sheet? When armies were growing, who but kings could afford the thousands of pikemen and arquebusiers and the hundreds of cannons which warfare now required? Medieval nobles were warriors, but their castles were no longer impregnable and a feudal levy of even 1,000 men drawn from their estates counted for nothing. Guns and *trace italienne* worked to undermine the independent military and political power of feudal magnates. The age of gunpowder helped tip the political balance of power between kings and their barons decisively in favour of the former. Still

Identify the factors that made the costs of war increase during the Habsburg–Valois conflict.

'Most important of all, success in war depends on having enough money to provide whatever is needed.' (The duke of Enghien, French commander at the Battle of Ceresole, 1544). From the evidence in this section, explain what the duke meant. Illustrate your answer with examples from the Habsburg–Valois Wars.

The **financial** effects of war were also felt in England. For the first 20 years of her reign, Elizabeth I was paying off loans incurred by her father Henry VIII to fund his wars.

common in 1450, noble 'private' armies had all but disappeared by 1600. At the same time, the enlarged royal forces that emerged between 1525 and 1559 could only serve as potent symbols of enhanced royal power.

The relentless impact of inflation on the largely fixed incomes of Europe's magnates only added to the political subordination of the nobilities. When their revenues were totally inadequate, they had little choice but to seek service. Employment in the army of the king became an attractive option for impoverished yet proud aristocrats. Noblemen could thus remain warriors, but winning glory henceforth as captains and generals in the pay and under the command of their king. Medieval chivalric notions of the loyal knight were skilfully adapted by monarchs to this new environment. Medieval codes of military honour now had grafted onto them the concept of service to the prince and the state (termed by scholars 'national chivalry'). Henceforth, noblemen would fight not by right of birth as they wished, but by licence of the king, serving as career officers.

Explain how the rising costs of war helped to undermine the military and political independence of the nobility.

The shift was not, however, all one way. Kings continued to rely heavily on the military tradition, experience and talent of their noblemen. Kings in 1560 also still remained dependent on the political loyalty of their nobles. The French Wars of Religion (1562–98) and the Dutch Revolt (1568–1609) showed that the ability of great magnates to raise large forces of their own had not yet vanished. The process of subordinating aristocrats to the royal will was, inevitably, very gradual, taking at least two centuries. Still very much warriors in 1500, they had not been extracted from their armour and fitted out with the satin and lace 'uniform' of royal courtiers until about 1700. But when assessing the costs of war for rulers in the first half of the sixteenth century, we must be careful not to lose sight of the political windfall that accompanied the financial ruin. Changing fashion had nothing to do with it. The costs of war bit even more savagely on barons than on kings. As Maurice Keen puts it in *Chivalry* (1984), 'harsh necessity was the midwife of the change . . . secular power tended to crystallise around the best paymaster'.

Military developments and the cult of chivalry

Chivalry was an essential part of the beliefs of the later medieval world. The concept portrayed the ideal way of life for a man in the world, as opposed to a priest or a monk. But religion lay at the heart of chivalric ideas. Alongside the quest for honour and glory through heroic and military feats lay an indelible emphasis on piety and virtue. The medieval knight was a Christian knight.

Use the illustration in Chapter 1 of Charles V at the Battle of Mühlberg (page 25) and that in Chapter 3 of Francis I (page 88), together with your own knowledge, to explain the late-medieval theory of the chivalric knight.

Tales of knights and their gallant Christian behaviour were endlessly popular. The invention of printing created a massive new market for epic stories like those of King Arthur, his knights and their quest for the Holy Grail. During the fifteenth century, such ideals acquired an even greater following.

The fashion began at the court of the dukes of Burgundy, but soon spread everywhere. New orders of knighthood were created. Tournaments and jousts flourished. Chivalry had originally been developed to promote the cause of **crusade** against the power of Islam; it was now hijacked to redirect political loyalties, focusing the allegiance of noblemen on their prince. Of course, chivalry had always been constructed around and for the nobility. It offered a way of distinguishing and maintaining the superiority of an elite aristocracy against the vulgar world of townsmen and peasants. But this was an illusion.

Nobles were living out a pantomime in which war was portrayed as a pure, often bloodless contest between individual knights fighting for noble motives: the glory of God, the honour of a woman. But medieval tales were also filled with robber barons and black knights. Mercenaries in the Italian Wars were condemned for their pillage, yet medieval armies, supposedly steeped in chivalric codes of honour, regularly employed scorched-earth policies, looting, raping and murdering at will. While medieval battles could be leisurely games of chess in which barely a handful of knights were killed, these were always atypical. Most were real contests and some were bloody affairs. Single combat was another myth. Knights invariably operated in groups of 10 to 40, employing tactics that made heroic, individual contest almost impossible. Some were conscious of these contradictions at the time, aware that, as Philippe de Commines put it, 'in war as in politics, the quest for honour will bring only failure. Success alone is what matters.' No one spotlighted the contrary nature of this world better than Commines. Employed by the duke of Burgundy, the greatest patron of late-medieval chivalry, he understood the contradiction between the jousts he watched and the growing stockpiles of arquebuses and cannons for which the Burgundian state was equally famous. Fair play rarely came into it. Chivalry had been developed for the tournament and belonged in jousts and books, not on the battlefield.

How then did the cult of chivalry, promoted as never before, cope with the military developments of the first half of the sixteenth century? At one level, nothing changed. Many were the authors who argued that the true knight could still be a noble hero within the disciplined ranks of the large armies of the Italian Wars. Throughout these campaigns, aristocratic prisoners were sometimes released without ransom if they had fought valiantly. Before the Battle of Ravenna (1512), the king of Navarre challenged the Spanish commander to personal combat instead of a contest of their armies. In 1528 and 1538, Charles V in all seriousness proposed the same with Francis I to resolve the territorial claims underpinning the Habsburg–Valois Wars. Personal combat was not the only part of the code to live on. During the joint French–imperial siege of Padua in 1509, Emperor Maximilian I suggested the French cavalry should join his infantry on foot to storm a breach in the walls. Medieval

Yet **crusading** ideals lived on. As late as 1578, King Sebastian of Portugal was killed in battle leading a crusade in Morocco.

How did developments in warfare between 1476 and 1525 threaten the knight? What evidence is there that the ideals of chivalry lived on during the Habsburg–Valois Wars?

knights often fought on foot, especially from the fourteenth century, but the French commander was outraged at the suggestion: 'Considers the Emperor it to be a just and reasonable matter to imperil so much nobleness together with his infantry, of whom one is a shoe maker, another a farrier, another a baker and suchlike mechanics who hold not their honour as do we gentlemen?'

Aristocratic reactions to the pike phalanx and the arquebus are similarly instructive. Like the bow in an earlier age, these increased the ability of armies to kill. Some noble anger and fear was directed against the weapons themselves, but fury was primarily targeted at the social consequences of what these weapons did. Armed with an arquebus, a peasant could kill a brave knight at long range. Such a contest was unfair. Armed with a lance or sword, the noble was out of reach of the arquebusier and could not defend himself. Until now, knights had been able to ride down and slaughter common soldiers, but now the contest had been levelled. In consequence, the new weapons were condemned as unchristian and ungentlemanly. Where was there now scope for individual courage? When battles were to be won and lost by the corporate ranks of massed infantry, chivalric notions built around the single heroic knight seemed redundant. Two early modern writers sum up below the passionate feelings stirred up by the arquebus.

Source A	Source B
O wretched and foul invention, how did you ever find place in a human heart? Through you the soldier's glory is destroyed; through you the business of arms is without honour; through you valour and courage are brought low, for often the bad man seems better than the good; through you, valour no more, daring no more can come to test in the field.	An invention which allows a base and cowardly hand to take the life of a brave knight in such a way that, without his knowing how or why, when his valiant heart is full of courage, there comes a random shot – discharged perhaps by a man who fled in terror from the flash the accursed machine made in firing.
Ludovico Ariosto (d. 1523), court poet at Ferrara, *Orlando Furioso*, xi.26, translated by Allan Gilbert (New York, 1954), vol. I, p. 156.	Miguel Cervantes (d. 1616), *Don Quixote*, book 6, stanza 40.

On what grounds did knights condemn the use of guns?

Suggest reasons why many in the early sixteenth century were in two minds about the desirability of guns.

This was an old rhetoric. Similar complaints had been made against earlier new weaponry from the catapult to the longbow and the crossbow. The armoured knight had been an endangered species for a long time. In the early days of firearms, captured arquebusiers were invariably killed – as had been bowmen before them. Yet even before 1500, knights were using the new weapons themselves. No attempt was made to ban these devilish weapons; their usefulness was all too plain to see. Instead, as ever with late-medieval chivalry, they talked up the lost nobility of war in some nostalgic distortion of the past, while simultaneously adapting with all speed to the realities of modern warfare.

It was the same story with the use of mercenaries. Contemporaries in Italy looked at the casualties and pillage of the Italian Wars and talked of a new barbarism. Medieval Italian war had been characterised by the manoeuvrings of armies of mercenaries. Often they did not clash in open battle. In consequence, Italian commentators like Francesco Guicciardini looked at the forces battling at Pavia and lamented the passing of the old ways 'in which commonly died but very few'. But Guicciardini misunderstood what was going on. As we have seen, mercenaries were as much a part of the armies of Charles V and Francis I as they had been in earlier centuries. The battles of the 1520s were bloody because siege artillery had liberated commanders from position warfare. Armies no longer spent their time manoeuvring because they could strike out in bold moves. That led to pitched battles, and casualties.

Contemporaries undoubtedly had difficulty adjusting to the escalation in warfare between c.1470 and c.1530. Never before had soldiers been so praised and abused. Guns represent the confusion better than anything else. Charles V described them as 'more vile than the plague', yet he named one artillery battery 'the Twelve Apostles' and gave guns as wedding presents. The papacy had tried to ban the crossbow when new in the twelfth century, but never condemned the gun. Rather, several popes praised their power as God-given, to protect Christendom from the Turks and Christian rulers from rebels; they even offered gunners the protection of a patron saint, St Barbara. For all their inconsistencies and uncertainties, our early-modern ancestors themselves understood that the cult of chivalry was a tinsel-coated hoax.

What evidence is there that a 'military revolution' occurred during this period?

How profound were all these military changes? The concept of a 'military revolution' was proposed in 1956 by Michael Roberts. He argued that major changes in tactics and organisation so altered war and warfare between 1560 and 1660 that they constituted a revolution. Further, these changes exercised so profound an impact on European history that they stood 'like a great divide separating medieval society from the modern world'. Since 1956, scholars like Geoffrey Parker and Jeremy Black have argued over and modified many of Roberts's details, extending the dates of the revolution back to 1530 and onwards to 1760. In a different direction, there is now also a growing demand to recognise the profound changes in medieval warfare, and thus to push the start date to cover at least the fifteenth if not the fourteenth century. But most historians still accept the general concept, even if the 'revolution' has become something evolutionary, developing over a long period of time.

This grand debate falls outside the scope of this book. None the less, we can assess the revolutionary nature of the changes identified as occurring during 1499–1560. The notion of the military revolution is built on the following four interlocking ideas:

- There were major changes to the types of weapons and fortifications used.
- Those new weapons and fortifications forced fundamental changes in the way battles and wars were fought.
- Those new tactics meant that war had to be fought on a broader scale, with larger armies and at greater cost.
- This new scale of war had a significantly greater impact on society, both in terms of the physical destruction caused and the financial burdens imposed (through taxation and other measures) to pay for it.

Most of these have already been examined in the context of that clash of empires known as the Habsburg–Valois Wars. We should not be surprised to see that this epic 65-year struggle led to an arms race between the superpowers, or to observe that the only response they could make was military expansion. Remember, however, that we are talking of the primary impact of war only in territory disputed between Habsburg and Valois: parts of Italy, the Pyrenees, the southern Netherlands, Luxembourg, Alsace and Lorraine. If a military revolution was generated by the Habsburg–Valois Wars of 1494–1559, it remained confined geographically to a small part of Europe for a long time. There was some spread across France during the Wars of Religion (1562–98). The Netherlands bore its full impact during the Dutch Revolt (1568–1609). The Spanish employed Cordoba's arquebus and pike tactics against Aztecs and Incas. Like the **Portuguese**, they also built *trace italienne* fortifications around their overseas territories. But central and eastern Europe did not see the impact of these developments until the seventeenth century; even Germany remained almost totally untouched until the Thirty Years' War (1618–48).

Before an assessment can be made of the extent to which the Habsburg–Valois Wars were affected, even in part, by a military revolution, it is necessary to consider further the impact of war on society. Mention has already been made of looting and murder by both mercenary and militia forces. Towns were sacked with some frequency during the Italian Wars; eight were victims of major massacre and destruction in the first three campaigning seasons. Mercenaries were notorious for their pillage, but looting was standard behaviour in all armies. Pay and conditions were so poor that **loot** was seen universally as part of a soldier's terms of employment. When the authorities could not feed or pay their own troops regularly (let alone well), they had no option but to connive at plunder. But it was more than an unavoidable necessity.

Fine **Portuguese** *trace italienne* coastal forts survive at Dill (Gujerat, India) and Mombasa (Kenya).

'In this cruel action, there was no moderation in killing and the taking of **loot**. No age or sex was spared. Nobody escaped. Nothing was left free from the violence and fury of the soldiers. Their lust for gold, for sex and for blood were such that it is impossible to say which was their main goal.' (Francesco Guicciardini, a contemporary account of the Sack of Ravenna in 1512, in his *The history of the wars of Italy*)

Commanders and ministers of the crown alike saw **looting** as a means to encourage their troops and maintain morale. The prospect of booty kept armies together, especially during long sieges; desertion rates rose sharply if the possibility of marauding seemed poor. The rewards could be massive and the pickings were easy. On the fall of a town, everything in it became the property of its captors. Soldiers dreamt of the gold and the diamonds they would loot. In reality, much booty was more ordinary but, to poorly paid men from peasant backgrounds, it still represented wealth. When Charles V's Spanish army left Rome after sacking it in 1527, they carried away 5,200 tonnes of loot.

Such opportunities were, in fact, rare. As Pescara noted dryly in 1522, 'if there is one man who grows rich through booty, there are 100 who gain nothing from war but injury and disease'. The sack of towns grabbed attention (then as now), but armies did far more extensive damage every day of a campaign. Troops went for weeks without pay or supplies reaching them so they were forced to live off their wits and plunder the neighbourhood, whether from friend or foe. We have already seen the scale of the supplies needed every day by an army in the field. Early in a campaign when a commander's funds were intact, most armies bought their supplies as they marched. As campaigns dragged on and war chests emptied, armies stole from the unfortunate civilian population close to hand. With the emergence of long sieges caused by the development of *trace italienne*, commanders began to administer the countryside around their stationary forces, imposing 'taxes' and regular quotas of requisitioned food on each surrounding village – under threat of turning the soldiers loose and burning it down. **Landsknechte** had a term for this: 'fire money'; the modern historian Borislaw Geremek calls it 'military gangsterism'.

No wonder then that war was seen as a scourge comparable to plague and famine. As armies approached, civilian populations deserted their villages. Even if there were no massacres, homes and farms were destroyed, and property and animals were stolen. As armies passed by and emptied the land of grain stocks and animals, they left a swathe of destruction, creating localised famines. They also spread all sorts of fevers, plagues and syphilis. The human misery caused by the presence of an early-modern army cannot be exaggerated. And when the campaign season closed or war ended, the misery did not cease. Roving bands of soldiers were cast upon the countryside, swelling the already large numbers of vagrants. Some made their way home. Others roamed, living the life of brigands. Vagrancy was already a major problem and the most easily identified group among those vagrants was ex-soldiers, demobilised at the end of a campaign or discharged due to age or wounds. No wonder bands of soldiers were compared to swarms of locusts.

As in earlier eras, wars were fought over limited areas. In the Italian Wars, most of the fighting centred on the plains around Milan. After 1515 there was

Pescara attacked the French at Pavia in 1525 because, with money running short to pay his troops, the promise of **looting** Milan seemed the only way to hold the imperial army together.

Landsknechte were German mercenaries.

The ambush, by Pieter Bruegel, 1567. The central soldier, kicking the woman and tearing a purse from the man's neck, holds a pistol; the soldier on the right wears an expensive (if now damaged) jacket – presumably earlier loot.

little activity south of Florence. To some degree, the impact of war remained harsh, but limited. On the other hand, those areas subjected to the march of armies suffered on a new scale. Intriguingly, scholars now suggest that the use of chivalric ideas in the Habsburg–Valois Wars represents a conscious attempt by commanders to re-educate captains and tame soldiers in the age of the gun.

In addition, kings imposed financial burdens on their own people. Taxation continued to fall on that part of the population that was numerically the largest, politically the weakest and economically the poorest: the already over-burdened ordinary people. In France, during the Habsburg–Valois Wars, the tax burden rose by 80 per cent. Charles V's son and heir Philip is likely to have been an objective observer. In 1545, he wrote to his father that 'the common people who have to pay the *servicio* are reduced to such distress and misery that many walk naked'. Five years before, the imperial viceroy in Naples had argued that the emperor's constant tax demands were turning the people into mere 'brute animals'. Even with slowly rising living standards and faster growth in population, both of which should have offset the load to some degree, the weight of the burden was unyielding.

To what degree was there a military revolution between 1499 and 1560?

Task
- Look at the list of four features identified on page 116 as signs of the military revolution.
- In turn, consider the evidence for and against each one and decide whether you think that aspect of the case is valid.
- Finally, look over your four separate conclusions and make an overall decision about whether there was, or was not, a military revolution during those years.

Points to consider
1 What is meant by the term 'revolution'? Must the change happen fairly fast? Remember, many historians now still support the concept of a military 'revolution', even though they have stretched its dates to cover at least two centuries, if not three or more.
2 For the idea of the 'military revolution' to be valid for the period 1499–1560, how many of the four features need to be judged valid?
3 While this chapter does focus on changes that occurred during the years 1499–1560, you may want to extend your research either side of the period. Where changes took place very slowly, 1499–1560 may be too short a period in which to see clearly what was going on.

Summary questions

1 (a) Explain how the role of the infantry changed during the Habsburg–Valois Wars.

   (b) How accurate is the term 'military revolution' in describing the changes in warfare between 1499 and 1560?

2 (a) Identify and explain any *two* reasons for changes in warfare between 1499 and 1560.

   (b) 'After c. 1530 neither side could win in the Habsburg–Valois Wars.' How far do you agree?

3 (a) Explain why developments in guns had such an impact on European warfare during the years 1499–1560.

   (b) Why did the Spanish and Imperial armies do so well in the Italian Wars before 1530?

4 (a) Why were mercenaries used so much by both sides in the Habsburg–Valois Wars?

   (b) To what extent was the escalating cost of war the most important factor influencing the outcome of the Habsburg–Valois Wars?

Document study
The German Reformation 1517–30

Focus questions

◆ What were Luther's main ideas?

◆ How did the authorities react to Luther's ideas 1517–21?

◆ What was the impact of Lutheranism in Germany from 1517 to 1530?

Significant dates

c.1515 Luther resolves his personal crisis over his own salvation. In doing so, he develops distinct ideas about the human–divine relationship and how the process of salvation works.

1517 Luther writes the Ninety-Five Theses in response to Tetzel's preaching on indulgences.

1519 At the Leipzig Dispute, Luther and Eck clash over papal authority – Luther is pushed into denying the absolute authority of the pope.

1520 Luther writes *An appeal to the Christian nobility* and *On the Babylonish captivity*, which together serve as the manifesto of the German Reformation.
Luther's ideas are condemned as heretical by Pope Leo X in the Bull *Exsurge Domine*.

1520–22 The Prophets of Zwickau, led by Nicholas Storch, campaign for religious changes far more radical than those approved by Luther.

1521 Luther is excommunicated by Leo X by the Bull *Decet Romanum*.
Luther appears before the Diet of Worms, and in the Edict of Worms is declared an outlaw by Emperor Charles V.

1521–22 Luther is hidden in the Wartburg by Elector Frederick the Wise. During his absence, Melanchthon and Karlstadt reform Wittenberg (the Wittenberg Movement).

1522 In the Wittenberg Ordinance, the town council organises local religious reform. The smashing of religious art (iconoclasm) by evangelicals begins in Saxony. In response to both, Luther leaves the Wartburg, returns to Wittenberg and attacks both the Wittenberg Movement and the Prophets of Zwickau.

1522–23 The Knights' War, led by Franz von Sickingen, attacks church property but is crushed by the Swabian League.

1523 Luther has Karlstadt expelled from Saxony and abandons his original belief that each church congregation should choose its own minister.

1523–25	Albert of Hohenzollern makes the duchy of Prussia the first officially Lutheran state.
1524	Luther abolishes Latin as the language of church services in Wittenberg (he does not allow the rest of Saxony to change to German until 1529).
1524–26	The Peasants' War disturbs much of the empire.
1525	The Twelve Articles of Memmingen, the most influential of Peasants' War manifestos, is published anonymously. Thomas Müntzer's followers gain control of Mühlhausen. Luther publishes *Admonition to peace*, criticising both sides in the Peasants' War and calling for a negotiated settlement. Müntzer's followers are crushed at the Battle of Frankenhausen. Luther publishes *Against the robbing and murdering hordes of peasants*, urging the princes to crush the peasants without mercy.
1526	Philipp of Hesse introduces Lutheranism into his state. The first Diet of Speyer authorises religious problems to be settled state by state (a freedom known as 'territorialism'), until a general council meets.
1529	The second Diet of Speyer cancels the freedom allowed by the first diet (1526), bans further religious innovations and orders all to enforce Catholicism. In response, some evangelical cities and states, appealing to conscience, refuse to change their ways (the 'Protest' – coining the word 'Protestant').

Luther in disguise as 'Junker George', engraving by Lucas Cranach the Elder, 1521. In hiding in the Wartburg, Luther was disguised as a German nobleman.

Overview

Document exercises covering some of the issues in this chapter are to be found between page 156 and page 166.

Historians work to interpret the past through study of the evidence the past has left behind: written, printed, oral, visual and physical sources. Scrutiny of sources is the working process of the historian and that scrutiny must always be undertaken with a sceptical attitude. Historians may work with first-hand ('primary') evidence, but that evidence has been filtered in several ways. Not everything that happened was recorded; not everything recorded has survived. The surviving evidence is thus incomplete. It is also partial. Sources must not be thought of as neutral. Some material was produced deliberately to deceive, to misrepresent reality. Most evidence contains half-truths, coloured in some way to exaggerate, generalise or underplay in a way that suits the author's purpose. In using evidence, historians must always therefore establish how 'credible', how 'reliable' each source is. But credible or reliable for what? Historians are concerned with far more than asking 'Is the author making a fair comment?' The authors of many sources do not make a fair comment, yet what they say is still of great value as historical evidence – because it reveals so well the assumptions, attitudes and prejudices of their era. Forget that misleading GCSE concept of a source as 'biased' and instead think of a source as 'subjective'. Neither a letter written by Luther in 1521 on the role of the pope nor a Protestant woodcut from the 1520s attacking the Catholic clergy is a neutral, unbiased source. Both are highly subjective and present a very one-sided view. In the middle of a great struggle like the Reformation, most people could not think or look objectively; they did not want to. They were involved in (as they saw it) a life-and-death contest between the forces of good and evil, wrapped up in the passions of one side or the other. That does not make their testimony worthless. On the contrary, their subjective perspective is exactly what historians need if they are to get under the skin of our sixteenth-century ancestors and understand them – and thereby understand the Reformation more clearly in all its complexities and subtleties.

In seeking to understand the Reformation, historians take the mass of evidence available and arrange it into a pattern that not only makes sense but reflects the sixteenth century as realistically as possible. Yet the jigsaw they seek to complete must remain incomplete. Historical judgements must be rooted in good evidence, drawn from a wide range of sources and subjected to critical assessment. In the end, however, historians' judgements are only hypotheses – 'guesstimates' limited by the survival of evidence and the scholarly ability to interpret that flawed evidence. The conclusions historians reach cannot be definitive. Debate is the lifeblood of history. Through scholarly debate, historians think and rethink their lines of argument and interpretation. In the memorable image used by Christopher Haigh, historian of Tudor England, debate is to the historian what experiment is to the scientist. Dramatic discoveries of new evidence are rarely the cause of historical debate. Rather debate is generated and sustained by historians asking new questions of old material, or taking a fresh angle on an old question. Debate keeps history alive because it keeps history moving.

What were Luther's main ideas?

Luther's ideas grew out of his work as a professor of biblical theology and his own personal crisis. The first made him study the texts of the Bible in great detail while the second forced him to examine head on the problem (as he saw it) of the human relationship with God. In time, the first provided the solution to the second – the core Lutheran idea of **justification by faith** – and the reason for his rejection of Catholic teaching on the subject. As Luther confronted other aspects of Catholic belief and practice, the authority of the biblical text provided the yardstick by which he judged the contemporary church. Where the two were in disagreement, he was insistent that the biblical view must be right. The **scriptures** were the source and norm of his teaching. The Lutheran Reformation was driven by the Bible.

In the Middle Ages, the term 'reformation' meant the correction of corrupt practices and the renewal of spiritual life. This was the image used for centuries to explain what happened in the Reformation. Indeed, it was an image the Protestants themselves adopted. This 'abuses thesis' of the origins of the Reformation is today seen not just as a misrepresentation of what occurred, but as a distortion of early Protestantism and of early-sixteenth-century Catholicism. Research has demonstrated that levels of corruption, inadequacy and indifference among the clergy of *c.*1500 were no higher than in other medieval centuries (across much of Europe, the condition of the church was significantly better).

Failings were plentiful (as ever), but complacency was not one of them. 'Reform' was a word in daily use, not as part of some derogatory attack but in campaigns to renew the church by a generation who wished her well – and who believed that time was short. Almost everyone seems to have thought that the Last Judgement was close. Preachers pointed to the impending **Apocalypse** and the horrors (and glories) it had in store. The end of the world gave a dark twist to their definition of 'reform': crusading against the Turks, hunting witches and driving out Jews were elements of Christian renewal.

What of Martin Luther? His criticisms of the papacy, for example, went beyond calls for modification to demands for total abolition. This takes us to the heart of the nature of the Reformation. Its primary concern was with corrupt theology, not corrupt organisation. Luther argued that the church's

For an explanation of **justification by faith** see pages 124/125 and 127.

'For Luther, **scripture** testified directly to the original gospel. Therein lay its signal and unique authority, since what it contained was the very Word of God.' (Bernard Reardon, *Religious thought in the Reformation*, 1995) Luther's own contribution to the use of the Bible was to translate it into readily understandable, everyday German: the New Testament published in 1522, the Old Testament in stages, 1523–34. Protestant reliance on the Bible meant followers always looked back to the origins of Christianity.

The **Apocalypse** is the name for the end of the world, the return of Christ and the final fate of everyone (living and dead) – when God will judge them and send their souls to heaven or hell.

organisational faults resulted from its **false** teaching. In seeking the recovery of 'pure' biblical Christianity, the magnitude of the changes Luther judged necessary meant that he had to destroy the medieval church. At first, he did not realise the implications of his own ideas. By 1519, however, Lutheranism was a revolutionary movement.

Luther's thoughts c.1512–17

The Reformation and Protestantism were triggered and shaped by Martin Luther (1483–1546). Both could have appeared without him, but the Reformation without Luther would have been very different. His personal imprint is to be found everywhere. To understand the direction the Lutheran protest took, a start has to be made with Luther himself and the major spiritual crisis he experienced. As a student, he began to show a growing fear of death. In an era when most diseases were fatal, this was not surprising. Two-thirds of children died before they were 10; most adults did not see their 45th birthday. In the young friar Martin Luther, these anxieties developed into a deep despair. The great question hanging over him was: 'What must I do to be saved and go to heaven?' Most medieval theologians taught that God had established a pact with mankind; anyone who makes their best effort to obey God will be saved. Direct human action was required – the initiative had to be taken by the individual.

But Luther asked how anyone could live by God's laws when human sinfulness led to **evil** and guaranteed perpetual failure. Human effort simply was not good enough. God was just and divine law was just, so – in justice – God the righteous judge must punish Luther for his sin and condemn him to hell. In Luther's personal experience, the traditional remedies of medieval Catholicism (regular confession, taking of communion, regular prayer to the saints asking for their help, the regular doing of good deeds) were of no comfort. No matter what he **tried** to do, he kept on sinning. The gospel of Christ was supposed to bring good news, but Luther could only see the righteousness of God as a threat.

What is almost unbelievable is that the late-medieval church had no definitive answer to this fundamental question. To make matters worse, the topic was subjected to so much debate that any hope of reliable guidance was lost in the mass of variant opinions. A solution to Luther's anguish thus had to be worked out for himself. It came gradually, through his work as professor of biblical theology at Wittenberg University. During research for his 1515–16 lectures on St Paul's Epistle to the Romans, the 32-year-old professor made crucial discoveries. Exactly when he made his final breakthrough has long been debated by scholars – most experts put it in 1515, but some argue for as late as 1518. The pieces of the jigsaw fell into place, however, when Luther understood Paul to be saying that the justice of God was not an avenging demand to punish but a gift already given and there to be enjoyed. People could indeed never merit God's forgiveness; they carried on sinning. Self-justification was impossible. But that did not matter because God chose to save them, even though they did not deserve it. God gave people the trust ('faith') to obey divine law and because of that faith he then justified them. At every stage, God took the initiative.

Luther termed this process of the gifts of faith and righteousness 'justification by faith'. It was, in his view, 'a marvellous work' and 'the article by which the church stands or falls'. Luther had turned his understanding of the justice of God on its head. Once it had been a menace. Now it was a deliverance. 'Immediately', he later wrote, 'it was as if I had been born again; as if I had entered into paradise itself through open gates.' From that moment, justification by faith has stood as the seminal Protestant belief.

In your own words, explain:
- justification by faith;
- how justification resolved Luther's personal crisis.

Luther had not yet started to think about the pope or the church. The Reformation had not yet happened and, indeed, was not inevitably going to happen. This chapter examines the historical context in which Luther's Reformation started to emerge. At the beginning, Luther's ideas evolved gradually and unevenly. Their impact and influence was a complex process. In the early days, Luther's thinking developed in reaction to events around him. The first such stimulus was provided by Dr Johann Tetzel who, using all sorts of dubious claims, was promoting a papal **indulgence** in Germany in 1517. Church law was clear. Indulgences could not be sold and were valid only if the individual had been to confession and, being genuinely repentant, had performed the penance imposed by the priest. Luther determined to take Tetzel to task, and not merely for his dishonest salesmanship. Everything Luther had come to understand about salvation was challenged by this 'donkey from Rome'. Thus it was that the Ninety-Five Theses were written, in the heat of his fury against the notions that 'Man can climb a ladder to God' and that 'God's forgiveness can be sold like a sack of cabbages.'

The medieval church had never established an official position on indulgences. In consequence, they had been controversial for over a century. As a professor of theology, Luther rightly felt entitled to debate an area of church life and teaching not yet controlled by formal doctrinal decrees. In fact his arguments in the Ninety-Five Theses were often far from clear and much of the content was repetitive. In essence, he made the following claims:

- An indulgence cannot be sold or bought. Divine forgiveness and salvation are not commodities to be traded.
- An indulgence cannot commute the penalty due for sin because the punishment is imposed by God, and the church has no power over God. The church can only forgive what the church itself has imposed.

Catholic priests claimed the power to forgive sins on God's behalf, but temporary punishment after death would still be due in purgatory for those sins (as opposed to eternal punishment in hell for unforgiven sins). **Indulgences** were developed as a means by which the church could commute that punishment, and so speed up the process of moving on to heaven. Initially restricted to exceptional service to the church (such as crusading), they became universally available – and from the 1350s could also be obtained on behalf of those already dead. Cardinal Albert of Brandenburg, archbishop of Mainz (who organised Tetzel's promotional tour of 1517), himself held indulgences worth a combined value of 39,245,120 years' remission from purgatory.

Briest fiestu bailiges antlit vnlers bebalters · Jn dē
da schinet die geslalt des gótlichen glanezes. Gedru
ket in ain schne wisses diechlin · Vñ gegebē veronice
ezū ainem zaichen der liebe. Briest fiestu geezierd der
welte ain spiegel der bailigen · Den da begerend ezū
schowen die hymelschē gaiste · Rúnige vns von allē
finde · Vnd fieg vns zū der selige gesellschafft. Briest
fiestu vnser gloz in disem hertten bintliessenden vnd
schwachem leben · Fier vns ezū dem vatterland o du
selige figure · Zū sehend das wōneuglich antlit cristi
vnsers herren · Bis vns ain sichere bilff ain siesse erkie
long trost vnd ain schirme. Das vns nit schadē múg
die beschwerong vnser fúnde · Sonder das wir nicl;
send die ewige rúo amen
    So fil sind gegeben tag applas vnd karen disem
gebet das ich sy bie nit kúnd wol begriffen

Left: Rosary bead, made in the Netherlands or France, *c.*1530. A skeleton embraces a dying man (*left*), behind whom is a devil disguised as a beautiful woman.

Right: The holy face with an indulgence, printed by Dinckmut, Ulm, *c.*1480–82. The illustration shows an image of Jesus known as 'The man of sorrows'. Very popular in late-medieval Christianity, it portrayed the suffering Christ, wearing the crown of thorns, on his way to be crucified. Below the picture is a prayer which encourages the owner of the indulgence to feel personal guilt for Jesus' crucifixion, and personal gratitude for the remission of punishment (due in purgatory) which the indulgence has delivered.

The issue of **repentance** illustrates perfectly Luther's method of work. His test was always to compare contemporary practice with the biblical text. Brought up in the Christian Humanist principle that the true meaning of early Christian writers could only be found in the original Greek, Luther always accepted the meaning of the text in Greek if it conflicted with the meaning of the (later) Latin translation used by the medieval church. In the Latin, the words used by St Paul for 'repentance' were *poenitentiam agere* ('to do penance'). The Greek, however, was *metanoia*, meaning 'change your heart and mind'. Luther

- Not even the pope has authority over the dead. The dead are in God's hands and, although the living can help them with prayers, an indulgence cannot assist them.
- The pope has no power to use the 'merits' of Jesus and the saints for the benefit of individuals. Their holiness and goodness are beyond the control of the church. Indulgences claiming to commute penalties, because the pope has wiped them out by applying the surplus merits of Jesus and/or the saints, are thus a hoax.
- Indulgences are not necessary because God's forgiveness is available automatically (and only) to an individual who is truly **repentant**.
- True repentance has nothing to do with doing penance (good deeds – 'works of repentance'), including obtaining an indulgence. Biblical teaching is clear that true repentance requires a change of heart in the individual, and that can never come by human effort (such as obtaining an indulgence).

In other words, the medieval system of penance, dependent as it was on human action, was built on false foundations. Indulgences were a fraud. Beyond indulgences, however, Luther had not thought. He did not yet deny the role of the pope or the function of the institutional church. Such ideas were to be born later. The Ninety-Five Theses was a very limited document because, in 1517, Luther's protest was very limited in scope and scale.

Justification by faith may have been a revelation to Luther, but it was no novel interpretation. Luther stood on ground occupied 1,100 years earlier by the great theologian St Augustine. His bleak view of humanity and mankind's utter dependence on God had never been forgotten, but it was very much a minority view during the medieval centuries. The fifteenth century then saw a renaissance in the study of Augustine. How far Luther was aware of (and influenced by) this remains uncertain, but he was not teaching anything heretical. In 1517–18, Luther was an obedient son of the Catholic church.

could therefore only see repentance as an entirely inner process, requiring no going on pilgrimage, giving money to charity and so on. The demand for action was only in the Latin, but the Greek was written first. In translation, a fatal error had crept in.

Luther's evolving thought after 1517

In the Ninety-Five Theses, Luther had questioned the authority of the pope to make the claims underpinning the recent indulgence. At once, he was accused of heresy and, in consequence, forced to consider the papal position. The Leipzig Dispute (1519) between Dr Luther and Dr Eck came back repeatedly to papal power, not indulgences. Leipzig forced Luther to confront the issue of authority in the church.

At Leipzig, Eck had pushed Luther into stating that popes could be wrong and there were limits to their powers. Where then lay authority for the church and the Christian faithful? For Luther, there could be only one answer: the Bible, the word of God himself. The second pillar of Protestantism thus emerged to sit alongside justification by faith: the teaching authority of the Bible. Eck had made Luther question the Catholic system. In a phase of enormous creativity, sermons and pamphlets poured from his pen in the 20 months after Leipzig. He wrote and published as he thought, so, like the Ninety-Five Theses, the content of these works overlapped and was repetitive. But then, he was the pioneer, hacking a rough path through the jungle.

Two essential pamphlets of this phase served as the manifestos of the German Reformation:

- *An appeal to the Christian nobility of the German nation*, published in August 1520, in German. Addressed to all Germans (from the emperor to the peasants), it:
  - called on the princes to reform the church;
  - set out the doctrine of the priesthood of all believers;
  - classified the pope as the antichrist.
- *On the Babylonish captivity of the church*, published in September 1520, in Latin. Addressed to the clergy, it:
  - redefined the nature and number of the sacraments;
  - redefined the role of the church and clergy.

Why might Luther have written *An appeal* in German, but the *Babylonish captivity* in Latin?

Most scholars regard the publication of the second of these as the defining moment when Lutheran reform turned into Lutheran revolution.

An appeal was too long, overloaded with ill-digested lists of old German complaints against papal taxes draining away hard-earned German silver and papal interference in German affairs. None of it was new, but anti-papal feeling was stronger in Germany than anywhere else. The pamphlet set Luther firmly in the role of national champion, exploiting the developing sense of 'German consciousness'. Theology had little to do with any of this. It was shrewd politics. At the very moment Luther was in direct confrontation with Rome, he gained defenders all over Germany.

An appeal did, however, contain one vital theological idea: 'the priesthood of all believers'. Against the medieval view that allowed the laity only a passive, subordinate role (and defined the church as a hierarchical institution almost entirely in terms of the clergy), Luther argued for a universal **priesthood**. There was no special elite among Christians; all were one. To draw a distinction of status between the clergy and the laity was meaningless because all Christians were priests. This provided the theoretical justification for Luther's call in *An appeal* for princes to take on the task of church reform. The pope and bishops refused to do it, so the princes must step in. From then on, Luther always regarded the princes as 'emergency bishops'.

The core of **The Babylonish captivity** was a redefinition of the system of sacraments. This was of the utmost practical importance because the sacraments were the main point of regular contact between the people and the church. Sacraments were seen as a series of divine signs (or gifts) by which God acted to influence the soul through an indelible implant that infused goodness into each individual. How many sacraments there were was a matter of medieval debate, but a definitive list of seven had emerged. Luther's Ninety-Five Theses had attacked not just indulgences but their role in the sacrament of penance. The theology of justification by faith propelled him into challenging contemporary understanding of the sacraments, which was incompatible with everything Luther had come to understand. A person was not gradually made holier, becoming a better individual able to do genuinely good deeds and so co-operate with God in their own salvation. In Luther's eyes, justification depended on God's intentions and actions.

Luther judged the sacraments against the measure of biblical evidence. By that yardstick, four of the seven collapsed – the church had no authority to invent sacraments. Baptism and eucharist had clear New Testament authority. What of penance? Luther's thinking evolved on this vexed problem. *The Babylonish captivity* taught that it was a full sacrament (and therefore Lutheranism had three). He knew from his own dark experience the therapeutic value of oral confession. Yet the biblical evidence was weak. After 1520, he no longer

The title **On the Babylonish captivity of the church** refers to the period when ancient Israel was conquered and enslaved by the Babylonians (597–539 BC). In the Middle Ages, the phrase 'Babylonian captivity' was applied to the period when the papal court lived not in Rome but at Avignon in France (1309–77), and more generally to the idea that the popes and/or the church were under the control of the devil.

In Luther's eyes, what was wrong with the church's view of sacraments?

described it as a **sacrament**. No other Reformation leader accepted its sacramental validity. But Lutheranism continued to offer voluntary confession of sins to a minister.

The **eucharist** is the central Christian ceremony. In *The Babylonish captivity*, Luther proposed a very different eucharist. The Lutheran eucharist was to be a communal celebration of God's promise of forgiveness, in which everyone must be able to take part. Luther therefore demanded that the service must be in German (not Latin). Since it was a community event, held by divine command, and every believer was their own priest, wine as well as bread must be given to everyone (as opposed to medieval practice which restricted the wine to the clergy). So influential was this point that offering wine to the people became *the* visible badge of the Reformation.

Theologically, Luther was equally radical, denying as unbiblical contemporary teaching on the value of mass and the explanation of what happened to the bread and wine during the service. The following lists set out his views alongside the traditional Catholic view.

The seven **sacraments** defined in 1439 by the Council of Florence were: baptism, confirmation, mass, penance, extreme unction (anointing of the dying with holy oil), ordination and marriage. Theologians often called them 'The Lord's seal'.

The terms '**eucharist**', 'mass' and 'communion' refer to the same religious service. No other theological problem (not even salvation) was debated more keenly during the Reformation than what happened during the eucharist and what it represented.

The sacrifice of the mass?

Catholic teaching	Luther's teaching
• Jesus sacrificed himself on the cross. The church commemorates and repeats that sacrifice when mass is celebrated.	• Jesus sacrificed himself on the cross. The church commemorates but cannot repeat that sacrifice.
• A sacrifice, mass is a good work offered to God, thus gaining merit and so of benefit to the living and the dead.	• The eucharist is not a good work. People cannot offer anything of value to God – that is an offence to the unique role of God in the process of salvation.
• Mass is offered to God by a priest on behalf of the people.	• Every believer is their own priest – no special intermediary is necessary (though not every believer may officiate at the eucharist). The clergy cannot therefore have special power and status.

What happens to the bread and wine?

Catholic teaching	Luther's teaching
• Jesus is present in the bread and the wine.	• Jesus is present in the bread and the wine.
• By miracle performed by a priest, the bread and wine become literally the body and blood of Jesus. The bread and wine retain their external form (look, smell, taste) but, behind that, is the crucified Christ.	• By miracle performed by God, the body and blood of Jesus are present 'in, with and under' the bread and wine. But real bread and wine remain.
• Only one reality is present: Christ. This explanation is called the doctrine of *transubstantiation*.	• Two realities are present simultaneously: Christ, and the original bread and wine. This explanation is called the doctrine of *the real presence*.

If you find it hard to distinguish the **real presence** from transubstantiation, you are in good company. No other Protestant leaders accepted Luther's interpretation. To Zwingli, Calvin and others, Luther had failed to purge the eucharist of its Catholic notions – there could be no real presence. But Luther's position was based four-square on the biblical text. The actual words of Jesus were, in his view, so clear as to bear no other meaning: 'This is my body . . . This is my blood.' To suggest that by 'is' Jesus meant 'represents' or 'symbolises' was, for Luther, to introduce unnecessary complexities. There was a real presence; Catholics were wrong only in how they explained it.

Catholic mass and Lutheran eucharist

In rejecting priests as an elite with special sacramental powers, Luther dug away the foundations of a hierarchical church led by the clergy – which he

The mass of St Giles, by the Master of St Giles, painting, c.1500. The scene takes place in the church of St Denis, Paris.
Note the position of the priest at the altar, and his robes (see first note on page 131); the statues of saints nearby; the cross above the altar which contains a relic of Christ's cross; the shrine behind the altar, containing relics of St Louis.

The supper of the evangelicals, by Lucas Cranach the Younger (detail from *The supper of the evangelicals* and *The damnation of the papists*), woodcut, c.1540.
Note the positions of the Lutheran ministers, and the clothes they wear (compared to those of the congregation); the ministers give wine as well as bread; the decorations in the church (confined to a large crucifix and the pulpit – in which Luther himself is preaching).

called 'a detestable tyranny'. Instead, he taught a different ethos for the church, rooted in the priesthood of all believers. Since all Christians became priests at baptism, the church was a community, a brotherhood. Each congregation must choose its own **minister** to preach and celebrate with them (rather than have a higher authority impose a 'priest' to act on their behalf). In Luther's words, the church was 'the living voice of the gospel'. The true office of the clergy was in preaching and therefore teaching, which in turn required them to be well educated. Protestantism set a new standard for the clergy.

One practical step had an especially dramatic impact: Luther's rejection of clerical **celibacy**. As ever, his guide was the biblical record and clearly the early church had no ban on clerical marriage. The clergy were, according to Luther, no different from the laity. Their function might be different, but in status they were identical – all were priests. So why should marriage be forbidden to some? Of all the reformers, none wrote with such joyful enthusiasm about marriage, about being a husband and a father (a reflection of his own very happy marriage in 1525 to Katherine von Bora).

Luther rejected the papacy. At Leipzig in 1519, Eck had pushed him into denying the absolute power of the pope. In *The Babylonish captivity*, Luther launched a frontal assault on the papal office as the human head of the church, God's deputy to be obeyed as we would obey God. There was no biblical justification for it so, he argued, it was a human invention, not an office of divine foundation. Since medieval popes had persecuted earlier attempts at church reform, and popes now did so again, Luther identified the office of the pope (not just the current holder of it) with the antichrist, the devil's chief disciple. Once excommunicated and thus cast out of the church by the pope (1521), Luther was increasingly violent and crude in his attacks on the papacy. Luther had dethroned the pope and enthroned the Bible in his place. He believed passionately in authority, but it had to be the right ('true') authority.

On monasticism Luther did not set out his views until 1522–23. None the less, the position he adopted had a profound impact for, wherever Protestantism became influential, monasticism collapsed. Luther's attitude illustrates well an additional dimension to his method of judgement by reference to the Bible. Obviously, monasticism did not exist in the days of Christ so the New Testament was silent on the subject. Unlike some Protestants, Luther never took the narrow view that only those things positively allowed in the New Testament could be allowed. But he was convinced (in part, from personal experience) that the monastic way of life could not offer the higher, purer form of Christian faith which the medieval church claimed. That would contradict the notion of the priesthood of all believers and make inadequate the religious life of most Christians. Luther was none

In a deeply symbolic change, Luther directed in his *German mass and order of worship* (1526) that the **minister** should stand behind the altar, facing the congregation – in contemporary Catholic practice the priest faced the altar, his back to the congregation.

In rejecting compulsory **celibacy**, Luther rejected the long-held idea that virginity was a higher spiritual state than marriage (a foundation of monasticism); if that was so, celibacy was a good work earning merit. Many Protestant clergy married in the 1520s. It has been suggested by historians that this was a deliberate demonstration of their rejection of the Roman church. Popular reaction varied enormously – for several generations, rural populations in Protestant areas were often openly hostile, calling ministers' wives 'priests' whores'.

How Luther saw the papacy

Lucas Cranach the Younger, woodcuts from *Against the papacy, founded by the devil* (1545). Under each woodcut were quotations written by Luther to accompany them. A translation only is given here.

'Just reward for the most satanic pope and his cardinals. If they were to receive punishment on earth, their blasphemous tongues would deserve what is rightly depicted here.'

'Pope, doctor of theology and master of the faithful. Only the pope can interpret scripture and sweep away error, just as a donkey can pipe and sound the right notes.'

'How the pope, obeying St Peter, honours kings.'

the less unwilling to deny it to anyone who saw value in its disciplined life. He would not ban monasticism, and himself continued to wear his friar's habit until *c*.1525. Furthermore, he opposed all suggestions that monks and nuns be expelled from their cloisters (a tolerance rarely accepted by most of his followers).

In the silence of the Bible, Luther allowed great latitude because the matter was clearly *adiaphora*. For that reason, he was, by comparison with other Protestant reformers, remarkably indifferent to the format of church services. Certain matters were essentials: a service in German and the central teaching role of readings from the Bible and of the minister preaching regular sermons. But, as will be seen later when we look at Luther and the radicals (pages 151–53), he opposed virtually every one of the changes they demanded. What should a minister wear? Should churches use candles? Was there a role for religious art? The biblical record was, on such matters, either silent or ambiguous. To Luther, they must therefore be *adiaphora*. His own conservative instincts, reinforced by his fear of direct action by the crowd, led him to move slowly. Lutheran churches kept quite elaborate ceremonies, retained candles and a crucifix on their altar, and employed paintings of biblical subjects. This was not theology, but public order. What Luther termed 'the need to consider the weak' controlled such matters. Visitors to the churches of other Protestant groups (e.g. Zwinglian or Calvinist) could never be in any doubt about the religious allegiance of the congregation. By contrast, there are many references to those entering a church in Germany not being certain from its visual appearance whether it was Lutheran or Catholic.

Luther was conservative for another reason. He never accepted the idea that he had split away from the church. To Luther, breaking from the church was unthinkable. Whatever difficulties we have in believing that Luther was a good Catholic **reforming the church** from within, that was how *he* saw things. The Reformation was only temporary. This is why Luther never produced a full-scale scheme defining the theory and practice of a church.

Remember also Luther's anchor in the authority of the Bible texts. Repeatedly he offered to withdraw his ideas if it could be shown that they contradicted the Bible. When he wrote the Ninety-Five Theses or when he stood before the emperor and princes at the diet in 1521, he was not defending his own ideas conjured from his own imagination. That was why he always rejected the contemporary labels of 'Martinists' or 'Lutherans' applied to his followers. For Luther, those who accepted his view were 'evangelicals' because both he and they followed the gospels. Luther could never see that he had created a new **church**. He believed that all he had done was re-create the link to the pure days of original Christianity – and thus restored the true church, not of Martin Luther but of Christ.

What does Luther's attitude to monasticism tell us about his attitude to reform?

Adiaphora is a Greek word meaning 'something indifferent'. Beliefs and practices categorised as *adiaphora* were neither commanded nor forbidden by the Bible. They could not thus be virtues or vices, so Luther saw them as optional.

'It seems that the evangelical faction in Wittenberg believed that the Catholic church would indeed reform itself, perhaps through convening a reforming council, within a matter of years, thus allowing the Lutherans to rejoin a renewed and **reformed church**.' (Alister McGrath, *Reformation thought: an introduction*, 1988)

'Luther had no notion of placing himself outside the institutional **church**, or of disowning the historic tradition of christendom, and still less of founding some new body. Rome herself possessed the scriptures and the sacraments of baptism, the eucharist and absolution, while saintly lives had been and continued to be lived under the old system.' (Bernard Reardon, *Religious thought in the Reformation*, 1995)

How did the authorities react to Luther's ideas 1517–21?

The Luther affair began with the Ninety-Five Theses in October 1517. Three years or so later, he stood excommunicated by the church and declared an outlaw by the state. In 1517 nobody had heard of Martin Luther. By 1519, his was a household name all over Europe. He had become a leader – God's prophet to some, the son of the devil to others. Yet he turned out not to be a nine-day wonder, burnt at the stake and forgotten as yet another obscure heretic. Instead, he died in bed aged 63 (in 1546), an international figurehead. This section looks at the first four years of the Luther affair. That was the time when Luther counted most, when his protest and the infant movement were at their most vulnerable. Had he compromised or retreated then, the German Reformation would have been stillborn.

The Ninety-Five Theses should not have provoked a fuss. They were written in Latin in a formula to initiate academic debate among university scholars. Luther was not looking to pick a fight. Indeed, if Pope Leo had acted swiftly to correct the abuses of indulgence salesmanship, the Luther affair would have been over rapidly, settled to everyone's satisfaction. The same day that Luther produced the Theses he wrote to his own bishop and Cardinal Archbishop Albert of Brandenburg, pointing out how the errors spread by Tetzel were misleading the people (and enclosing a copy of the theses). Throughout, he was respectful, claiming only his duty as a doctor of theology and a priest to be concerned with the safety of souls. Well into 1520, he continued to treat the church authorities (even the pope) with honour and consideration. This was hardly the behaviour of a revolutionary. Albert did not reply. He was himself compromised because he had commissioned Tetzel to promote the papal indulgence. In a secret pact, he had also negotiated with Pope Leo X to keep half the proceeds as a way of recovering some of the 24,000 ducats' purchase price he had paid Rome in 1514 to keep his archbishopric of Magdeburg while becoming archbishop of Mainz as well.

Others were not so indifferent. Dr Tetzel, the indulgence preacher Luther attacked, was a Dominican friar. The Dominicans were great hunters of heresy, and the sworn enemies of the Augustinian friars to which Luther belonged. Out of tribal loyalty and rivalry, the German Dominicans set out to destroy Luther. They took the issue to Rome and agitated for action against the new child of Satan. While the Augustinian chapter (parliament) of 1518 heard Luther with approval, the Dominican chapter declared him a heretic and obtained the appointment of a papal judge to examine the case. The Dominicans had from the start spotted Luther's weak spot. Victory could never be theirs on indulgences; they were too controversial for any charge to stick. In the Ninety-Five Theses, however, Luther had questioned the authority of the pope to grant indulgences to souls in purgatory. Dominicans were the champions of expanding papal power. To deny the authority of the pope was heresy. This was the ground on which they chose to fight. It was a major escalation of the issue.

Why were the Dominicans such determined enemies of Luther?

Not everything went their way. Just as papal proceedings were beginning, Emperor Maximilian I became ill (he died in January 1519) and began working to secure his grandson's succession. Heresy was a matter for church courts. The Luther affair was of no concern to the state. But the **new emperor** would be chosen by just seven German electoral princes – one of whom happened to be Luther's own prince, Elector Frederick the Wise, duke of Saxony. The papacy was deeply involved in European power politics and Leo was anxious to prevent the election of Maximilian's grandson, Charles. Frederick was a devout Catholic with his own gigantic collection of holy relics, to which one of the most valuable indulgences in Europe was attached. But Frederick protected the star professor of his beloved university and had rejected all requests to have Luther arrested. It was far from clear that Luther was actually a heretic. Rather, Frederick saw Luther as the victim of a Dominican–papal plot. Desperate not to offend the Saxon elector, Rome reined in the Dominicans.

For the constitution of the Holy Roman Empire, see Chapter 1, pages 5 to 6.

The new mood of papal conciliation was seen as early as October 1518 when, thanks to Frederick's diplomacy, the great theologian Cardinal Cajetan was sent to Heidelberg to meet Luther. A further conference with another papal representative took place in January 1519. Neither saw real progress. Luther would not withdraw anything, unless proved wrong from the Bible. Leo's political manoeuvrings also failed and Charles was elected emperor in June 1519. The German Dominicans had, however, grown impatient and, on their own authority, challenged Luther to a debate. This was held at the University of Leipzig in June–July 1519. Luther's challenger was the noted theologian Dr Johann Eck, who in 1518 had published an attack on the Ninety-Five Theses. The theses had been written for debate, but the Leipzig Dispute was not what Luther had in mind. Luther's attitude to papal power was Eck's constant interest. As he probed, he cleverly introduced the anti-papal ideas of **Jan Hus**. Luther was cornered and at several points manoeuvred into agreeing with Hussite ideas. Above all, Luther denied that the pope was the head of the church and always to be obeyed. Eck was jubilant. He had all the evidence he needed for a papal trial. Simultaneously, he sent minutes of the dispute to the Dominican-controlled universities of Cologne and Louvain, both of which obligingly judged Luther to be guilty of heresy. Eck seemed to have won.

The Bohemian **Jan Hus**, the most notorious late-medieval heretic, was a professor at the University of Prague. He was condemned by the Council of Constance and burnt in 1415. To brand Luther as a Hussite was more than a theological move. Hussite armies had ravaged Saxony in 1430, so many Saxons regarded them as no better than thugs.

After Leipzig, Eck became Luther's most determined opponent and the most influential anti-Protestant theologian, devoting the rest of his life (he died in 1543) to combating the rising forces of Protestantism. Yet the papal court moved slowly. Not until January 1520 was Luther's case reopened, with Eck and Cajetan as two of the judges. Their findings led to the publication on 15 June 1520 of the Bull *Exsurge Domine*, condemning 41 of Luther's ideas as heretical and giving him 60 days to withdraw his teachings. But the Bull was not the triumph Eck had hoped for. Because much of its content was vague, many in Germany thought it was a forgery. Eck himself made things worse by inserting the names of several personal enemies after he arrived in Germany to enforce *Exsurge Domine*. Luther's books were burnt in public ceremonies. In response, Luther in December 1520 publicly burnt Eck's writings, books of papal law and the Bull. It was a deeply symbolic act of defiance.

Why did *Exsurge Domine* fail to end the Luther affair?

The 60 days came and went. A new Bull, *Decet Romanum*, excommunicating Luther, was eventually prepared in January 1521. Simultaneously, papal ambassadors went to the imperial diet meeting in Worms to petition that it be enforced by the secular authorities. The new young emperor, a devout Catholic committed to the maintenance of the Catholic church, wanted to order this straight away. But Frederick persuaded him that Luther must be given a hearing in Germany by Germans before being outlawed merely on the say-so of Rome. Charles bowed to domestic German influences. An imperial safe conduct was issued and Luther summoned to appear. This he did in April 1521, refusing to withdraw anything 'unless I am convinced by the testimony of Scripture or evident reason . . . My conscience is captive to the Word of God. I cannot revoke anything for it is not safe to act against conscience.' Compromise would have been possible even at this late stage. The diet was strongly anti-papal and key figures, including the emperor's chaplain, urged him to put theology aside and concentrate on the abuses of papal power in Germany. But for so long prepared to negotiate, Luther now sought confrontation. Trusting to the imperial pass, Luther left Worms. One month later, Eck published *Decet Romanum* and Charles V declared Luther to be an outlaw as well.

For the rival **Saxonies**, see Chapter 1, page 12, and the map on page 137. Frederick had himself founded Wittenberg University in 1502 to rival Leipzig, and it was catching up.

Frederick had one final scheme to set in motion. Throughout 1518–20 he had rejected all calls to arrest Luther. A proud imperial prince, and as anti-papal as any German, he was not going to be dictated to by a figure he dismissed as 'that Italian bishop'. Equally, he resented the way his cousin and rival George, duke of the other duchy of **Saxony**, had sided with Eck and the Dominicans. George had hosted the 1519 dispute. Leipzig and Wittenberg were competitor universities. But cousin George's interference threatened more than the success of Wittenberg: it threatened the sovereignty of electoral Saxony. Frederick had plenty of reasons to protect his most famous subject and he was determined not to stop now, at the point when Luther was most vulnerable. In the past, the state could always be relied on to hand over a condemned heretic. As Luther had defied the pope by burning *Exsurge Domine*, so Frederick now did the same, arranging for Luther to be 'kidnapped' on his

	Number of students attending	
	Leipzig	Wittenberg
1501–10	1529	835
1511–20	1524	964
1521–30	506	629
1531–40	557	957

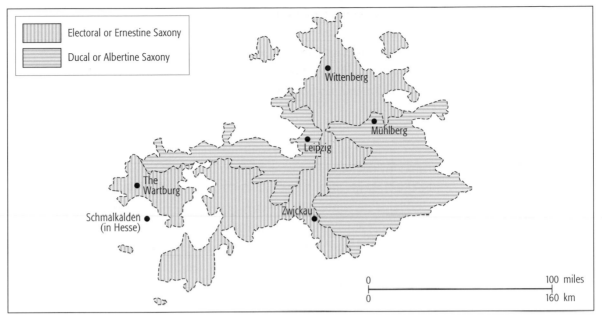

The divided House of Wettin – the rival duchies of Saxony.

return journey. His whereabouts was a closely guarded secret. When the news broke, most assumed he had been murdered by papal agents or carried off to Rome for execution.

In fact, Luther was in safety in the Wartburg, one of Frederick's remote castles, where he stayed until March 1522. Further, Frederick once more exploited the large debts owed him by the late Emperor Maximilian to persuade Charles that, by an administrative error, the Edict of Worms and *Decet Romanum* would not reach electoral Saxony. They would not therefore be published in Frederick's territory so, by a legal technicality, he would have no knowledge of them and could not be expected to enforce them. The conduct of Frederick the Wise was critical to Luther's personal survival and, therefore, to embryonic Protestantism putting down strong roots. From 1517, he guaranteed Luther the priceless advantage of a safe haven. Without it, Luther would have been burnt before 1520.

What was the impact of Lutheranism in Germany from 1517 to 1530?

Luther's ideas spread far and fast. By word of mouth, through sermons and via the (still fairly new) medium of print, his voice was heard across Germany and all over Europe. As Luther modestly put it in 1522, 'I simply taught, preached and wrote God's word; otherwise I did nothing. And while I slept or drank beer with my friends, the Word so greatly weakened the Papacy that no prince or emperor ever inflicted such losses on it. I did nothing; the Word did everything.'

This section examines the early reception of Lutheranism in Germany. Who supported it, and why? What factors were required before a state decided to establish Lutheranism as the official faith?

The German princes

Most of northern, central and south-eastern Germany was ruled by territorial princes. In all, there were about 250 princely states in the empire. Some rulers, like the Hohenzollern in Brandenburg and the Wittelsbach in Bavaria, governed large states. Others, like the counts of Reus and Sayn, were sovereigns of postage-stamp-sized countries. As a political class, however, their attitude was vital. Without their endorsement, the disciples of Wittenberg would remain persecuted minorities. Textbooks tend to lump the princes together and, ignoring the chronology of what happened when, have generalised inaccurately on the central role played by the princes in the early triumph of Lutheranism. This is wrong. During the 1520s the princes of a mere ten states of any political significance (of whom two were not German) introduced Lutheran reformations; in the 1530s, just another eight. Six made the legendary 'protest' at the Diet of Speyer in 1529, while only five were founder members of the Lutheran military alliance, the Schmalkaldic League, at Christmas 1530.

The Lutheran princely reformations of the 1520s were essentially phenomena of northern and central Germany. As a group, the German princes were politically cautious. Unlike the cities (as will be seen shortly), they were remote from popular pressures and generally resisted demands from the people for religious change. Instead, they hesitated to break with the emperor and risk provoking his wrath. Those determined to develop Lutheran ways moved warily, only starting to organise reformed churches in the wake of the 1526 **Recess of Speyer**, which gave them legal protection to introduce Lutheranism. Saxony and Hesse, the leading Lutheran states, were four years behind the cities in setting up official Lutheran systems. The princes played a 'softly, softly' game in the 1520s, tolerating changes and refusing to crush them, but hesitating to endorse them overtly, let alone authorise them. To defy the pope was one thing. To defy the emperor was quite another. Of the early Lutheran princes, only Philipp of Hesse dared to challenge Charles V openly.

Another factor that made princes nervous of adopting too public a position was the endless squabbling over inheritances which plagued German princely families. Almost everyone was split by dynastic rivalries. If one adopted Lutheran heresy, the real danger was that, with imperial backing, his rival

For the 1526 Diet and **Recess of Speyer**, see Chapter 1, page 9.

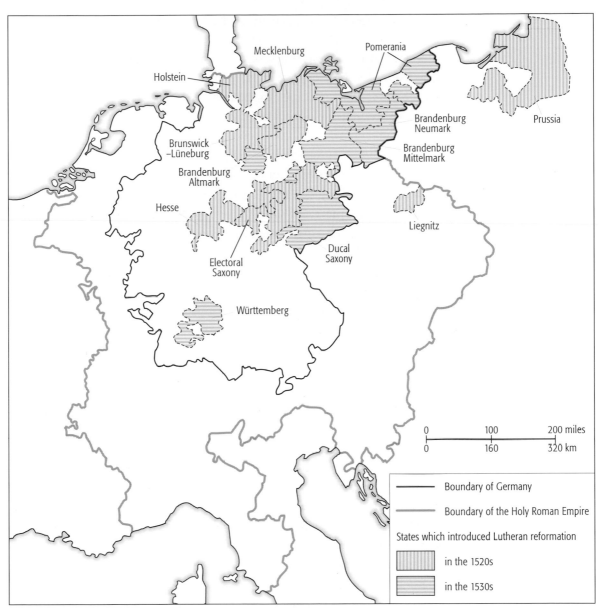

The princely Lutheran Reformation (to 1539).

would invade, depose him and seize his territories. The gradual move to Lutheranism by Elector Joachim II of Brandenburg in the later 1530s is the best example of this restraining fear. Rapid action could jeopardise dynastic interests.

One element was certainly age. We have long known that the appeal of the early Reformation was linked to the generations. Few among those born before *c.*1480–99 became Protestant, while the majority of its initial disciples came from among those born in or after the 1490s. This factor alone helps to explain the limited number of princely defections from Catholicism in the 1520s and, conversely, the rush to the Lutheran faith that occurred in 1534–45. Among the staunchest supporters of the old religion were George the Bearded, duke of Saxony (b. 1471) and Joachim I, elector of Brandenburg (b. 1483). Yet on their deaths (in 1539 and 1535 respectively) their successors adopted the Lutheran cause. That raises another significant lever – the influence of Lutheran wives and mothers. The new Brandenburg elector, Joachim II, had, against his father's wishes, been brought up a Lutheran by his mother, the Electress Elizabeth. Count Johann of Anhalt-Dessau introduced Lutheranism to his state in 1532–34 after being converted by his wife in 1529. If on the surface the 1520s seem to have been the slack decade of Lutheran princely reform, sub-currents were preparing the way for more spectacular developments.

None of this has explained *why* some princes wanted to support Luther. Historians have long understood that no single explanation can cover the complex motives of so many different people (even within a single 'class' like ruling princes). The only clear-cut case of the 1520s is Albert, grand master of the order of the Teutonic Knights. An elected prince, he was a monk administering church lands. In 1523–25 he established the first officially Lutheran state (ahead even of electoral Saxony). In the process he carved out for himself a personal state which, by marrying, he could pass on to his own newly founded dynasty. This he did, taking the order's Baltic lands and turning them into the duchy of Prussia. Political and material explanations must always be borne in mind as possible factors in helping to sway a prince. In no other case, however, were these selfish motives so blatant or so all important. Nevertheless, the example of the new Duke Albert of Prussia set a powerful temptation in front of every other European prince. If the Reformation was adopted, great wealth could be seized from the church. Yet if the exploitation of church lands and valuables was so seductive, barely a prince in Christendom should have been left in the Catholic camp – which patently was not the case. Above all, we must be wary of so simplistic an explanation of motives. Princes on *both* sides of the religious divide were busy looting their church. The Catholic dukes of Bavaria (like the Catholic kings of France and Spain) were successful in forcing popes to surrender substantial church wealth and grant extensive authority over the church in their territories. In other words, a prince did not have to go to all the trouble (and run all the risks) of becoming a Lutheran just to plunder the church. Indeed, he would almost certainly be better off pillaging as a Catholic because, as a Protestant, he would have to spend vast amounts on **mobilisation** against possible Catholic attack.

If financial self-interest will rarely provide a satisfactory explanation for German princes, where are we left? Count Philipp of Hesse offers an excellent

By 1530, ten princely states were officially Lutheran. Was that a small or a large number? Justify your answer.

'Hesse and Electoral Saxony embarked on military **mobilisation** and frantic diplomatic activity to defend their confessional position, which swallowed up the increased income which they received from the Church, and quite possibly more.' (Euan Cameron, *The European Reformation*, 1991)

case study. Openly sympathetic to Lutheran ideas from 1524, he began to introduce an official Reformation in 1526. From that date he became the primary Lutheran statesman – so much so that William Wright has classified him as 'a lay counterpart to Luther'. His Protestant credentials are first rate. A considerable theological scholar in his own right, the count must be classified as a genuine convert. He risked his life and his throne out of conviction. While recognising that, we can be equally clear that his vigour in the Lutheran cause was fuelled by dynastic concerns. Count **Philipp** was the arch-opponent of the Habsburg family. The quarrel was in origin an inheritance dispute from the 1470s between the counts of Hesse and Nassau over Upper and Lower Katzenellenbogen, Rhineland counties which generated major toll revenues from traffic on the Rhine and Main. Emperor Maximilian had sided with Nassau in the dispute, a stance continued by Charles. The quarrel really took off, however, when the new emperor invaded the duchy of Württemberg in 1519. For one thing, the duke Charles deposed was Philipp's cousin. More important probably was this direct Habsburg move into the Rhineland, upsetting the political balance between the Rhenish states and threatening the dominant position Hesse enjoyed. From that moment, Philipp became Charles V's sworn enemy. His dynastic and religious quarrels with the emperor fitted seamlessly together. The secular pre-dated the ecclesiastical, but that is not in itself significant. We ignore the religious dimension at our peril.

For **Philipp** and his opposition to Charles V, see Chapter 1, pages 20 to 23.

Assess the motives of Count Philipp of Hesse.

The imperial knights

The Knight's War (1522–23) was a curious affair. The imperial knights were minor nobles, concentrated in those western parts of Germany where major princely states had not developed (the Rhineland, Franconia and Swabia). Since the mid fourteenth century, they had been in economic decline. Since the early fifteenth century, their political influence had been falling as that of territorial princes grew. Even on the battlefield, the shift to **infantry** meant that they belonged to the past. Their position was degraded. Squeezed from all sides, many were reduced to the life of 'robber barons'. Revolt began in response to the banning of 'feud' by the 1521 Diet of Worms. Until then, imperial law had allowed a noble to declare war on a fellow noble, a town or even a prince. That was a traditional part of the knights' way of life, and this latest attack on their standing provoked the creation of 'fraternal associations' of knights under the leadership of Franz von Sickingen.

See Chapter 4, pages 96 to 100, on the rise of the **infantry**.

Alongside the 250 or so German princes were about another 80 ecclesiastical states, ruled by prince bishops or abbots. These the knights resented with a special loathing and the fraternal associations began to pillage church territory. From the lands of the bishops of Bamberg, Cologne and Würzburg, however, the marauding knights moved into the duchies of Brunswick and

'Only one incident, Sickingen's attack on **Trier**, raises the Knights Revolt above the level of a group of minor disturbances.' (Thomas Brady, 'The knights revolt', *The Oxford encyclopaedia of the Reformation*, vol II, 1996) Von Sickingen's ally Ulrich von Hutten proclaimed this campaign *Pfaffenkrieg* (war against the priests).

'**The two men** exercised considerable influence on one another.' (Eckhard Bernstein, *Ulrich von Hutten*, 1988)

Why should the Knights' War be seen as relevant to the Lutheran Reformation?

Cleves-Jülich. At once, the territorial princes mobilised to crush this challenge not just to order but to their own position. Many gave up without a fight. With the rest, the princes were ruthless, burning castles and hunting down knights without mercy. As for von Sickingen himself, he attacked the lands of the electoral prince archbishop of **Trier**. Caught between the armies of the elector palatine and Count Philipp, von Sickingen was killed in battle.

What this has to do with the Lutheran Reformation is still disputed by historians. Traditionally, the knights' championing of Luther has been seen as the result of a mixture of their own ignorance and selfishness. They heard Luther attack the pope and the power of priests, and in their own minds thought they heard an invitation to loot church property. At best, therefore, theirs was no more than a militant outburst of anti-papal, anti-clerical feelings. At worst, the Knights' War was a blatant misuse of Luther's name to justify thuggery. However, in the words of Euan Cameron, 'the knights have suffered the double stigma, for modern historians, of being both aristocrats and failures'. Recently, scholars have indicated that the links between Lutheranism and some of the knights were genuine. In his own territory, von Sickingen implemented a Lutheran Reformation in 1520–21 (*before* any princely state or city), while he was the active patron of important Protestant leaders, including Philipp Melanchthon. Another knight, Harmuth von Kronberg, wrote and published several of the very earliest pamphlets defending Luther. After the war, he converted Duke Ulrich of Württemberg to Lutheranism. Intriguingly, there was a cross-influence in the other direction. Loudest among the knights was Ulrich von Hutten, a noted scholar and champion of German national identity against the 'foreign' power of the papacy. In 1519–20 he was regarded, equally with Luther, as leader of the anti-papal party in the empire. He was certainly never a Lutheran. Equally, after the Leipzig Dispute, he saw himself as Luther's ally in the battle against the power of the clergy. Whether or not von Hutten understood that Luther was really talking about something else remains a mystery. Yet **the two** knew of each other and read each other's works. Textual analysis shows that Luther drew heavily on von Hutten's political, nationalistic views in devising both the general shape and some of the specific content of *An appeal to the Christian nobility* (1520).

Minor nobles were crucial to the success of the Reformation in France, Poland, the Netherlands and Scotland. In Germany, however, that potential link was never allowed to develop. The story of the Knights' War is a reminder of what might have been. Some territorial princes may have understood Lutheranism no better than some imperial knights. Even by 1520, the Reformation was no longer a purely religious matter. Historians need to study failures as well as successes.

Towns

Germany in 1520 had about 2,000 towns. The urban Reformation has been the subject of intense historical research. Historians have come to portray the German Reformation as essentially an urban phenomenon. This can be misleading. Protestantism could be successful in the countryside, where the great majority of the people lived and worked. **Towns** were not always the most significant centres of Reformation activity. But, in the words of Euan Cameron, the point is that towns 'possessed the concentration of people, the literary awareness and the political sophistication to propel the ideas of preachers and pamphleteers to the forefront of the political agenda in the early 1520s'. Generalisations are dangerous. Each town had to make its own decision for its own reasons. Nevertheless, the Reformation began in a town (Wittenberg) and every significant Protestant leader was essentially an urban reformer (notably Martin Bucer in Strasbourg, Andreas Osiander in Nuremberg, Ulrich Zwingli in Zurich and Johannes Bugenhagen in a series of north German and Danish towns). The focus so far has been exclusively on Martin Luther. His was never the only voice. Although Luther held a pre-eminent position and virtually every Protestant preacher was inspired by him, by no means all agreed with him on everything. It is a great error to think of the Reformation as a coherent movement with a single message. Rather, we are rediscovering, as Bob Scribner has commented, that 'the Reformation was a many-sided affair with many variants'. In the **German urban Reformation**, the southwestern cities like Strasbourg tended to look south to the religious leadership of Zürich, rather than north-east to Wittenberg.

Obviously, Wittenberg itself saw the very first religious changes, although they were made by others while Luther was in hiding. Luther disapproved of what was being done in his name (especially when riots and violence broke out), and the initial Wittenberg reforms were the cause of his emergence from the Wartburg, to *put a stop* to change. Over the following five years, he deliberately retarded the pace of innovation. But Luther's reluctance was too frustrating for many and the years 1522–26 saw over a dozen Saxon towns acting on their own, introducing their own Reformations, tailor made to their own circumstances. Only very slowly (often well into the 1530s) did Luther and Wittenberg establish a general control and impose a common 'Lutheran' form of worship.

This story of reform in little Saxon towns reveals the central point about urban Reformation: decision-making was local. Enthusiastic and eloquent Lutheran preachers usually set the process moving, and the start of evangelical preaching soon led to demands for evangelical action. The direction and pace of events were almost invariably determined, however, by the town's authorities. Rarely was the town council itself so swept up in the new fervour that full

In 1500, Germany had a population of *c.* 12 million. Of these, at most 400,000 lived in **towns** of 10,000 or more inhabitants. Perhaps 10 per cent of the total population was urban – and the *typical* town had a population of 500–2,000 people.

'Recent work on the **German city Reformation** has re-emphasised the powerful attraction of Zürich even within the Empire ... After around 1530, it appears that Luther was losing ground to the other reformers.' (Andrew Pettegree, *The early Reformation in Europe*, 1992)

Reformation was authorised at once. At the same time, councils could not ignore sizeable factions; effective government required some degree of assent by the **people**. The more common pattern was to allow the new faith to operate alongside the old, and thereby avoid direct confrontation with the forces of both sides; public order and social harmony were as crucial to town councils as they were to princes. Above all, urban authorities aimed to prevent (or at least contain) direct popular action. From the start, the Reformation was never a movement under control. Heady enthusiasm was an especially prominent feature of the early days of the urban Reformation. Following Nuremberg's lead in 1522, many councils tried to cool passions by regulating preachers. In instructions called 'scripture mandates' they sought to control sermon content by limiting preachers 'only to what could be proved from scripture'. Ultimately, however, such mandates were ambiguous and, whatever controls were attempted, the cautious encouragement given to the new ways could rarely prevent escalating tensions. Every authority had ultimately to face the moment of truth and decide. Often this was done by organising a formal **debate** between Lutheran and Catholic preachers, which the council would adjudicate in a legally binding judgement. The following time-table for the independent city state of Nuremberg illustrates this process well:

1520	Lutheran preachers at work
1524	Lutheran services officially tolerated
1525	The dispute, judged in favour of Lutheranism; monasteries closed

Even then, Nuremberg did not rush. Monasticism was very much out of fashion in the early sixteenth century, so its formal abolition was unlikely to provoke mass protest. A ban on Catholic worship was, however, a very different matter and Nuremberg only gradually made itself Lutheran between 1527 and 1533. The city magistrates kept control of events because peaceful, orderly change was their ultimate concern.

In north German cities, that pattern was broken in one essential way: popular enthusiasm clashed with unsympathetic councils. Evangelical preaching unleashed deep-seated hostilities in the citizens against their ruling authorities. Struggles developed between the mass of the people (excluded from power and influence) and the narrow elites monopolising power (which, of late, had been tightening their exclusive grip on decision-making). In a string of cities like Bremen, Brunswick, Hamburg and Lübeck, Lutheran preachers organised 'citizen committees' to campaign against the magistrates. They did more than protest. They took direct action, inspecting the council's financial and other records for irregularities – which were then used to justify the expulsion of current office holders (in Hanover, the entire council). In their place, new councillors were elected who (of course) favoured Lutheranism and, forming a new majority, authorised Reformation. A political and social (as well as religious) coup had been engineered. Yet in no case was there major violence. Once the new regime was in place, the changes were then made in an orderly and peaceful way. Who can say whether in north Germany the chief objective was a shift in the political balance or a change in religious practice?

Luther's pamphlets found a ready audience in the disproportionately literate **urban** populations. Towns were communication centres and Protestantism can be shown to have spread along (and then outwards from) the trade routes. Towns were also the centres of printing and natural centres in which ideas were exchanged. Clergy, themselves inspired by Luther's message of personal salvation (and encouraged by the slow, incompetent response of the Catholic authorities), brought his sensational platform to their urban churches. The written and the spoken word were the vehicles of Protestant expansion. Pamphlets and pulpits made Germany Lutheran. The papacy and clergy were criticised openly from the official pulpits of the official **preacherships**, funded from communal funds by town councils. They were agents of Reformation, and their role must never be under-estimated.

The Protestant message had economic and political potential. Furthermore, the confidence it gave allowed the converted to speak with an authority and assurance that could be charismatic. In the confined world of a town, the consequences were often dramatic. In several south German and Swiss cities, the attack on the power of the clergy and the banning of the mass led to the **expulsion** of the ruling prince bishop. Everywhere, it led to the urban clergy being stripped of their legal immunities and being subjected (alongside all other residents) to the municipal laws. The Reformation cause allowed urban governments to strengthen their control over the *whole* community.

Some, however, turned down that possibility. Bamberg and Würzburg expelled the preachers, kept their bishop and stood firm in the Catholic camp. In the case of Bamberg, a key element seems to have been their deep-seated rivalry with Nuremberg. Since it had gone Lutheran, they were determined not to. Comparable in size and status to Nuremberg, the mighty city state of Augsburg resisted throughout the 1520s all pressures to change. The eloquent preachers were hard at work while the discontented craftsmen dreamt of a new order in their city. But the force of the reformist message broke on the rival versions offered by Lutheran and Zwinglian ministers. Exposed to so conspicuous a display of Protestant divisions (and thus weakness), the council determined to do nothing against the laws of the empire. Catholic worship was supported and in 1529 the city signed the Recess of Speyer, cancelling the temporary tolerance of Lutheran practices. This line did not, however,

A very high literacy level would mean that 30 per cent of the inhabitants could read. The **urban** norm is likely to have been 5–10 per cent. About 4,000 Protestant pamphlets were printed in Germany and Switzerland between 1517 and 1530.

'Any reasonably eloquent and plausible reformer soon found an enthusiastic and sometimes raucous following ... Preaching usually, but not invariably, was the starting point for vigorous popular involvement. Such mass popular enthusiasm was neither rare nor surprising: fifteenth-century **preachers** often had a similar cult following.' (Euan Cameron, *The European Reformation*, 1991)

Constance ordered Protestant preaching in 1524, **expelled** its bishop in 1526 and banned the mass in 1528. Basle drove out its bishop in 1529.

represent a ringing commitment to Catholicism. When the diet met in the city in 1530, Charles demanded the expulsion of all its Protestant preachers. Augsburg might not have permitted official recognition of reformed ways, but it had not silenced them either – and flatly told the emperor that there were no heretical clergy to send away. The city of Augsburg provides more than just another example of civic caution in the face of the divisive religious squabble. Zealots everywhere pushed individuals and institutions to choose the side on which they stood. Augsburg is an example of those (too frequently overlooked by historians) who refused the choice and declared their **neutrality**.

The profound influence of the Peasants' War (1524–26) on the Reformation must always be borne in mind. The evangelical message had naturally spilled over from town to countryside. As in the thirteenth and fourteenth centuries, urban and rural protest could march comfortably together. The strength of radical urban Protestantism was one important factor influencing peasant attacks on the clergy and feudal lords. Just as important were the ongoing influences once the peasants had been crushed. To moderates and conservatives (as well as reactionaries), peasant actions had shown a gospel of social unrest. Popular pressure had been revealed in its true colours – as the gateway to anarchy. Everywhere, the hand of all in authority was strengthened. In some towns (notably Freiburg-im-Breisgau, Schwäbisch-Gmünd and Wangen), councils abandoned a previously tolerant stance and crushed Protestantism mercilessly. Elsewhere, the war made councils delay the implementation of reform. The year 1525 turned out to be a critical one for the urban Reformation. Fear of disorder meant the pace of change was regulated closely. Until 1525, Lutheran Reformation was a haphazard affair. After 1525, tight regulation meant Lutheranism was reorientated. Luther endorsed that too. The Peasants' War allowed rulers to take greater control of the church in their territories, and forced Lutheranism to establish in the ranks of its own clergy the very hierarchical authority so denounced in *An appeal* and *The Babylonish captivity*.

The other fundamental point about the urban Reformation during the 1520s was that it was more important than the princely Reformation. The towns and cities of Germany committed themselves to Lutheranism sooner than the princes. Towns and cities allowed people their first opportunity to adopt the evangelical faith in safety. And the public support of urban Germany gave Luther his first official endorsement. The scale of that is indicated by a brief glance at the following table, showing the conduct of the elite group of German cities – the imperial cities independent of every prince and bishop.

As Germany (and Europe) increasingly divided, **neutrality** was a difficult position to maintain. Augsburg itself moved into the Lutheran camp between 1533 and 1537.

Endorsement of Lutheranism		
	Imperial free cities	Imperial princes
Signed the 1529 Protest at Speyer	14	5
Signed the 1531 Schmalkaldic alliance	11	5

Note that four of the cities that signed in 1531 had not signed in 1529. Towns were the nurseries of the Reformation.

The peasants

The term **peasant** cannot be defined precisely, but it covers that broad mass of the population employed in agriculture, either on their own self-sufficient farm or by others as wage labourers. Peasants were also defined by their social position. Medieval society saw three social groups: those who prayed (priests and monks), those who fought (nobles and knights) and those who laboured (peasants). This social hierarchy was seen as God's creation and God's will. The clergy and nobility were defined by their privileges, the peasants by their lack of legal rights and their subjection to the other two groups. More than 80 per cent of the population were peasants and the variations in economic positions among so many people were considerable. Some owned their own land and enjoyed a comfortable prosperity. At the other end of the scale, some were landless, unskilled and permanently close to starvation.

See Chapter 1, pages 15 to 19, for the German **peasantry** and a brief discussion of the economic grievances involved in the Peasants' War.

Rural discontent was strong in early-sixteenth-century Germany. Uprisings had been a regular occurrence for nearly a century, and were becoming more frequent, as the following table shows.

Number of major peasant uprisings	
1400–50	7
1450–74	6
1475–99	8
1500–24	18

Late medieval lords, squeezed by declining revenues and a shortage of tenants, had been working to tie down their peasants. Ancient rights to the use of woods, rivers and commons were overthrown by lords seeking exclusive exploitation of these economic resources. Simultaneously, lords imposed new obligations on peasant labour. Together, these changes represented a major attack on peasants' liberties and livelihoods.

Since the 1980s, historians have talked of the 'peasant Reformation' with growing frequency. The Reformation was a mass rural phenomenon. The 'pure gospel' was just as attractive a proposition to the 'common man' in the countryside as in the town. Urban literacy levels have already been noted, and the position in villages would have been lower. Book owning would have been rare. As in the towns, pamphlets would have been read aloud. Similarly, those who had been to market and been read to or heard a sermon would have spread reports of what they had been told. To an even greater extent than in the urban Reformation, the rural Reformation therefore involved a general awareness but a secondhand knowledge of the specific ideas of Luther and others. With direct experience of the reform message so slender, the peasants had greater scope than other groups to misunderstand and misinterpret Protestantism. But before dismissing out of hand their shading and adapting of Lutheran ideas to their own social, economic and political context, remember what imperial knights, Baltic townsmen and some princes did with the evangelical gospel.

The Peasants' War, which lasted from April 1524 to July 1526, was one of the largest peasant risings in European history. It was a series of revolts of varying sizes in different parts of Germany, Austria and Switzerland. Some were interlinked. Others seem to have stood alone.

'The introduction of evangelical ideas by preachers produced a revolutionary principle: the Word provided the means to judge what was just in a Christian society and decide the problems of daily life.' (T. Scott and B. Scribner, *The German Peasants' War*, 1991) Since the **Twelve Articles** were anonymous, the major problem with them is to know how far they represent the views of the peasants, rather than the plans of one or more of their educated leaders.

Of the many lists of grievances produced by peasant armies, the **Twelve Articles** of Memmingen, produced anonymously in Swabia in March 1525, was the most influential at the time and is now seen as the most significant document produced by the rebellions. One of only two peasant manifestos published, demand for it was so high that 28 editions sold out in 2 months. In some areas, the Twelve Articles were adapted, rewritten and supplemented; their widespread use makes them *the* manifesto of the Peasants' War. They served as the basis for political negotiations with individual lords and were even discussed by the diet in 1526. In summary, the Twelve Articles argued:

- communities must have the right to appoint and dismiss their clergy;
- tithes are an oppression – some must be abolished, while the rest must no longer be paid to the clergy but used for the benefit of the community;
- serfdom must be abolished;
- free access to hunt in forests and fish in rivers and lakes must be restored to local communities – lords must not steal these rights for themselves;
- the use of forests and common land must be restored to the community – lords have no legal right to take these for their exclusive use;
- peasant services owed to lords (paid in cash, in goods or by labour) must be reduced to the sensible levels of the past – currently they are too oppressive;
- tax rates on land are too high – farming no longer allows peasants to earn enough to keep their families and pay their taxes; taxes must therefore be lowered.

They ended in the twelfth article with the decisive claim that each point could be tested against the evidence of the Bible. Custom and law counted for nothing. The gospel had become the court of appeal for peasant grievances – and legitimised peasants' current actions in seeking to rearrange the peasant–lord relationship. This was explosive.

In Thuringia, a different revolution was proposed by Thomas Müntzer. From 1521 he was in dispute with Luther and was expelled from three successive parishes in Saxony. His faithful following believed him to be a prophet, whereas Luther saw him as an arch-devil. In the medieval tradition of fiery preachers, **Müntzer** stressed the imminence of the end of the world and offered guidance to the 'last generation' through the interpretation of dreams (the medium through which he declared God spoke directly to people, rather than through an official, organised church). As Luther had done in 1520, he first called on the princes to reform the church. When in 1524 they failed to adopt his revolutionary Reformation, he denounced all lords as agents of the devil because they had stolen the land and its wealth from the people, God's children. The peasants must therefore rise up and, in God's name, slaughter the rich for their wickedness, just as in the Old Testament the prophet Elijah had massacred the prophets of Baal. Then, a holy commonwealth could be established, where God's servants would live in purity, governing themselves in New Jerusalem as they waited to be lifted into heaven at the Last Judgement. Briefly, Jerusalem was created in the towns of Mühlhausen and Frankenhausen, where new councils were established. They claimed that God had transferred political power to the **people** and authorised them, 'the children of light', to march against 'the children of darkness in these last dangerous days'. Under the banner of a rainbow, the Eternal League marched out to enforce the new order, under Müntzer's stirring guidance: 'We cannot sleep any longer. Go to it; go to it now! Show no pity and do not let your sword grow cold. March while the fire is hot and throw down the towers of the mighty. Go to it, while it is still day. God goes before you. Follow!' Within days, the armies of the count of Hesse and the elector of Saxony had given their reply. At Frankenhausen in May 1525, the Eternal League was destroyed. For the cost of six men, more than six thousand peasants were killed.

Müntzer is currently the subject of major research. For a long time, he was claimed by Marxist East German historians as an early prophet of the class war and an early political revolutionary. Scholars now point to the wide gap between his own goals and those of the peasants. He was not primarily concerned with taxes and land rights. He did not fight ultimately for a better tomorrow; he fought for no tomorrow – his concern was with the end of the world and life in heaven, not a better life on earth. Few of his followers seem to have understood this.

All the uprisings which make up the Peasants' War were to some degree provoked by economic and political grievances. The peasant way of life was

Where Luther looked to the Bible as the ultimate authority, **Müntzer** saw it only as a code of law and stressed the 'inner light' as a *higher* source of guidance. God's message was not yet complete. The Bible alone was therefore inadequate and, in Müntzer's opinion, Luther had erected it into a barrier that concealed God.

'The Godless have no right to live, unless God's chosen **people** allow it' was a favourite statement of Müntzer, based on his reading of Deuteronomy, chapter 13. He saw himself as a second Gideon – the first was a charismatic Old Testament general (see Judges, chapters 6–8). 'It is the division between God's chosen elect and the ungodly which underlines his whole programme.' (Gordon Rupp, *Patterns of Reformation*, 1969)

'**Müntzer**'s concerns were religious and pastoral. He believed that extreme poverty weighed so heavily upon many people as to debar them from religious thinking and hence from salvation.' (A. G. Dickens, *The German nation and Martin Luther*, 1974)

getting harder. Problems in the rural economy, whether in taxes or tithes or labour services, stand out from the Twelve Articles. The other secular issue that jumps out of all rebel manifestos is the feudal relationship between peasants and their lord. The peasant sense that things had become too one sided cannot be mistaken. Neither can their rosy view of some mythical past when all was once well. All peasant armies invited the lords to explain what *they* did for their peasants. Many took the next logical step and tore up the feudal contract, arguing it was unjust because the peasants did everything while the lords did nothing. But, as was seen with Müntzer's two Jerusalems, it is misleading to think only of the countryside.

All these points accepted, there can be no doubt about the important role of Protestant ideas in the Peasants' War. Lutheran ideas like the **priesthood of all believers** and the right of every congregation to elect its own minister were taken up with enthusiasm. Lutheran reform of the church and the clergy met with popular approval. The involvement of the people in Lutheran services, symbolised by the giving of communion wine to everyone, was eagerly adopted. Luther struck many chords, and not just when playing the nationalist tune in *An appeal to the Christian nobility*. Lutheran sermons attracted huge audiences. The little pamphlets Luther (and others) wrote in ordinary German, often illustrated, were passed around and discussed with passion. From the start, Lutheranism was often a popular cause.

Whereas many historians once questioned the link between the Reformation and the Peasants' War, scholarly opinion now asserts vigorously the validity of the connection. If the peasant movements were only about land rights and taxes, why did Luther react the way he did? He turned all his attention to the peasants. At first, his attitude was quite encouraging. In his *Admonition to peace* (April 1525), he called for negotiations, criticising the lords as much as the peasants for the current situation, while praising the treaty signed between the archbishop of Mainz and the rebels. During April and early May, he travelled extensively in Saxony, preaching to peasant groups and doing nothing to silence them. If anything, his surviving letters suggest that he had himself caught some of their enthusiasm.

Everything changed with Müntzer and the outbreak of violence in Thuringia. In mid May, Luther published his second Peasants' War pamphlet: *Against the robbing and murdering hordes of peasants*. He was in panic. Peasants were finding political and economic implications in his views. They had understood that the gospel had social implications and was a call to **action**. In bloodthirsty language, Luther urged the princes to take merciless action to crush the rebels; their Christian duty to God demanded nothing less. He was running as fast as he could to distance himself and the cause of the fledgling Reformation from any association with the peasants. The people must not

'**The priesthood of all believers** was Luther's most original, most imaginative and most vote-catching concept.' (A. G. Dickens, *The German Reformation and Martin Luther,* 1974)

'The evangelical movement unwittingly provided the common man with a new vocabulary and basis of **action**.' (Andrew Pettegree, *The early Reformation in Europe,* 1992)

be allowed to decide for themselves what evangelical freedom meant – it was too powerful a weapon of protest. If the idea caught on that Luther inspired social and political revolution, the cause was doomed. This was the **greatest crisis** Luther ever faced (far more dangerous than the pope and his excommunication).

Most fellow Lutherans, notably Luther's own lieutenant Philipp Melanchthon, thought that Luther over-reacted. Among the peasants, Lutheranism was dealt a mortal blow. Luther, the son of a peasant, was seen as having betrayed the people and encouraged the barbaric slaughter. Some returned to Catholicism, while others turned to more radical Protestant leaders. Few showed much enthusiasm after 1525 for Lutheranism. That popular alienation was reinforced during the later 1520s as Luther and his senior assistants adopted an openly conservative position. Lutheranism cuddled up to the ruling authorities, simultaneously allying with princes and town councils, while demanding strict obedience by the people. From Lutheran pulpits, the evils of rebellion became a regular theme.

The Luther of *Admonition to peace* had recognised the religious vigour at large in Germany in 1525. Seven years of preaching and publishing had created evangelical movements. Luther might well shift his ground and claim the Peasants' War was the result of false preaching, distorting the true gospel of Christian liberty. But that view demands the belief that there was only one Reformation. As we have seen with the princes, the knights and the towns, people reacted to the evangelical campaign in their own ways. They attempted to understand it, but also to interpret and integrate its message into their environment.

> Yet the Reformation *did* survive this **great crisis** (which must indicate the early strength it had gained); in 1526–30 there was significant recruitment among princes and cities; and the 1526 Diet of Speyer agreed the liberal religious formula in its Recess.

> 'A creed which allows each person to interpret the faith according to their own taste must breed civil disobedience and ultimately rebellion.' (Duke William of Bavaria, 1527) How far would Luther have agreed with the duke? Explain your answer.

Luther and the radicals

1520–22	The Prophets of Zwickau.
May 1521–March 1522	Luther in hiding in the Wartburg.
October 1521–March 1522	The Wittenberg Movement.
25 December 1521	Karlstadt's evangelical communion.
January 1522	The first act of iconoclasm; the Wittenberg Ordinance.
March 1522	Luther's Wittenberg sermons.

There was always more than one form of Protestantism, more than one version of the Reformation. This final section focuses specifically on the emergence of alternative voices: the radicalisation and fragmentation of the evangelical movement. In the apt phrase of Bob Scribner, Protestantism did not 'spring fully formed from the head of Luther'. The Reformation had not happened when Luther was excommunicated in 1521; it had barely begun. A firm label 'the Reformation' is wholly inappropriate for the unstructured happenings of those early years. So too is a single label. Diversity, division and disunity were the hallmarks of the very broad movement we call 'Protestantism'.

The earliest sign that the evangelical cause was pluriform came during 1520 in the Saxon weaving town of Zwickau. From among the wool weavers, recently subjected to heavy new taxes and town laws, emerged an eloquent voice claiming to be inspired directly by God and called to the role of prophet. He was Nicholas Storch and, although uneducated, an articulate, charismatic personality. Storch was taken seriously by Zwickau's new supply preacher, appointed on Luther's personal recommendation: Thomas Müntzer (the future firebrand of 1525). When Müntzer was expelled from Zwickau in 1521, Storch seems to have taken over as preacher to Müntzer's followers. Details are thin, and come from hostile sources, but Storch was assisted by a student and a blacksmith, and permitted women to lead prayers and preach. His supporters were nicknamed 'the Prophets'; we know that they stressed God's direct communication with them and their interpretation of the Bible under his inspiration. They required adults to be baptised if they were true believers and they thought the **Last Judgement** was imminent.

In itself, the belief that the **Last Judgement** was close was almost universal. Luther himself was convinced that he was living in 'the last days' (see page 123).

Luther and Melanchthon worried primarily about the Prophets' hostility to baptising babies. The town council of Zwickau, by contrast, was alarmed by the politically subversive idea of individuals organising themselves. Arrests were ordered, and the Prophets fled to Wittenberg, where for some months the visions of these unlettered craftsmen caused quite a stir (and impressed not a few, including Melanchthon). Storch spent the next 14 years as a wandering preacher, talking to all who would listen. The Prophets were obscure and apparently of marginal significance, but are worth some attention. First, this is because they had no initial links to Martin Luther. Instead, their core ideas came from fifteenth-century heretical groups and thus pre-dated those of Luther. Second, even allowing for the subsequent influence of Müntzer (and thus, perhaps, Luther), the Prophets developed their own teachings. Third, they were not priests or monks but lay men and women, essentially uneducated but confident and missionary in their beliefs. Luther questioned specific details, but for a long time delayed condemning their ideas. The Prophets of Zwickau are important because they demonstrate that the Reformation had more than one source, and was never simply a set of variations on the themes of Martin Luther. From the beginning, two very different Reformations competed for the hearts and minds of the Christian faithful. One was led by professional theologians like Luther, who organised the people and kept control of authority within the church. The other tended to be a collective in which non-professionals, ordinary men (sometimes women), organised themselves and shared responsibilities. The first allied with the state and demanded the membership of all citizens. The second stood apart from the state and invited consenting adults to join their community – hence the demand that, as the sign of voluntary membership, adults submit to baptism. Historians call the first type 'magisterial Reformation' and the second 'radical Reformation'.

Explain the features which made Luther a 'magisterial' rather than a 'radical' reformer.

Luther accused the Prophets of being subjective, of making up their own interpretation of the Bible to suit themselves. Yet Luther too claimed a personal revelation from God. His key ideas, drawn from his understanding of the meaning of the biblical texts on justification, could also be said to have been highly subjective. Luther called the Prophets fanatics, but they had raised a core problem for Protestantism: once the authority of the pope to rule on all matters had been transferred to the Bible, who was to decide which interpretation of the Bible was correct? This was Protestantism's Achilles' heel.

Karlstadt and the Wittenberg Movement

Where the story of the Zwickau Prophets is one of alternative evangelical thinking separate from Luther, the Wittenberg Movement illustrates another Reformation phenomenon: the divergence of views that split a group (in this case, the circle around Luther himself). For ten months after the Diet of Worms, Luther hid in the Wartburg. Yet the previous four years had seen the creation of a powerful dynamic. Excitements and expectations had been raised. Against that momentum stood the emperor's edict condemning religious innovation. All eyes were on electoral Saxony, but none looked more anxiously (or greedily) than Duke George of Saxony. Any excuse could be used to invade; the duke of Württemberg had been deposed for less in 1519.

By temperament, Luther was conservative. He was as keen as his prince to maintain public order. Both wished to keep control of events, especially with details filtering through of prophetic weavers and women preachers, but Luther's supporters were fired up. After *An appeal to the Christian nobility* and *The Babylonish captivity*, how could they mark time? Luther's senior lieutenants were his university colleagues **Philipp Melanchthon** and **Andreas von Karlstadt**. Both wanted to turn words into deeds and initiated a series of changes in Wittenberg during 1521. Three stand out:

- permitting the clergy to marry;
- allowing monks, friars and nuns to give up the monastic life;
- giving wine as well as bread to everyone at communion.

Luther's publications of 1520 had called for all three.

By mid 1522, however, Luther and Karlstadt were locked in an escalating feud. Luther would soon brand his former friend a rebel against God. What had gone wrong? Initially, the answer is 'nothing'. Regular correspondence

Melanchthon (d. 1560) was professor of Greek; **Karlstadt** (d. 1541) was senior professor of theology, and Luther's assistant at the Leipzig Dispute.

It appears that, **marrying** in January 1522, Karlstadt was only the third Catholic priest in Europe to claim that Reformation teachings allowed him to marry.

Giving wine as well as bread to the laity is known as **communion in both kinds**. It had been a central belief of the Hussites, the fifteenth-century heretical movement in neighbouring Bohemia. Karlstadt's act opened Protestantism again to the charge of Hussitism (the same charge Eck tried to pin on Luther in the Leipzig Dispute).

For all **Melanchthon**'s enthusiasm, he could not have conducted the Christmas Day service because he was a layman.

'It is worth considering whether, had **Luther** been in Wittenberg during those weeks [of 1521], he might not have done the same.' (Gordon Rupp, *Patterns of Reformation*, 1969)

between Wittenberg and the Wartburg kept Luther closely informed. If he never formally sanctioned the 1521 changes, he certainly raised no objection. When he heard that Karlstadt was to be **married**, Luther sent his warmest congratulations. As for Karlstadt's now legendary Christmas Day evangelical **communion** service, judged ever after as revolutionary, Luther made no complaint against the various changes involved. Indeed, Karlstadt was only doing in public what the Lutheran circle had already done in private. The only negative comment it drew from Luther was a certain discomfort with the fact that Karlstadt had worn his ordinary clothes rather than a priest's robes – that he had not taken off his hat, Luther thought particularly ill advised.

The theological justification for these changes was not in dispute. And in the light of what was about to occur, it is intriguing to see that the figure impatiently pushing all three issues forward was **Melanchthon** (while the cautious voice ever trying to enlist the support of the magistrate and warning of possible direct popular action was Karlstadt's). **Luther** too was uneasy; the reasons are set out in the following diagram.

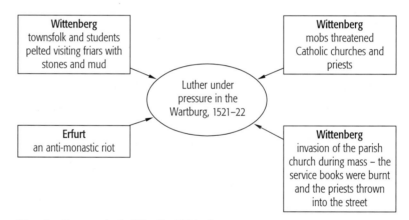

Direct action sparked off by the Wittenberg movement.

Order and discipline seemed to be breaking down. Events were moving too fast. What eventually forced him to quit the Wartburg and return to public life were the consequences of the Wittenberg Ordinance, published by the town council in January 1522. This linked closely religious and social reform, legalised the recent ecclesiastical changes, banned prostitution and begging (but established a new system of civic charity) and ordered the official removal of all religious images from the town's churches. Written by Karlstadt, the ordinance was a milestone in the Reformation because it was the first official attempt to implement evangelical teachings. As such, it was used as a blueprint for urban Reformations across much of central Europe. Everything in it was drawn from Luther's pamphlets of 1520 – except the ordinance's ban on religious art. Yet Luther disowned the entire package. Underlying the feud over paintings were two fundamental issues that rapidly became fault lines in Protestantism:

- Should reform happen cautiously so that as many as possible could be recruited gently to the cause, or should reform rush ahead (because it was 'right')?
- Did reform have to wait for the permission of the secular authorities, or should clergy and people make it happen regardless (because it was 'right')?

For Luther, the answer to the first part of both questions was 'yes' and to the second parts 'no'. Karlstadt, however, would wait for nobody. Conservative and radical were thus defined and divided first by their positions not on theology but on practical considerations: the pace of change and the tactics for reform.

Paintings and statues played a central role in Catholic worship, especially in the cults of the saints. Karlstadt did not mince his words, denouncing them in harsh Old Testament terms as false idols and promoters of perverted religion: 'I tell you that God has not less diligently and truly forbidden pictures', he wrote in 1522, 'than murdering, robbing and adultery.' Wittenberg council set a date when it would purge all the town's churches. Gabriel Zwilling, a fellow friar with Luther and Melanchthon's close assistant, could not wait and removed every statue from his monastic chapel. It was as if he lit a fuse. The subsequent days saw waves of populist action as bands of townsfolk **attacked** the artwork of their local churches.

Suddenly, on 9 March 1522, Luther reappeared in his Wittenberg pulpit. For eight days, dressed in his friar's robes and with his tonsure freshly shaved, he preached a set of counter-sermons, distinguishing between 'true Reformation' and fanaticism (by which he meant the Zwickau Prophets and the Wittenberg Movement). On the particular issue of **images**, he rejected Karlstadt's zeal as legalistic and lacking the authority of scripture. His reasoning deserves attention because it explains much of the subsequent gulf between the two great wings of Protestantism. Karlstadt believed that Old Testament law remained fully in force. God had spoken to Moses and the ancient commandments must be obeyed. Against that, Luther drew a distinction between the authority of New and Old Testament teaching. While the Old Testament could offer useful advice, the law given by Jesus replaced the law given to Moses. Thus on matters (such as religious art) about which the books of the New Testament were silent, the requirements of the Old could no longer be binding. What mattered was not external rules but the inner condition of the soul. The real idols, Luther argued, were the bad habits in people's hearts. There must be no popular direct action. Iconoclasm was a breach of the peace.

A notable characteristic of such **attacks** was the personal way in which statues were abused: their eyes gouged out, their hands cut off.
'The relationship with the saints had encompassed fear and aggression as well as love and respect. The intensely personal tone of traditional devotion probably carried within itself the prospect of an equally intense reaction once the news had got around that the saints were unable to meet their obligations in this world or the next.' (John Bossy, *Christianity and the west*, 1985)

'**Images** for memorial and witness, such as crucifixes and images of saints, are praiseworthy and honourable, as were the witness stones erected by Joshua and Samuel.' (Luther, *Against the heavenly prophets in the matter of images*, 1525)
The term for the destruction of religious images is 'iconoclasm'.

In that wholly different approach to the Bible lay much more than rival conceptions of the place of art (or music) in religion. The way of Karlstadt, copied by the south German and Swiss Protestants, was driven by the Old Testament legal code. From it came a form of religion more austere, moralistic and narrow minded: a religion controlled by firm rules of do's and don'ts. This was the form of religion we call 'puritanism'. During 1522–23, Luther used his influence with Elector Frederick to restrict Karlstadt. In 1523, **Karlstadt** therefore moved away to a country parish where he preached and published on a grand scale. As a result, his influence on the developing evangelical movement in southern Germany and Switzerland was conspicuous. In frustration, Luther had Karlstadt expelled from Saxony.

The Prophets of Zwickau and the Wittenberg Movement made clear there must be rival forms of Protestantism. A handful, like the Prophets, pre-dated Luther. Most, like Karlstadt, started with Luther as their base but then drew more radical conclusions. In the words of Bob Scribner, 'radical religious thought was a coat of many colours'. Luther's attacks on the Prophets and Karlstadt were linked by a common theme. Reformation was a slow process, involving the winning of the hearts and minds of the people; mere changes to the outward form of religion achieve nothing. The people must be persuaded, and abrupt imposed action will only make people hostile.

The Ordinance was suspended. For a while there were no religious changes in Wittenberg. No further clerical marriages took place. The **communion** cup was withdrawn from the laity. Monks and friars wishing to live by their vows could do so. Religiously, this curious limbo allowed Luther to reassert his authority. Politically, it helped Elector Frederick state categorically that law and order operated in Saxony, and that the emperor's ban on religious innovations had not been broken. From 1522, however, both were having to wage war on two fronts – against the rival Protestants as well as the Catholics.

In the years from 1521 to 1525, **Karlstadt** stood second only to Luther in the sheer volume of books and pamphlets he wrote in German: 90 separate works, in 213 editions (Luther wrote 192 new works, in 1,281 editions). It is often said that the Peasants' War made Luther abandon his original belief in the right of congregations to choose their own minister. This is not so. He changed his mind in 1523–24 because of his war with Karlstadt, who had the support of his parish and had been appointed to the post by Wittenberg town council.

Full **communion** was restored late in 1522, but the old Latin mass was not abolished until 1524 and Luther provided a full service in German only in 1525. And these restorations applied only in Wittenberg. Other parts of Saxony were not allowed to do the same until 1529. Even in its heartland, therefore, the Lutheran Reformation was *very* gradual.

Document study: What were Luther's main ideas?

1 Luther's thinking on justification and indulgences

1.1 Luther remembers the dark days of his personal spiritual crisis and the moment of revelation

I hated the thought of the righteousness of God because I had been taught to understand 'righteousness' to mean the punishment which God must inflict on every living man and woman. I could not love the righteous God, the God who punishes and adds suffering to our suffering . . . for we are all sinners and must be damned . . . But I continued my studies. Must God threaten us with his righteousness? Eventually I came to see the great truth. St Paul writes in the gospel 'the just shall live by faith'. That moment I understood.

Source: adapted from 'The autobiographical fragment', written by Luther, 1545

1.2 Luther criticises indulgences the day he wrote the Ninety-Five Theses

[I] regret the false meaning which the simple folk attach to it [the **indulgence**], the poor souls believing that when they have purchased such letters they have secured their salvation; also, that the moment the money jingles in the box souls are delivered from purgatory, and that all sins will be forgiven through a letter of indulgence, even that of reviling the blessed mother of God, were any one blasphemous enough to do so.

Source: Luther to Cardinal Albert of Brandenburg, 31 October 1517, in E. G. Rupp and B. Drewery (eds), *Martin Luther*, p. 17

Tetzel is reported as saying 'as soon as a coin in my chest rings, a soul from purgatory springs', and claiming the **indulgence** was powerful enough even to save someone who had raped the Virgin Mary.

1.3 Luther explains justification by faith

We are still sinners but we have been justified, by God's mercy. Our sin is still with us and we commit new sins for we are corrupted creatures. But God in his great love cloaks us in his righteousness. We have not earned it. Indeed, we never could. It is his gift. He has chosen to accept us. He can justify us because he has shielded us with his righteousness against our sin.

Source: Luther, *Against Latomus*, 1521

1.4 An early Lutheran woodcut attacking indulgences

Source: 'The devil and her indulgence', German woodcut, 1520s. The devil sits on an indulgence and holds a collecting box for indulgence sales. The pope is brought to join friars and cardinals in a feast in the devil's mouth. In that feast, being prepared on the devil's head, the pope and the clergy will dine on the Christian laity who are deceived into pinning their hopes and efforts on a lucrative trick.

1   From 1.2 and your own knowledge, explain the reference to 'the moment the money jingles in the box' (lines 3–4).

2   How reliable is 1.1 as evidence for Luther's thinking c.1511–16?

3   Compare 1.2 and 1.4 as evidence for Protestant hostility to indulgences.

4   Using all these sources and your own knowledge, examine the view that in 1517 Luther attacked Tetzel's claims rather than indulgences themselves.

2 Luther's ideas in 1520

2.1 Luther demands wine for the laity at communion

The first captivity of this sacrament is its incompleteness for the tyranny of Rome has stolen it from us . . . They are the sinners who forbid the giving of both kinds to those who wish to exercise this choice. The fault lies with the priests because the sacrament does not belong to them. Rather, Christ gave it to all men.

Source: Luther, *On the Babylonish captivity of the church*, 1520

2.2 Luther and the authority of the Bible

For my part, although I cannot understand how the bread is the body of Christ, I will nevertheless cling simply to Christ's words and believe not only that the body of Christ is in the bread, but that the bread is the body of Christ. My warrants for this are the words of Scripture and of Our Lord himself: 'He took bread and, when he had given thanks, he broke it and said, "Take, eat, this [that is, the bread which he had just taken and broken] is my body." '

Source: Luther, *On the Babylonish captivity of the church*, 1520

2.3 Luther attacks the roots of Catholic authority

The Romanists have very cleverly built three walls around themselves . . . In the first place they have made decrees and declared that the temporal power had no jurisdiction over them but that, on the contrary, the spiritual power is above the temporal. In the second place, when an attempt is made to contradict them with scripture, they raise the claim that only the pope may interpret the Bible. In the third place, if threatened with a council, they say that only the pope may summon a council . . . May God help us, and give us one of those trumpets with which the walls of Jericho were overthrown to blast down these papal walls of straw.

Source: Luther, *An appeal to the Christian nobility of the German nation*, 1520

1   From 2.1 and your own knowledge, explain the reference to 'sacrament' (line 1).

2   How useful is 2.2 as evidence of Luther's method for deciding which Catholic beliefs and practices should be kept?

3   Study the woodcut by Cranach (page 130) and 2.1. Compare these sources as evidence of the changes Luther made to the mass.

4   Using all these sources and your own knowledge, examine the view that Luther's demands in 1520 were moderate.

Document study: How did the authorities react to Luther's ideas 1517–21?

1 Luther and the Catholic authorities

1.1 Luther alerts his archbishop to Tetzel's claims

With your electoral highness's consent, the papal indulgence for the rebuilding of St Peter's in Rome is being carried through the land. I do not complain so much of the loud cry of the preacher of indulgences, . . . but regret the false meaning which the simple folk attach to it . . . Reverend father, it has gone abroad under your name, but doubtless without your knowledge, that this indulgence is the priceless gift of God, whereby the man may be reconciled to God, and escape the fires of purgatory . . . What else can I do . . . than beg your serene highness, carefully to look into this matter?

Source: Martin Luther to Albert, archbishop of Mainz, 31 October 1517

1.2 Luther gives his view of the Leipzig Dispute

Eck debated with me . . . concerning papal primacy . . . He emphasised exclusively the council of Constance, where the articles of Hus asserting that the papacy derived [its authority] from the emperor had been condemned. There he stood quite boldly, as If on a battlefield, and reproached me with the Bohemians and called me publicly a heretic and a supporter of the Hussite heretics . . . The third week we debated concerning repentance, purgatory, indulgences . . . Indulgences were thrown out of the window and he agreed almost completely with me . . . Eck conceded all this so that even the common people observed his disregard for indulgences. He is even said to have admitted that he would have agreed with me in all points had I not debated about the authority of the pope.

Source: Martin Luther's report of the Leipzig Dispute, 20 July 1519

1.3 An independent observer gives his view of the Leipzig Dispute

Luther followed Karlstadt to sustain the thesis that it was only by recent [decrees] that the Roman church was proved to be superior to other churches, against which stood the authority of scripture . . . Eck left no stone unturned to overthrow this opinion . . . doing his best especially to make his opponent invidious by dragging in some Hussite articles. Luther at once understood the snare and raged as though inspired by some spirit.

Source: Peter Mosellanus to the dean of Meissen Cathedral, 7 December 1519

1.4 Luther protests his innocence in spreading the Ninety-Five Theses

It is a mystery to me how my theses . . . were spread to so many places. They were meant exclusively for our academic circle here. This is shown by the fact that they were written in a language that the common people could hardly understand . . . Had I anticipated their widespread popularity, I would certainly have done my share to make them more understandable. What shall I do now? I cannot recall my theses and yet their popularity makes me hated. Unwillingly I must enter the limelight.

Source: Martin Luther to Leo X, 1520

Document-study questions

1 From 1.1 and your own knowledge, explain the reference to 'the fires of purgatory' (line 7).
2 Assess the reliability of 1.4 as evidence for the circulation of Luther's Ninety-Five Theses.
3 How far does 1.3 confirm 1.2 as evidence for what happened at the Leipzig Dispute?
4 Using all these sources and your own knowledge, examine the view that Rome had to prosecute Luther as a dangerous heretic.

2 The role of Frederick the Wise

2.1 The pope tries to win over Elector Frederick

It has come to our ears . . . that a certain son of iniquity, Friar Martin Luther, sinfully vaunts himself in the church of God, and, as though relying on your protection, fears the authority or rebuke of no one. Although we know this is false, yet we thought it good to write to your Lordship, urging you in the Lord, that for the name and fame of a good Catholic prince such as you, you should retain the splendour of your glory . . . unsoiled by these allegations. Not only that we wish you to avoid doing wrong, but we desire you to escape the suspicion of doing wrong.

Source: Pope Leo X to Elector Frederick, 1518

2.2 Luther reports the outcome of his second negotiations with a papal ambassador

Most illustrious, high-born prince, gracious lord!

Let me humbly inform your grace . . . that . . . the papal **nuncio** and I have finally reached an agreement . . . Both sides will be forbidden to preach, write and dispute further about this subject.

A **nuncio** is a papal ambassador.

Secondly, [the nuncio] is to write shortly to the holy father, the pope, describing all aspects of the situation as he has found them, and also to see that his holiness the pope commissions some learned bishop to adjudicate the question and to point out the erroneous articles, which I should withdraw. And when I have thus been informed of my error, it will be my duty and pleasure to recant them gladly and to do nothing to diminish the honour and power of the holy Roman church.

Source: Luther to Elector Frederick, January 1519

2.3 Reaction to the news that Luther has vanished

Last Sunday the news arrived here that Martin had been arrested, and it was widely rumoured that we were the instigators of this deed. We found ourselves in the greatest danger, for the supporters of Luther incited the people by pointing out how Luther was a man filled with the Holy Spirit and how we had broken the safe-conduct . . . The emperor, all the territorial rulers, and virtually the entire court agreed with our view so emphatically that the elector had to make a statement before the diet that he knew nothing about this matter . . . However, one can trust neither his glance, which is always directed down to the ground, nor his words.

Source: Papal Nuncio Aleander to Leo X, May 1521

2.4 Luther defies the elector and returns to Wittenberg from hiding

Your electoral grace's writing reached me on Friday evening, the night before I began my journey. That your electoral highness had the best intentions towards me is evident. And this is my answer. Most gracious lord, I desire to make it known that I have not received the gospel from men, but from heaven, through our Lord Jesus Christ. I have done sufficient for your grace this year in remaining in my forced seclusion . . .

I write all this to let your grace see that I come to Wittenberg under higher protection than that of the elector, and I have not the slightest intention of asking your electoral highness's help. For I consider I am more able to protect your grace than you are to protect me.

Source: Luther to Elector Frederick, March 1522

Document-study questions

1 From 2.4 and your own knowledge, explain the reference to 'my forced seclusion' (line 6).

2 Assess the reliability of 2.3 as evidence of attitudes to Luther.

3 How far does 2.2 confirm 2.4 as evidence for Luther's attitude to the Elector Frederick?

4 Using all these sources and your own knowledge, examine the view that Frederick the Wise was vital to the development of Lutheranism in the period from 1518 to 1522.

Document study: What was the impact of Lutheranism in Germany from 1517 to 1530?

1 The forces of German nationalism

1.1 Von Hutten encourages the rise of German national feeling

Ernhold: There are plenty of other things we must suffer: settling for arch-bishops' appointments, paying annates and other exactions. When will the Romans moderate their demands? I fear we Germans will not stand them much longer. Things are getting worse and there is no end to their robbery.

Hadron: As you well say, unless they are more reasonable and show some restraint, this nation of ours will finally have its eyes opened. It will recognise the deceptions which have been employed to delude a free people and bring into contempt a strong nation. Many are beginning to act as if we were about to cast off this yoke.

Source: von Hutten, *Vadiscus or the Roman Trinity*, early 1520

1.2 Von Hutten criticises papal Rome and its theft of German wealth

We see that there is no gold and almost no silver in our German land. What little is left is drawn away daily by the new schemes invented by the Roman curia. Leo gives some to his nephews and relatives . . . These in turn draw after them, at untold expense, copyists, beadles, messengers, servants, scul-lions, mule drivers, grooms, and an innumerable army of prostitutes and of the most degraded followers. They maintain dogs, horses, monkeys, long-tailed apes, and many more such creatures for their pleasures. They con-struct houses all of marble. They have precious stones, are clothed in purple and fine linen, and dine sumptuously, frivolously indulging themselves in every form of luxury by means of our money.

This money might be put to better uses as, for example: to put on foot great armaments and extend the boundaries of the empire; to conquer the Turks, if this seems desirable; to enable many who, because of poverty, now steal and rob, to earn honestly their living once again; to give contributions to those who otherwise must starve; to help scholars, and to advance the study of the arts and sciences and of good literature.

Source: von Hutten, letter to Elector Frederick, September 1520

1.3 Luther and von Hutten as the champions of Germany

Source: 'Champions of Christian liberty', German woodcut, 1521. Copies were on sale in Worms during the diet.

1.4 Von Hutten interprets Luther's condemnation

Behold Leo X's Bull to you, men of Germany. Here he tries to stamp out Christian truth which he attacks and opposes, as our freedom raises its head after long repression. It is not just Luther who is involved in this business. It affects us all. They do not want to be deposed from their tyranny; they do not want their frauds to be detected. Do you want advice? If you will heed mine, remember that you are Germans. This alone should be sufficient motive for you to justify these acts.

Source: von Hutten, foreword to his translation of the Bull *Exsurge Domine*, 1520

Document-study questions

1   From 1.1 and your own knowledge, explain what is meant by 'their robbery' (line 4).
2   Assess the reliability of 1.4 as evidence for the relationship between the papacy and Germany in the early 1520s.
3   How consistent are 1.1 and 1.2 as evidence for the aims of von Hutten?
4   Using all these sources and your own knowledge, examine the view that the Lutheran Reformation was an expression of German nationalism.

2 The urban Reformation

2.1 Luther hears how fast copies of his books sell

Balsius Salmonius, a printer of Leipzig, gave me some of your books bought at the Frankfurt Fair, which I immediately reprinted. We have sent six hundred copies to France and Spain . . . We have sold out all your books except ten copies, and never remember to have sold any more quickly.

Source: Johann Froben, a printer of Basle, to Luther, 1519

2.2 Practical difficulties in the way of reform for a city state

Action against your parish priest, who serves you poorly, can only be taken by the bishop. His is the authority to act against negligent clergy and we have no power to remove your priest. Neither can we transfer him to a parish where the city is the patron [with the right of appointment] because none of ours is vacant at present . . . If your pastor wants to stay put, a virtuous Christian preacher might be appointed to work with you as well or, if your priest will not agree to that, it would not be a bad idea to provide your own evangelical preacher at your own expense, since you value so highly the word, through which alone we can be saved.

Source: the city of Nuremberg to its village of Herzogenaurach, December 1534

2.3 A city council moving towards reform faces up to some of the consequences

Two points concern Nuremberg . . . The first is the divisive preaching of those opposing the word of God . . . A large number here have not been turned . . . but rather these preachers have strengthened them in their old human errors. Some who turned to the word after hearing Christian preaching have even been corrupted again by secret and public sermons, and then by going to confession . . . Second, such divisive preaching must create disunity among the magistrates, the fracturing of civic unity and public disturbances against the clergy and the city authorities.

Source: memorandum of the secretary of the city of Nuremberg, March 1525

2.4 The spread of Protestant ideas did not just depend on the official clergy

An old man, a weaver, came through the city gate and there offered hymns for sale while he sang them to the people. The burgomaster, coming from early mass and seeing the people, asked one of his servants what was going on. 'There is an old scamp over there,' he answered, 'who is singing and selling the hymns of the heretic Luther.' The burgomaster had him arrested and thrown into prison; but two hundred citizens interceded and he was released.

Source: from a chronicle written in the city of Magdeburg, c.1524

1   From 2.2 and your own knowledge, explain what is meant by 'the word, through which alone we can be saved' (lines 8–9).

2   How useful is 2.3 as evidence for the issues that mattered to city councils when adopting the Reformation?

3   Compare 2.1 and 2.4 as evidence for the way Protestantism spread.

4   Using all the sources and your own knowledge, explain how far you agree with the view that the urban Reformation was a popular movement uncontrolled by the authorities.

3 Luther and the Peasants' War

3.1 Luther explains the need for princes and nobles

The children of Adam divide into two groups: the first belong to the kingdom of God, the second to the kingdom of the world. Those who belong to the kingdom of God are true believing Christians, obedient to Christ, and therefore in no need of secular law or authority. And if all the people of the world were true believing Christians, there would be no need for princes, kings, lords or law because Christians have the Holy Spirit in their hearts and he teaches them to do no wrong and to love everyone.

Source: Luther, *Secular authority: to what extent it should be obeyed*, 1522

3.2 Luther criticises both sides, and calls for negotiation

Since, dear sirs, there is nothing Christian on either side, and there is no Christian issue pending between you, but both lords and peasants are concerned about heathen or worldly justice and injustice, and about temporal goods; since both parties are acting against God and stand under God's wrath: for the sake of God's will let yourself be counselled and advised, and grasp these issues as such issues deserve to be grasped – that is, with justice and not with violence, so that you do not produce endless bloodshed.

You lords have against you both scripture and history, describing how tyrants are punished. You peasants also have scripture and experience against you, declaring that no rabble has ever come to a good end . . .

Accordingly, my faithful counsel would be that some counts and lords should be chosen from the nobles, and some councillors from the cities, and the issues dealt with in a friendly fashion and resolved.

Source: Luther, *Admonition to peace*, April 1525

3.3 Luther calls on the authorities to crush the peasants

I think that all the peasants should perish rather than the princes and magistrates, because the peasants have taken up the sword without divine authority. They have been false to the gospel which they profess to follow. No mercy, no toleration is due to the peasants; on them should fall the wrath of God and of man. The peasants are under the ban of God and of the emperor and may be treated like mad dogs. Therefore strike, throttle, stab, secretly or openly, whoever can, and remember that there is nothing more poisonous, more hurtful, more devilish than a rebellious man . . . Their ears must be opened with musket balls, so that their heads fly into the air.

Source: Luther, *Against the robbing and murdering hordes of peasants*, May 1525

3.4 The revolutionary implications of the priesthood of all believers

Source: woodcut published in Leipzig, 1522. In the world turned upside-down by evangelical ideas, the priest and friar work in the fields while the peasants take the services in church.

Document-study questions

1 From 3.3 and your own knowledge, explain what Luther meant by 'the peasants have taken up the sword without divine authority' (line 2).
2 How useful is 3.1 as evidence for the way the peasants could misunderstand Luther?
3 Compare 3.2 and 3.3 as evidence for Luther's views on the Peasants' War.
4 Using all these sources and your own knowledge, discuss the claim that Luther had no choice but to call for the peasants to be crushed.

Further reading

Chapter 1

Useful short introductions are Stewart MacDonald, *Charles V: ruler, dynast and defender of the faith 1500–58* (Hodder, 1992), and Martyn Rady, *The Emperor Charles V* (Longman, 1988). Important articles on Charles and on the Habsburg–Valois Wars by Professors Koenigsberger and Rodriguez-Salgado respectively are to be found in *The new Cambridge modern history*, volume 2 (2nd edition, Cambridge, 1990). The weaknesses of Charles V are laid bare by J. M. Rodriguez-Salgado in *The changing face of empire: Charles V, Philip II and Habsburg authority 1551–1559* (Cambridge, 1998), while Paula Fichtner, *Ferdinand I of Austria: the politics of dynasticism in the age of the Reformation* (New York, 1982), shows clearly just how important Ferdinand was during the long reign of his brother.

Chapter 2

MacDonald and Rady (listed above under Chapter 1) offer accessible general discussions of Spain during the reign of Charles I. Excellent fuller treatments are to be found in John Elliot, *Imperial Spain, 1469–1716* (Pelican, 1970); Henry Kamen, *Spain 1469–1716: a society in conflict* (Longman, 1983); and John Lynch, *Spain 1516–1598: from nation state to world empire* (Blackwell, 1991). The critical value of los Cobos is made plain by Hayward Keniston's meticulous *Francisco de los Cobos: secretary of the Emperor Charles V* (Pittsburg, 1960).

Chapter 3

Brief treatment is offered in Robert Knecht, *French Renaissance monarchy* (2nd edition, Longman, 1996). For thorough and critical considerations of France during these years look at the same author's masterly *Renaissance warrior and patron: the reign of Francis I* (Cambridge, 1994), and Frederic Baumgartner's superb *Henri II, king of France, 1547–1559* (Durham, North Carolina, 1988).

Chapter 4

Sixteenth-century warfare is not well served by modern publications. Geoffrey Parker, *The military revolution: military innovation and the rise of the west, 1500–1800* (Cambridge, 2nd edn 1996), has useful ideas. So too do John Hale, *War and society in Renaissance Europe, 1450–1620* (Fontana, 1985) and Jeremy Black, *The Cambridge illustrated atlas of warfare: renaissance to revolution 1492–1792* (Cambridge, 1996). The effort should be made to track down John Hale's brief *Renaissance fortification: art or engineering?* (Thames and Hudson, 1977), for its text as much as for its illustrations. One work is, however, indispensable – David Eltis, *The military revolution in sixteenth-century Europe* (I. B. Tauris, London and New York, 1998).

Document study

Students of the German Reformation and of Martin Luther are spoilt for choice in books to read. The handiest single-volume collection of sources is Gordon Rupp and Benjamin Drewery, *Martin Luther* (Edward Arnold, 1970). Pamela Johnston and Bob Scribner provide by far the best short introduction for sixth-form students in their *The Reformation in Germany and Switzerland* (Cambridge, 1993), a book doubled in value by its regular use of extracts from contemporary documents. Among other A-level topic books, outstanding is Andrew Johnston, *The Protestant Reformation in Europe* (Longman, 1991). For first-rate studies of Reformation ideas, see Alister McGrath, *Reformation thought: an introduction* (Blackwell, 1988), and Bernard Reardon, *Religious thought in the Reformation* (2nd edition, Longman, 1995). A comprehensive but rich study of the Reformation is Euan Cameron, *The European Reformation* (Oxford, 1991). This is excellent, as is the brief overview given in Bob Scribner, *The German Reformation* (Macmillan, 1986). On the Peasants' War, see Tom Scott and Bob Scribner, *The German Peasants' War: a history in documents* (Atlantic Highlands, New Jersey, 1991). For Luther and the radicals, read Mark Edwards, *Luther and the False Brethren* (Stanford, California, 1975). Finally, students should at least sample Steven Ozment, *Protestants: the birth of a revolution* (Fontana, 1993), and Heiko Oberman, *Luther: man between God and the devil* (New Haven, Connecticut, 1986).

Index